"Society sells us the idea that we could ever be alone, unworthy, and powerless. Patricia Walker shared those beliefs—until life blasted her free. Her story shows what can happen when you get those beliefs out of your way."

—FRANK DeMARCO, author of *The Cosmic Internet*

"Pat Walker's memoir is a joy. It is *Eat, Pray, Love* for the common woman — you know, the vast majority of us who can't travel the world because we're stuck at home, doing laundry and driving kids around. I laughed out loud, but I also discovered that serious transformation can occur when one is open to it. In other words, it gives me hope."

—LAURA PRITCHETT, winner of PEN/USA Award and Milkweed National Fiction Prize

"*Dance of the Electric Hummingbird* is rich with symbolism, feeling, and message. It's alive with it. It gave me goosebumps. Some of the scenes just took my breath away. Such a powerful, powerful story. It's about finding God and we all want that in our lives."

—KRISTIN HUNGENBERG, certified in Epona: Equine Facilitated Experiential Learning

"A smoky, crowded bar in Cabo San Lucas, Sammy Hagar and his guitar, and one woman ready to begin her spiritual journey . . . *Dance of the Electric Hummingbird* is an irresistible combination. A great read."

—PATRICIA STOLTEY, author of *The Prairie Grass Murders* and *The Desert Hedge Murders*

AN ORDINARY WOMAN'S ACCIDENTAL JOURNEY
TO ENLIGHTENMENT, THE SUPERNATURAL,
AND ROCK STAR SAMMY HAGAR

Dance of the Electric Hummingbird

PATRICIA WALKER

RAINBOW RIDGE
BOOKS

Cover and interior design by Frame 25 Productions
Cover painting © Aaron S. Hagar
Song Lyrics for "Eagles Fly" and "Open" © Sammy Hagar

Published by:
Rainbow Ridge Books, LLC
140 Rainbow Ridge Road
Faber, Virginia 22938
434-361-1723

If you are unable to order this book from your local
bookseller, you may order directly from the distributor.

Square One Publishers, Inc.
115 Herricks Road
Garden City Park, NY 11040
Phone: (516) 535-2010
Fax: (516) 535-2014
Toll-free: 877-900-BOOK

Visit the author at:
www.bajarockpat.com
www.bajarockpat.net

Library of Congress Cataloging-in-Publication Data applied for.

ISBN 978-0-9844955-7-3

10 9 8 7 6 5 4 3 2 1

Printed on acid-free recycled paper in the United States of America

For Lovey:
You are the wind beneath my wings

You were born with ideals and dreams
You were born with greatness
You were born with wings
You are not meant for crawling, so don't
You have wings
Learn to use them and fly

—Rumi

Contents

CHAPTER 1

Supernatural Euphoria

*There came upon me what was far more than elation or exhilaration; I was
beside myself with an intensity of joy, and with this indescribable and almost
unbearable joy came a revelation of the essential goodness of the world....*
—Sir Frances Younghusband

Cabo Wabo Cantina
Cabo San Lucas, Mexico
October 11, 2003

I'm trying not to focus on how insanely hot it is in here, how
badly my knees ache, or that I'm much too old to be standing for so long amongst all these sweaty, drunk people, so to
take my mind off my self-pity, I watch all the young girls bounce
through the crowd. They're wearing too much makeup, their
breasts are disproportionately large for their bodies, and the
cheeks of their little, round butts peek out from the bottoms of
their colorful sundresses as several of them climb up and dance
on the platform that rises above our heads and to the left of
the stage. The men below them erupt in thunderous cheers, so
I look more closely to see what all the commotion is about—
those sweet little darlings aren't wearing any panties.

Wow. I never would have acted like that when I was that age. Of course, I didn't *look* like that when I was that age either. Now they're throwing their hair around as they slither and wrap their legs around the platform poles. Oh, and the dark-haired one is undoing the straps of her top and flashing everyone while the men fall all over themselves and snap pictures like the paparazzi.

The people near me seem to find all this perfectly acceptable, so I pretend I'm not shocked either, as if this is something I see every day. Man, am I a prude. I've been clipping coupons and mending holes in socks for far too long.

Everything about this place reeks of sweat and booze. Even the palm trees. Even me. My hair is stuck to the back of my neck. I'm cursing my faded orange tank top with the white, built-in bra that I bought before we came on this trip because now it's drenched and hanging on me like a suit of armor. I'm sure the stains will never come out. And although there are huge fans in the room, the forest of people surrounding me blocks any movement of air while second-hand smoke looms overhead like a storm cloud. It makes my nose sting and my stomach churn.

How is it possible to be this miserable and still be vertical?

The rather small but well-worn stage is ready and waiting to come to life. Tiny red and green lights buzz on the amps and speakers and neon lights glow in the semi-darkness. Two large bars with palm-branched roofs take up the side and back of the room, while thousands of bras and panties dangle above like jungle snakes waiting in ambush. Bartenders pour tequila by the gallon.

This is Mexico, but it feels more like a testosterone-soaked American rock and roll museum. And everything is sticky. What's that saying I hear everyone using? Oh yeah, "What happens in Cabo, stays in Cabo." I'll have to remember that one.

The recorded mix blasting from the speakers has made a complete loop and is now replaying from the beginning. They're all songs I should know but don't, because I was too busy trying to get through each day as a single mom when most of them were popular, like Bon Jovi's "Livin' on a Prayer" and "Sweet Child O' Mine" by Guns N' Roses. Tonight, they make me want to dance—I like the music; it's fun and lively—and maybe I'd wriggle around in my little space if my legs didn't feel like someone beat them with a blunt club or if it wasn't so god-forsaken hot in here. I need water. Bad. But there haven't been any servers by for a long time and there's no way I'll be able to get through this unruly mob.

A chubby, balding man two rows ahead of me hoots at the top of his lungs and twirls a plastic cup of beer around and around above his head, showering those of us nearby. Brown-skinned men with the word "security" on the back of their shirts glare at him. I cringe. Now I'm even stickier and I smell like beer. Great. *What's taking them so long to start the show?*

Over the past week, there have been other concerts here, all featuring some famous singer by the name of Sammy Hagar. Apparently, he owns this place. My husband and I happened to walk in the other day and catch the end of the show and tonight there's another one, so we thought we'd come back and watch the whole thing this time. Besides, it's the last night of our vacation so we might as well make the most of it. Tomorrow morning we're going home.

Dee, my husband and fearless protector, has deserted me in lieu of the perfect spot to take pictures. I'm not afraid to be alone though; the people around me are friendly and chatting about the concert.

"I've been a fan since Montrose; that's . . . um . . . almost 30 years," a middle-aged woman next to me says. "My favorite song, I think, has to be 'Rock Candy,'" she continues with a big smile. "What's yours?"

Before I came on this trip, I'd never even heard of Sammy, but I don't want her to know I'm as clueless as I really am. Trying to fit in and be one of the "cool people" has been a rather delicate issue for me most of my life, so now I have to think fast. "Uh, that's my favorite too," I lie and reach down to rub my aching knees.

"Really? Way cool," she shouts and slaps me a high five. Then she tells me that she and her husband are from Detroit and they've been coming down to Cabo every year for the past ten years. That seems to be the story I'm hearing from a lot of these people. How can they care so much about a singer that they plan their entire vacations around him, year after year? Don't they get sick of hearing the same music? But I guess it's none of my business.

By this time, I've already drunk three blue Waboritas, Hagar's own recipe, I'm told, for what tastes at first like a super-sweet, pure-alcohol-kick-in-the-ass, because I guess that's exactly what they are. They're small. They look harmless enough and once you get over the initial shock, these drinks go down like soda pop, until you try to walk. By that time, you know the score and it's already too late. But I'm not to that point tonight—I don't think. Besides, I drank them over a period of several hours. I do feel pretty good though. Kind of wispy.

After what seems an eternity, the band finally emerges from upstairs and walks down a catwalk above the audience that leads to the stage. As soon as they see him, the crowd erupts, "Sam-my! Sam-my! Sam-my!" Sammy smiles, straps on his red Les Paul guitar, and kicks his band into high gear. It's so loud, my ears are doing this bzzzz, bzzzz, bzzzz sound, so I plug my fingers into them for a moment. Then Michael Anthony, whom I've been informed is Sammy's long-time friend and once fellow-member of Van Halen, joins the rest of them onstage and BAM! the music rises to an even higher level, like the difference between watching a video and actually being there. It's fearless, powerful, pounding, exhaling fire. It's sucking me in like it owns me or something. Maybe it's the way it's vibrating through me, shaking my ribs, or maybe it's more than that. Maybe it's being this close to a major rock band in such a small venue—eight or ten rows from the action, and it's slamming me from every angle—body, mind, and soul, with an "only-bad-girls-have-this-kind-of-wild, animal sex" sort of sweet poison. I don't know, but it's so hard-core, superficial-deep, and in-my-face real that I forget all about my aching knees or that it's nine thousand degrees in here. All I want to do is stand here—*am I standing or am I sailing?* —and let it take me.

But something else is happening.

Sammy's up there on the stage—he's bent over, cranking his guitar, his brow furrowed with intensity, and he's singing a song I've never heard before. Energy blasts from him like the flame of a blowtorch, ricocheting off all the zebra stripes, orange hands, lighthouses, and naked women with guitars for bodies that are painted on the walls. His playing grows harder-edged and more dynamic with each phrase and I can feel his passion building, like a storm brewing.

He's singing about getting higher and higher and about moving upward. He's singing about not crying anymore and something about dreams.

Dreams . . . I remember those. Barely. Somewhere down the line, my life had become plastic and routine. Well, not entirely, but in a spiritual sense. I didn't even notice that I'd allowed it to happen. I'd been too busy taking care of my family.

Now for some reason, the words he's singing are conjuring up memories I've been holding in for decades, as if the time is right to finally let them go, like lifting the lid off a big pot to let the steam out. And they come barreling out—I see myself twenty years ago, sitting on the floor in a puddle of my own blood, holding my hand to the side of my face and weeping from deep in my soul. My first husband, Rick, stands over me looking bewildered and rubbing his fist.

Tears come to my eyes. They're not tears of self-pity; I'm not sure *what* they're for. For mourning the innocence I'd lost to that terrible man perhaps? For the loss of my dreams? I watch the movie unfold in my mind and feel the pain and the desperation all over again, as I tried all my life, to cling to some sort of hope beneath it all.

Other memories start to surface too—of always being the new kid in school, because we moved around a lot while I was growing up, and the girls in my class calling me names while I lowered my head and tried not to let them see me cry. These thoughts then melt with the words in the song about dreams and I see myself as a little girl on Christmas morning, peeking into the living room and finding the Christmas tree dripping with silver tinsel and beneath it, the gifts I had asked Santa for. I can feel the sheer elation and shock all over again, as I was sure right then, that dreams really did come true. And I've never stopped believing that.

All these thoughts swirl in my mind like small flecks of iridescence inside a gray tornado—the good, the bad, and the ugly all at once. Before I can stop to wonder why a rock concert would elicit such intense emotions, something lifts me right up and out of them, as if an aperture in the sky is opening and two giant hands are emerging from it and picking me up. I actually see the words of the song Sammy is singing rise from their patent meanings because they're suddenly tangible objects—light blue and trimmed in silver. They blur and ripple like a still lake when you throw a stone into it, becoming a kind of phantom escort that's literally taking me higher.

Uh . . . what is this? I'm just watching a concert . . . .

My thoughts and perspective shift like a camera going out of focus, as something familiar and warm flows back and forth between Sammy and me. It looks like a thick conveyor belt of liquid golden light, but I don't see it; I feel it. My spirit welcomes it and absorbs it like a thirsty sponge.

The sensation of being an audience member falls away in slow motion, as my body suddenly becomes paralyzed, lighter than air, and I feel myself lift right up out of it.

I'm falling. *Up.*

When I look down, I can see myself about five feet below, as if the "me" in the audience is someone else. But how can I be "me" up here and "me" down there at the same time?

Jesus—am I losing my mind?

All sound disintegrates except for a muffled voice crying out in the distance, "*Oh . . . my . . . God!*" It's coming from somewhere on the ground, in the crowd. It's *my* voice—within me and without me at the same time, a rather alarming feeling. A pervading sense of universal peace then saturates my being. I'm floating on the breath of heaven. And I'm warm, protected, important, and loved beyond measure. *What is happening?* Maybe the heat's getting to me.

I pass through the roof of the building as if it's not even there and then I see that the ordinary scene of the concert below that I'm part of, is now bathed in an all-encompassing light. I can see minute details I didn't notice before, as if I'm looking through a magnifying glass: a small, jagged stone on the floor between my right foot and the woman next to me, a crack in the side wall that someone had attempted to cover with yellow paint. I'm still going up. And the higher I go, the more focused everything becomes. I swear I can hear Sammy's thoughts while he's onstage singing, as if they're my own, but that's not possible, is it? A thread of a thought pokes in from reality, *Oh, I get it, I must've had waaay too much to drink!* Then it fades.

An overwhelmingly pleasant sensation starts to grow within me, and the higher I go, the more pronounced it becomes, as if white light is pouring into my soul. *Did I just collapse during the show and now I'm dead?* But I don't *feel* dead—whatever that means. And I'm not afraid anymore either. I feel absolutely safe. Safe enough to let go of the tiny shards of hesitation and skepticism that still cling to my sides, the ones that tell me none of this is real—and surrender to whatever it is that's happening to me. I might as well. I can't fight it anyway.

The instant I have this thought, I see it all fall away like a launching rocket dropping its booster engines, and I become completely lost in the sensation.

My years of sadness are over, and I didn't even know I was that unhappy.

Where did that thought come from?

Everything is now moving in slow motion, like I'm floating in water. I feel my senses diminish, as if they are needed only in the physical world and are unnecessary here, *wherever* it is I am right now. The only sense that matters is the Supreme Sense— that which my soul is feeling: pure, unutterable joy. Unbridled, ubiquitous ecstasy. It's so enormous, it can't be humanly possible to feel this way. I've given birth to three healthy children and I thought nothing could top that, but this does. By far.

My mind keeps trying to rationalize all this and the only thing it can come up with is, *I wonder if somebody slipped something into my drink when I wasn't looking. That must be it.* Oh . . . God . . . It's taking more effort than I'm capable of to hold on to my thoughts any longer; something more important seems to be taking over. I—

I AM— It's like an absolute, blazing sunrise, a volcanic burst of euphoria into—

I am.

Everything.

I am.

Nothing.

I'm the question and the answer, the dream and the realization of the dream.

I am paradise. I am a celebration. I am perfect. Everything is perfect; it's exactly how it's supposed to be.

My spirit is now spiraling within something all-powerful, and I recognize an integral piece of my soul, something I didn't know was missing. I reach out in a daze, in a dream, like the starry blackness of space, and pluck it from midair. Then I pull it into me; and as I do, a sparkling mist of white light flows through me and plugs me into some gigantic force. Is it God? It must be God. What else would it be? It's so huge that I should be scared shitless but I'm not. It feels . . . *what are the words?* Beyond wonderful. This force then shows me that it isn't a race or religion, but an energy consisting of *all* races and religions, even the lack of these. Neither is it a gender, but some kind of dual persona, each half as vital as the other and constantly moving, evolving, and sharing dominance. And it is also me. I am God/God is me in a great circle of radiance that's alive, breathing, and still rippling like that lake reacting to the stone. I don't think this; I *can't* think. I don't see it either, at least not with my eyes, I *know* it. Then I "see" with my soul, in great detail, how everything is connected—every human being, every grain of sand, every snowflake, plant and animal—every thought, every deed—all that has ever been and all that will ever be. I can see it all—even beings and non-beings in other dimensions that I can't identify—and within this connection, there is only love. No beginning, no end, no separation—nothing—but love. I'm so overcome that if I were in my body right now, I think I'd be crying, laughing, peeing my pants from sheer astonishment. But I'm not in my body. Of that much I am certain.

I inhale deep and feel all of this flow into my lungs like the pinch of microscopic grains. What is this sensation? I'm whole for the first time in my life.

It lasts only seconds.

Reality drifts back into my awareness, as if someone has turned a dial and raised the volume on a stereo until it's booming again. I bob like a cork on the threshold for a moment, then slowly become reintegrated back into my body, back into the crowd swaying to the beat of the music and crashing greedily into one another's space. I half expect that woman from Detroit to tap me on the shoulder and ask, "Are you all right?" as if I'd just regained consciousness after having passed out. But she doesn't. She's still rocking and screaming, caught up in the show. By this time though, I'm no longer tuned in to what's going on onstage. My head is spinning but not like when I've had too much to drink. And I'm gasping, as if I've just been taken off pure oxygen and now I'm forced to breathe the putrid air in the room.

I hold my hand in front of my face and spread my fingers to make sure they're all connected to me. I feel the movement of my hand, but there's some kind of dull light coming from it. *This didn't happen.* I bet somebody slipped something into my drink. What else could it be? But then, if someone drugged me, it would last for more than a few seconds, wouldn't it? *It must have been my imagination.* Either that or . . . Damn! That tequila must be some strong shit!

Before I can get my bearings, the band says goodnight and leaves the stage. Did I miss half the concert? *What's wrong with me?* My skin feels like it's fizzing.

The audience breaks apart, revealing thousands of discarded plastic cups and empty water bottles on the ground. As I attempt to find Dee in the throng, I'm trying to act normal but I feel so different, like I've just had sex with the Ultimate Ecstasy. I'm shaking all over. I'm elated. Excited. Energized beyond anything I've ever known. I can't wait to tell Dee about this, although he'll have a logical explanation, I'm sure. He always does.

After a few minutes, he saunters up to me, camera strap swinging from his arm and a big grin on his face.

"So how was that?" he asks, meaning the concert.

"Wow, I must be drunker than I thought," I confess, touching my hand to my forehead. "I don't even remember the last part of the show. Dee, something really weird just happened to me, like I left my body or something."

He just looks at me. "No more tequila for *you*. I think you need to go outside and get some air." He takes my arm and steers me toward the door.

"No, really." My eyes fill with tears and my heart begins to pound. "Something happened to me in there. I don't know how to describe it, but I went somewhere else."

"Okay." It's his sarcastic tone. In Dee's world, everything is literal. If he can't see it with his eyes, then it's not real and he doesn't want to hear about it. This has been an issue between us for decades. But maybe his more-grounded sense of reality is what I need right now.

I try to explain what just happened to me, but I'm not sure I know the words to convey any of this. How can I make him understand when *I* have no idea what happened myself? I have emotions I've never had before, emotions that have no equivalent on earth that I'm aware of. I'm definitely not the same person who walked into the concert a few hours ago. It feels as if I've been zapped by an electric explosion of joy and suddenly brought to life. I'm glowing from the inside out, walking ten feet above the ground. And I can't stop smiling.

Something wonderful and terrifying just happened. It wasn't the drinks or the heat though, because now that I'm outside, I should be back to normal and I'm not.

How can I possibly make sense of this? And why does it feel so *incredibly* important?

CHAPTER 2

Another Time

No one can make you feel inferior without your consent.
—Eleanor Roosevelt

Denver, Colorado
August, 1979

Rain runs down the outside of the window in great slices. It collects in puddles against the heavy wooden frame and leaks in around the edges where the wood doesn't quite line up. I can't remember when it's rained so hard.

My insides ache, and I feel as squishy as the weather, even though it's been several months since giving birth. Is it normal to feel this way after all this time? At 21, I have a three-month-old son who's asleep in his crib in the other room, and I'm sitting here in the living room, watching it rain and wondering where my husband is. I'd kept his dinner warm for hours, until I figured there was no longer any use, so I finally put it away. It's just beans and tortillas anyway. Homemade. We can't afford much else.

After a while, I grow tired of waiting and head down the hall to bed. I pass the baby's room and peek in. He's sleeping like . . . well, yes, a little angel. David, my beautiful baby boy. I love to hold him, feed him, and I could stand by and just watch him sleep for hours—his perfect skin, soft and warm, his tiny chest rising and falling, eyelids flittering in some baby dream. I put a kiss on my finger and touch it to his cheek. He doesn't stir. I tiptoe out and close the door.

Crawling between my cold sheets, I try to sleep but all I can do is toss and turn. For one thing, this isn't the best neighborhood in Denver. Every time I come home, I'm surprised to see that our stereo and TV are still in the living room. And there are always people doing drug deals in front of the red brick duplex across the street. Would they break in and hurt me if they knew my husband wasn't here right now?

It's 2 A.M.; where is he? Has he been in an accident? Hurt or killed? Why doesn't he call? Finally, comes the sound of the key in the lock and voices laughing and shouting from the front porch. Rick is wasted.

When he steps inside, I meet him in the hallway. "Where have you been?"

"Having beers with my bros, baby! Gettin' high with ma buds." He's slurring his words and there's a big, stupid grin on his face. His eyes are glazed and bloodshot and he's dripping water all over the floor.

He leans in to kiss me. I guess I'm supposed to play along, as if this is normal behavior for any 20-year-old husband and father. But his breath smells like rancid rats drowned in beer. I duck out of his reach and turn to face him, folding my arms across my chest.

"You're getting the floor all wet. Why didn't you call me?"

"Why would I call you?"

"I was worried about you." I feel the anger building and push it aside as best I can. Am I being unfair by feeling this way?

He wrinkles his brows and clenches his fists. "Hey, I'll do whatever I want; you got that?" He spits in my face.

"What? You don't think you owe me the courtesy to call and let me know you're gonna be late when you know I have dinner waiting for you?" I'm unaware that I am crawling into the pit of an alligator and inserting my head into its gaping maw. Stupid me. Stupid, stupid, girl-child. But I also see that he's too drunk to reason with, so I might as well go back to bed and talk to him about it in the morning.

As I turn and walk toward the bedroom, Rick follows me down the hallway and shoves me up against the wall, causing my head to bang against the doorframe. His hand strikes my right cheek with a throbbing sting. I suddenly feel sick. I don't know whether to be scared or shocked. I've never been in a situation like this before. I wasn't raised amid violence.

The man who just one year ago promised to love and cherish me, then pins me against the wall by my chin and glares into my eyes as if deciding what awful thing he can do to me next. My body is trembling. The palms of my hands begin to sweat, so I rub them over the side of my pink and white nightgown to dry them off, or maybe to distract myself from the fear I don't know how to process.

He finally releases me, as a different mood seems to sweep across his face. I take a breath of relief. *I'm safe!* I . . . I think. When I turn to leave, he moves in closer, then squeezes my breast so hard I'm sure it's going to leave a bruise.

"Come on, baby. Give your man what he needs. You gotta take care of your man!"

Whose sense of reality is skewed here? Mine or his? I can't think.

"Leave me alone," I lean toward him and shout into his face.

Without warning, his fist makes contact with the left side of my face and I hear something crack. All that registers with my brain is that a second ago, I was on my feet and now I'm on the bedroom floor. Did I pass out? How long have I been on the ground? Silver sparks whirl in front of my eyes as I look up at my husband. He's standing above me, as if he can't believe what just happened, as if someone else had done this to me. Or maybe he thinks I got what I deserved. I don't know.

I must be asleep and having a nightmare. I need to wake myself up. But there's something wet and warm against my cheek and the inside of my mouth tastes like blood. *I don't think I've ever tasted anything while dreaming before* . . . . It *is* blood—my blood—all over the floor and smeared against my face. When I try to speak, I can feel sharp fragments loose in my mouth and my jaw pops and twists at an odd angle. Pain shoots through my head like a stab of hot lightning. This is not a dream.

My brain says, "Get on your feet or you're going to die!" *Die?* Who ever thought of such a thing? That stuff only happens on TV; not in real life. When I put my hand down, something jagged and hard pierces my fingers from inside the shag carpet. Not wanting to step on it and cut my bare foot, I pick it up. The tiny, white bits in the palm of my hand slowly come into focus—several of my teeth. My stomach erupts in spasms.

What . . . has just happened? I look around the room for something solid to help me get my bearings. The bed, the dresser, the yellow-floral-print drapes, and the clothes hanging in the closet seem to mock me, as the room is warm and brutal at the same time. Warm, because when I was a teenager, my bedroom had always been my sanctuary—a place to escape with my dreams. Now it tastes like rusty metal.

I manage to stand up but the room starts to spin. Rick is still staring at me, as if he's waiting for my next move. I can't imagine what might be going through his mind. I hardly know what's going through *my* mind. Help—I need help. Call somebody. Mom and Dad.

I stumble into the hallway to grab the phone, but Rick beats me to it. He yanks the cord out of the wall and it leaves a hole in the plaster and a crumbled mess on the floor.

"You ain't fuckin' callin' nobody," he screams.

I'm sure now that I'm definitely going to die. For real. I have to run. Opening the locked door that connects our apartment to the one upstairs, I bolt up the steps to ask the neighbors to call the police. Rick clambers up the steps behind me, the keys in his side pocket jangling.

"What do you think you're doing? They're not gonna help you!"

He catches me before I reach the top. With one angry fist, he grabs my hair and drags me down the stairs and back into our apartment, scraping the skin off my arms and legs as they bang against the wall on the way down. I am now an empty shell.

I don't know how to accept this kind of reality. It doesn't seem that long since I was playing with plastic horses and Barbie dolls. How did I get from there to here?

Growing up, I was raised to be modest and demure, but after high school, my hormones began to protest. My mother's voice echoed in my head that sex outside of marriage was a sin, but my body had other intentions and I listened to it. I gave Rick my innocence. We were co-workers at dead-end jobs and he was just too good-looking to resist. But after months of having sex, I couldn't figure out what all the fuss was about. It didn't feel good. It hurt. Was this the way it was supposed to be? My vagina, my inner and outer lips, and my thighs swollen and black and blue? Rick bragging to his friends that he'd dumped ten loads into me the night before? It even hurt to walk sometimes. His friends said he was "the man," banging his girlfriend so hard she could barely walk.

I knew my religion would scorn me for having sex out of wedlock, so after two years, I figured I'd better marry him and make amends for my sinfulness. My parents would be so disappointed in me if they knew what I was doing. And God would surely punish me.

My mother always told me that after she married Dad, she wanted a baby right away, so I thought that was what I was supposed to want too. A few months after Rick and I were married, I got pregnant. I just knew that once he settled down, Rick would be an exemplary provider—handsome and all dressed up in an expensive suit, kissing me good-bye as he went to his nine-to-five job at a downtown office building while I stayed at home tending the children. I guess all of this came from those quaint little fairy tales they used to tell us when we were kids—the ones that always had a moral to the story and were laden with your classic knight-in-shining-armor and Prince Charming bullshit.

And now, my Prince Charming has me sitting defeated on the green, linoleum floor at the bottom of the stairs. There's a merciless pain in my jaw and my arms and legs are burning. My flannel nightgown is stained with blood, my jaw is swelling like a balloon, and it feels as if I haven't slept for months. Maybe I should have noticed the warnings when while we were dating— he punched two holes in the wall on either side of my head one night. At the time, I blamed his behavior on the fact that he was drunk, along with his hot temper and his uh, *love* for me—why were bad boys so exciting?

If I hadn't had such low self-esteem, maybe I wouldn't have gotten myself into this situation in the first place. I think it all started when the Catholic Church taught me that I was born a sinner, and that altruism was the supreme virtue, so I took all that to heart. The worst part about it was, although I was expected to live a life that would satisfy God—someone I'm not humanly capable of pleasing because I'm a sinner and would always *be* a sinner—the whole purpose of my life was to try anyway. All that did was make me beat myself up trying to be the ideal *everything* to everyone and ultimately end up feeling like a failure because I was fighting a losing battle. And I think others can sense it when you're down on yourself like that, as if you exude "I'm not worthy" or something, and like the baby chicks I had when I was a kid, they tend to peck the weak one until it dies.

Ohhhhhh, this isn't happening.

I begin to cry, "Somebody please *help* me! Please, God, please help me."

But no one hears. Not even God.

I collapse inward and sob into my hands. Roll me over and let me die. I'm done.

The next morning, with his shirt caked in dried orange vomit, Rick apologizes. He swears he will never hurt me again. I want to believe him. We've only been married a year; we have a son together. I'm an adult. I know what love is. He loves me . . . right?

Hours later, I'm sitting in the dentist's chair and wondering how we're going to pay for this.

"You should press charges against your husband," the dentist tells me. "Not only are your teeth broken, but so is your jaw." He shows me the x-ray.

But I can't imagine pursuing such a nightmare. I just want it all to go away. So I have the teeth fixed and decide to give my husband another chance. Maybe this won't happen again. Just please, don't let me smell the beer—it smells like a beating.

And then Rick finds Jesus.

On a late summer afternoon, he comes home from work with a big grin on his face.

"I have accepted Jesus Christ as my Personal Lord and Savior," he says, sitting at the kitchen table and waiting for me to serve him dinner.

After all this time, God has finally heard my prayers! He has delivered a means to help me. I feel a twinge of hope as, balancing the baby in one arm and Rick's plate in the other, I ask him to explain.

"I repented for my sins," he says, producing a small, black Bible from the pocket of his gray work pants.

He tells me how he's been studying the Bible for the past few weeks with a woman he works with and that today was his day of salvation. He makes it sound like trumpets blared and angels appeared in the sky to welcome him.

But something doesn't feel right. And yet, I tell myself that I should be grateful that he's finally found a positive influence in his life. Maybe all he needs is a little spiritual direction and he'll be kind to me. Besides, this is God's will; I trust in The Lord. He won't steer me wrong.

"I have been saved." Rick opens his arms wide and glances toward the ceiling with a light in his blue eyes. "I am guaranteed a place in the kingdom of heaven."

I don't get it. How come *he's* going to heaven and I'm not? I've never hurt anybody. On second thought, I don't think I want to know.

But things don't stay this way for long. Even though I want to believe it, people don't go from bad to good in one day like that. Besides, how can I trust my husband when he beats me, then tells me I'm going to hell and he's going to heaven? There's something really messed up about that. And in the first place, what gives him the right to judge me? Only God is worthy of passing judgment.

At first Rick only beats me when he's drunk, but then it starts happening more often, even though after each episode, he apologizes and swears it'll never happen again. He even brings me flowers sometimes, flowers we can't afford.

And then my dear husband, the one who's going to heaven because he's saved, starts raping me. I can't figure out if it's some sick, sexual fantasy of his or if it's his way of showing me who's boss.

In the middle of an argument, he throws me down on my back on the bed as if I'd been a bratty kid and I'm about to get my ass beaten. Do husbands really treat their wives like this? Maybe I just don't know anything about sex.

Before I can move or wonder which one of us is crazy, in what seems like one quick motion, he spreads my legs with his knees and kneels on them while he unzips his fly. His stiff penis bursts out of his pants like a thick, rubber sword as he pins my arms above my head with his hands. He's really getting off on this, because he doesn't need his hand to force himself under my skirt and inside me. But he can't get in very far because I'm dry. And I'm scared.

He thrusts harder. It feels like he's cutting me between the legs with a knife.

I feel like I'm spinning, spinning, falling down a dark well—and I'm trying not to think about how my skin feels like there are a million centipedes crawling all over me or how I can't breathe under his weight. And I'm trying not to focus on how I can feel the bruises and welts forming on my wrists and legs or that the sheer force of him might blow me apart.

Within seconds, he moans and comes all over me like a fountain of sludge.

The horrible, sticky wetness feels like acid burning me and my legs are pinched and cramping. I want to scream, but I don't want to wake up David, who's asleep in the next room. That's all I need is a crying baby right now. The only thing I can think of to defend myself is to spit in Rick's face, so I do. Big mistake. It makes him madder.

"You bitch!" he screams. Then he shoves himself into me again only this time it doesn't hurt quite as bad because now I'm wet with his slime. It hurts worse in another way. Tears roll out of my eyes and soak the sheets under me as I flail my head from side to side and wriggle to try and get out from under him. But it's no use. I'm no match for his strength. I finally give up and just let him finish. If I felt low before, now I feel sub-human, as if I'm being sucked into a version of hell I never thought possible.

Where is the ruler of heaven who's supposed to rescue me? He certainly doesn't dwell in rape and violence. My God is a loving God. I must be a horrible person to deserve this treatment, because obviously I deserve it or it wouldn't be happening. I must have pissed God off big time. Jesus, what did I do that was so wrong? All my life I've bent over backward to live up to the Ten Commandments and do what God wanted me to do—except that one thing—having sex before getting married. But what's so terrible about that, really? Why would God give us bodies that crave sex and then punish us for doing what's supposed to be so natural and beautiful? Maybe I'm just the worst kind of sinner for thinking these thoughts; I don't know, because none of this has ever been beautiful for me, although I've heard that's how it's supposed to be. Maybe it's beautiful because the act makes babies and babies are beautiful.

And where does my husband get the notion that being "saved" and abuse are on the same page? Maybe he doesn't even realize he's abusing me. Maybe he thinks he's taking from me what he's entitled to. Since he's my husband, I'm his property to do with as he pleases.

None of this is helping my relationship with God either—He supposedly blessed this marriage. *Oh, God, where are you? How can I please you? I'm so very sorry for everything; why don't you see that?* It seems like everything I've ever believed in has turned out to be a lie.

But everything looks so normal on the surface, I don't get it. The pots and pans in my kitchen don't care, my ironing board and laundry basket seem perfectly happy, and when we go out, Rick and I look so cute together—he's so good-looking. Maybe it's me. I feel like I'm on the wrong planet and everyone is acting according to some standard of behavior that's foreign to me. But then, I've felt that way all my life. Even when all those girls picked on me in grade school, I never fought back. I couldn't conceive of hurting anyone on purpose, even when they hurt me first. I thought God wanted us to love one another and get along with each other. Where does all that hate come from?

And now I'm afraid all the time.

Maybe I should leave Rick, but if I did, how would I support my son and me? I haven't worked outside the home since having David and I don't know who would hire someone like me. I don't know how to do anything. And what would my relatives think? As far as I know, none of them were divorced. The Catholic Church would turn its back on me if I did that. Then what would I do without my religious foundation to hold me up in times of trouble and sorrow? I was also taught that a divorced woman was an adulterer. Maybe they'd make me walk around with a scarlet letter "A" on my shirt like in the book.

And yet, my religion isn't helping me now, is it? All the dogma, all the rituals and the rules—all those men in power— where are they now? None of them, not even God is coming to my rescue. Is it worth it to suffer God's retribution for divorcing my husband or should I simply remain in the marriage and accept my fate? The saying "You've made your bed, now lie in it" keeps going through my mind. Other women do it; I can too. But then, what will become of me and my baby?

I keep hoping things are going to change—any day now— but they don't. They just seem to be getting worse. My marriage doesn't contain white lace and fancy cakes anymore. Now it smells like rotting malt and hops and tastes like burning flesh. My life is spinning out of control.

I approach Rick on a Saturday while he seems to be in an agreeable mood. His feet are propped up on the edge of the coffee table and he's drinking a beer and watching TV. The smell of the beer makes my stomach turn upside down.

"Maybe we should consider getting divorced," I suggest as sweetly as I can, thinking that if I'm nice about it, he won't lose his temper.

"Ha!" He doesn't even look up from the TV. "Nobody's ever going to want you. Look at you. You're fat and ugly. You're lucky to have me. No other man would ever even *look* at you." He tells me this all the time. In my heart, I know it isn't true, but after you hear something over and over long enough, for some stupid reason, it begins to sound like fact.

I feel myself sinking. Maybe he's right; maybe I am ugly and un-cool and he's doing me a favor by marrying me and smothering me with sex. Isn't this supposed to be love? What is it I don't understand about it? There's obviously such a thing as sex, but the concept of love is nothing but a farce. So is sex for that matter. Maybe even God, because He never answers me. I pray and pray and pray but God never pays any attention to me. There doesn't seem to be an easy solution.

But a solution comes on its own. I don't think God has anything to do with it.

Rick threatens to hurt our son. When it comes to standing up for myself, I'm sorely lacking, but when my child is threatened, a mother grizzly bear emerges with a fearlessness I didn't know I had in me. I would die before I let anyone hurt my baby.

Even if this is just a ploy by my husband to scare me into staying with him, which I think it is, I can't take the chance. I take David and move back in with my parents.

The marriage finally ends after months of terror, lawyers, restraining orders, and tears.

I've heard that when one is on the right path in life, the Universe will provide. She does.

I find a job working at an oil exploration company. For a woman in her early twenties, there isn't much excitement here, unless one finds satisfaction in monitoring black blips and grids on endless rolls of paper—which I don't—but it pays enough to support David and me.

On a Friday afternoon, a man I work with tells everyone that he has some friends in a band and they're going to be performing at a local bar. My friend, also a single mom, and I decide to check them out.

The cocky lead singer is a man named Dee. He sort of sticks his nose in the air when he refers to their brand of music as "rock'n'rollboogiewoogieandblues" as if it's something they invented. His band does a great rendition of J. Geils' songs, some Rolling Stones tunes, and some down-home, old-time, bare-bones blues. The music washes over me and through me like a dam busting loose. I can't sit still. I dance with anybody who asks me. I dance by myself. I dance all night long. Besides rock and roll, the blues is my favorite type of music. Oh yeah, mean, down and dirty, raw emotion blues. One of my dreams is to visit New Orleans someday.

"Caledonia, Caledonia, what makes your big head so hard?" The band spits into their microphones while rocking back and forth on the stage like lunatics. It makes me smile.

"Booze!" The bar patrons shout and raise their drink glasses. It shakes my bones. It releases my starved soul.

Dee has a face that looks tough and scarred, yet something warm and gentle moves behind his eyes. A draping mustache frames his lips, and it somehow coaxes a hint of tenderness from his face. Maybe it's corny, but I like it. I've never known anyone with a mustache like that before. And I love the way his light brown hair falls down the middle of his back in easy waves; I've just *got* to get my fingers all twisted up in it. Forget tall, dark, and handsome, long hair on men has always been a turn-on for me.

But why would the lead singer even look at me? I mean, the *lead* singer—the *personification* of cool. I've never been cool. Anyway, I didn't come in here looking for a man. Men can't be trusted. They use their cocks like weapons to hurt you.

But something between us clicks.

Dee and I can't get enough of one another. He makes me laugh. He makes me sing. He's gentle and patient and he teaches me that my body is not just a dumpster for a man's jizm, but that there exists a whole realm of joy I never knew about—orgasm after orgasm after orgasm. And most of all, he makes me feel safe.

We have so much fun together—dancing, making love under the sprinklers on the golf course one night, telling jokes, going to concerts, and playing music and more music.

Every now and then, his friends come over to his house and jam on guitar, keyboards, harmonica, or bass. Dee hooks up the mics to his PA system and everyone joins in. They play Uriah Heep, Starwood, and the Little River Band—songs I've never heard before. I love the sound of live music playing in the house, filling up the space between the walls, filling up the space within my heart.

Eventually we're married, but this time not in a church with walls, presided over by a priest. I don't see the point. The Catholic Church wants $500, personal details about my sex life, and mountains of paperwork to annul my first marriage. I don't have $500. And I don't think my sex life is any of their business. Why do they want to know anyway? I just can't get the picture out of my head of some old man sitting behind an ornate desk and getting off on reading about other people's sexual exploits. This thought makes me sick.

They're also encouraging me to respect God's laws and stay married to Rick, but I don't think these are really God's laws, but something devised by men in high ranks to control the rest of us. They know about the rape and beatings (although not all the sordid details they asked for in their reports) because I told them about that and yet, they refuse to condone an annulment.

So I'm choosing to willfully ignore the rules of the Church for the first time in my life. I know I'm not a bad person, nor am I turning my back on God. I'm a woman with a child who refuses to die at the hands of a cruel man.

And God isn't striking me down. On the contrary. Sunlight is shimmering on the soft currents of a small lake at the bottom of a hill and the sky is deep blue. The scent of the pine trees wafts clean and exhilarating on the warm summer breeze as Dee and I exchange our vows in a mountain park under a picnic shelter, the words "Lennon Lives" spray-painted in black graffiti over a massive stone fireplace.

CHAPTER 3

Beige

Who looks outside, dreams. Who looks inside, awakens.
—Carl Jung

Northern Colorado
November, 2002

The concept of time is often a relative thing. When I consider that it's been seventeen years since Dee and I got married, sometimes it feels like a hundred. Sometimes it feels like five. Either way, the clock keeps ticking. Our son David is 22 now, and has recently moved out into his first apartment with a friend, giving me a new set of worries to deal with. But we're not empty-nesters by any means. Dee and I had two more sons after we married—John and Michael—who are now 16 and 13 respectively, although sometimes I swear they act as if they're half that age. Like tonight. They're chasing one another around the house like wild animals, their shrieks competing with the sitcom that's blaring from the living room TV to which no one is paying attention.

"Gimme that remote or I'll pound you," yells John.

Michael giggles, and clutching the remote like a football, makes a beeline upstairs. He knows he's faster than his brother.

Even if John catches him, it's still worth the scene to get him really pissed off.

Why must they antagonize each other like this? Is it just a boy thing? Or do girls do this stuff too? I don't know, but it's been a long day and I've had enough. I let out a heavy sigh and turn to the sticky dinner plates and plastic cups stacked in my sink like a monument. I scrape the food off them as I do every night, and load the dishwasher—one of the chores that comes with my job of stay-at-home mom. The kitchen counters are cluttered with the remnants of dinner prep, kids' school papers, bills needing attention, various sundries such as AA batteries that no one knows whether are still good—nor do they want to take the time to find out—coupons, and a lone slice of chocolate cake I just hate to throw out.

The scents of garlic and spaghetti sauce linger in the air. It's only 7 P.M., but already dark outside as I look out the window, wishing it was spring instead of late fall. In Colorado, fall means having to wear warm clothes and shoes and socks. It means winter isn't far behind with its icy streets because the city snowplow never scrapes our cul-de-sac. I don't like the cold; sometimes I can't get warm no matter what I do. And I hate wearing shoes and socks; I'd rather go barefoot.

The boys' screaming rises to a point where I can't stand it anymore.

"Stop it!" I holler at them as I reach into the cabinet that holds all the Tupperware, searching for a lid and container that fit together. "Don't you two have homework to do?" Then, getting no response, "How 'bout you come help me clean up the kitchen?"

"Oh jeez, Mom, you're so boring." John at least makes an attempt to reply, then proceeds to tune me out. He's the master of selective hearing.

It's true, I'm boring, but I'm also too tired to press the issue.

Glancing out the window once more, the thought of the bite of the autumn air and its galvanizing scents stirs something in my soul—an elusive spiritual ache that has been a part of me for as long as I can remember. It makes me know that there is something critically important and obscure moving just above or below the pretense of everyday life—beyond what I see with my eyes. What is it? And why does it feel like it's very close right now? That's odd. I haven't thought about stuff like this in years.

In the past, its small spark would tease me like this, making itself known, then retreating to the sidelines for decades—scintillating like a silver sphere in the dark recesses of my basement—behind the dust-laden storage boxes containing my boys' outgrown baby clothes, my 45 and 33 1/3 record collection and scrapbooks filled with discarded dreams. I wanted to be an actor so I could see what it felt like to be somebody else. I wanted to taste the stars and the galaxies on my tongue; I wanted to be a wild, black stallion, my great mane whipping the wind as I ran, or a dolphin feeling the warm waters of the sea as they rushed past my sides. I wanted to climb to the top of Mount Everest, give all my possessions to the poor, especially the young girls who've been downtrodden like I was and are left to raise children without hope. I wanted to experience a sweat lodge and be indoctrinated into the Native American ways or a Buddhist monk and know all the holy secrets of life. I wanted to be a seagull and float high above the cliffs by the ocean or the little eddy that stirs beneath a waterfall—the place where only the smartest and biggest fish hide. I also wanted to know why some people were as rich as kings while so many in the world were starving. And I wanted to know about God. What if God wasn't what they'd always told me He was? What if there *wasn't* any God?

Whenever I allowed myself to pursue these notions—even just a little—it caused my heart to soar, as if there just might be an answer waiting for me somewhere out there, or maybe *in here*, if only I could figure out the meaning of what I was feeling. Because of this though, I've always believed that God isn't *out there*, God is inside of us. And I taught this to my kids, although I'd always felt a bit blasphemous saying it, as if it went against Catholicism, whose thick fingers were still entwined in my soul.

And yet, the moment my ambition would rise up to explore these kinds of thoughts, reality would stick its head in, usually in the form of Dee. He and I couldn't talk about stuff like that. He'd make it sound as if it were a character flaw in me he was obligated to tolerate. "You're always *searching* for something," he'd say. Then he'd go on to enlighten me to the fact that lofty thinking didn't pay the bills.

I wanted so badly to pursue what I needed, but I didn't. Dee wasn't going to understand anyway. Besides, it wasn't practical. I was raised to be practical. My dad was a design engineer and in our house, everything was always in order. And labeled. Neatly.

Maybe something was wrong with me for never being satisfied in a spiritual sense. Why couldn't I just accept things the way they were? In any case, it was just easier to drift along with the current, to shut up and function on autopilot. Mom who vacuumed. Mom who cooked. Mom who did the laundry. Mom the chauffeur.

That's what I'm supposed to do, right? Besides, moms aren't supposed to have needs. It's a funny thing about needs though; you can deny them all you want, but that doesn't make them go away.

Our dog Sam, a black and white lab-border collie mix, sits on the rug at my feet. She sniffs the floor and lets out a small whimper, hoping for a taste of pasta, then looks up and stares as if she worships me. I slip her a morsel and pat her bony, little head. At least I'm important to someone. Or maybe I'm kidding myself; maybe I look like one giant T-bone steak to her because I'm also "Mom who feeds the dog."

My life has a nice, smooth rhythm for the most part. I should be grateful for what I have and quit entertaining spiritual aspirations because it only makes me restless. What's there to get excited about anyway? That come Wednesday, pork roast will be on sale at the grocery store? I can hardly wait.

Reaching for the pan on the stove, I misjudge the distance and knock it to the floor, splashing spaghetti sauce all over my cream-colored T-shirt, the one Dee bought me in the "misses" section at JC Penney's. It's been doing its best to cover the rolls I've acquired on my sides over the past few years.

It's not that I don't notice the rolls or that I'm not bothered by them, or that attractive gray strings don't highlight my hair without any effort on my part; I just don't care. I've accepted my fate and don't see much point in doing anything about it—it's too much trouble. Besides, no one looks at 46-year-old Mrs. Frumpingtons who will never grow up to be black stallions or seagulls or Buddhist monks.

Wetting a paper towel, I attempt to clean up the mess.

"This red stain will never come out," I say more to myself than anyone.

Dee gets up from his perch at the computer, just around the corner in the other room and comes into the kitchen. His receding hairline is at this point, quite well established and he keeps his beard year round now because it helps hide the heaviness in his face. He hasn't heard a word I've said nor does he notice the mess all over the floor, which is typical.

"Hey, how'd you like to go back to Cabo?" His eyes light up as if he has just presented me with the opportunity of a lifetime.

Probably any normal wife would have jumped at the chance to go to Mexico for a much-needed vacation, but our first trip there wasn't pleasant.

"No way." I'm still trying to wash the spaghetti sauce out of my shirt. "Why would I want to go back to Mexico and get the shits for a week?"

Dee frowns the way he does when his feelings are hurt. "Well, I just won an auction for a trip to Cabo. We can use it any time within the next year."

I'm sure he means well, but he has incurred an expense we can't afford and he's done it without telling me. We've been together for so long now, it's kind of like this game we play—I move this way, he moves that—and I'm not sure either of us realizes when we're doing it. And God forbid that we ever *talk* about it, like the proverbial "rhinoceros in the living room."

"Good. Take a friend with you," I say. "I'm not going."

Wiping my hands on a towel, I give up on removing the stain.

Three years earlier, we took a trip to Cabo San Lucas, Mexico, our first vacation without the kids in seventeen years. We had the grandparents lined up to watch our three boys. It was going to be a dream vacation.

That year, as we arrived at our hotel on the beach, the bell-hop bowed and beckoned while opening the door of the shuttle van and saying, "Welcome to paradise," as if we had just landed on "Fantasy Island." Beyond the arched entryway to the hotel were green palm trees and carefully-maintained, white, brick walkways curving seductively toward the swimming pool with a swim-up bar overlooking the Pacific Ocean. On the walls were excruciatingly large, stuffed specimens of marlin, *dorado,* and sailfish, their glass eyes bulging. Fringed Mexican blankets in vibrant stripes of color hung on the opposite wall. The scent of the sea wafted through the foyer as fiesta music sprang from a mariachi trio. It was truly a dream for landlubbers like us.

But after a few days, we both got sick—"Montezuma's Revenge." No one warned us about other ways to contract this lovely condition besides "Don't drink the water." My digestive system protested violently against anything I attempted to put in it. All I wanted to do was stay close to the toilet in the hotel room.

It's bad enough being sick at home, but in a foreign country, it's much worse. Why would I want to go through that all over again? Besides, I'm not one of those prissy women who needs to be waited on hand and foot; I'm content with our usual vacations: a one-week annual trip to Steamboat Lake with the kids, camping under the pines in our second-hand, dinosaur RV (the one where we actually have to *add* lead when we pump the gas), and fishing from the aluminum boat we bought for $500 from the next-door neighbor.

Seeing he is getting nowhere with his argument, Dee lets the conversation drop. I guess he figures he has an entire year to convince me to go.

Several months later, Dee gets up from in front of his computer with more news.

"There's a big rock star who owns a bar down in Cabo," he announces. "He goes down there and plays once in a while."

Dee gave up his rock'n'rollboogiewoogieandblues lifestyle to settle down with me and raise a family. And although music was a big part of our lives and it still simmered in the background, we hadn't been to any concerts since our kids were born. Who could afford concerts when you needed to buy school supplies? But in our younger years, we went to as many live shows as we could. We saw performances from The Rolling Stones, Led Zeppelin, and The Eagles, to lesser-known acts such as April Wine and Tab Benoit and just about everything in between.

"He has his own website," Dee continues. "It says when he's gonna be there. How 'bout we go then?" He beckons to me to come and see for myself.

"Who is it?" Following him into the living room where the computer is set up, I trip over one of the boys' slippers and kick it aside.

"Sammy Hagar."

"Who?" I bend over to look at the screen. It doesn't mean anything to me.

"He used to be the lead singer of Van Halen."

I'd heard of Van Halen, but Dee and I didn't own any of their music.

"Sammy took over after David Lee Roth left the band." Dee shifts in his chair and suddenly sounds very well-versed on all things Van Halen, a talent I'd not previously seen in him. I'm not sure whether to be impressed or not.

"Oh. Never heard of him. I never listened to Van Halen."

I didn't listen to popular music in the '80s. I was too busy learning the words to Raffi's "There's a Spider on the Floor," and trying to survive as a single mom.

Dee shows me the website, which is full of color, pictures, and links to more information. I have to admit, it is kind of exciting.

"Yeah, so?" I don't get it.

He starts singing in his best Hagar-imitation voice. It's some song about not being able to drive the speed limit.

I look at him, puzzled, yet intrigued, not sure if I've ever heard that song before. No; I'm certain I haven't. "What else did he sing?"

Now he's crooning a song about riding a motorcycle. He's off-key, but he has a twinkle in his eye as he sings it and it makes me laugh.

"Nope. I'm sure I've never heard that one."

"You never heard of Montrose?"

"Nope."

"Ronnie Montrose?"

"No."

"Wow, you were sheltered. I have their records in that big box in the basement." But he never gets around to digging them out for me to hear.

In the meantime, Dee tells some friends that Mexico has some of the best sport fishing in the world and they want to meet us in Cabo. There isn't too much deep-sea fishing in Iowa or Colorado, and since our friends are going, combined with Dee's "we-can-go-and-see-a-rock-concert-while-we're-down-there" argument, I'm finally convinced to give Cabo one more try.

Life as I know it in "whiter shades of pale" is over.

CHAPTER 4

Nothing's What It Seems

Music is a special energy. It is of this world, but it also acts as a bridge to the spirit world. Music is our connection to the hidden world of the soul, the subconscious that lies beneath waking states. It becomes a universal language, a spirit language, with the power to change consciousness.
—Mickey Hart

October 8, 2003

As our plane lands at the small four-gate concourse in San Jose Del Cabo, I'm looking forward to lying on the beach, getting a tan, drinking margaritas, and doing some fishing. When we left home, it was 36 degrees out and looking like it might snow any minute, so when the flight attendants open the door of the plane, the hot and humid Mexican air hits me like a slap in the face. Even the air conditioning is getting a run for its money as it strives to comply, never quite accomplishing its task. The vents along the windows are now spewing steam. I suddenly and desperately wish I was wearing shorts, sandals, and a tank top instead of these heavy jeans and my long-sleeved shirt. And what am I supposed to do with the winter coat I brought along? Lug it all over Cabo?

Dee and I walk out onto the tarmac and follow the line of visitors into the building, then wait respectfully in line to go through customs, get our passports stamped, and claim our luggage on one of the three carousels. We then head to the exit where security guards with badges and machine guns stand around looking like they just can't wait for someone to cause trouble. I tell myself not to make eye contact with them—*machine guns in the airport?* What kind of place is this? I hope I don't accidentally do anything to draw attention to myself. *Just act normal,* I tell myself. Yeah well, normal and machine guns don't go together in my mind. I stay close to Dee. Real close.

Making our way into the *aeropuerto* lobby, we find hundreds of locals awaiting the opportunity to inundate unsuspecting tourists with their charm and their timeshares. I guess we must look like it's our first time here because it takes almost an hour before we're able to weed through them and find our way to the rental car building.

As I sit on a webbed chair waiting for Dee to do the paperwork, I become acutely aware of how different everything feels here—the vegetation and buildings seem to hug the ground as if they're timid bystanders. There are palm trees and cacti everywhere, so unlike the pines and aspen I'm used to. And there's a scent in the air I've never smelled before—heavy and pungent.

I watch the wind blow the parched earth into dirt-devils, and I feel like an intruder in a foreign land. I don't want anyone to notice me, so I attempt to blend in with the dirt and cacti while Dee does the talking. But he's not doing a very good job of it; he's having a hard time understanding what the locals are saying even though they're speaking English. Oh God, now he's assumed a fake Mexican accent and he's laughing in that forced way he only uses around other people. We must have flashing

neon signs on us: ¡*Turistas!* ¡*Gringos!* ¡*Estúpidas!* (stupid white
tourists.) I try to shrink smaller.

When I'm safely inside the car with Dee at last, and no one
is speaking Spanish—as long as we don't turn on the radio—
I relax a bit. But as we drive, we pass kids in parochial-school
uniforms waiting at dusty bus stops and people living in shacks
without walls. And then, there are huge hotels, one after the
other, with magnificent fountains and manicured lawns. There
doesn't seem to be any middle class here; you're either dirt poor
or movie-star rich.

The seat of the car suddenly feels a bit too hard on my butt.

After a while, our little car rounds a bend and before us lies
the Sea of Cortez, shimmering as if it has diamonds for waves.
Then the world-famous rock formation known as The Arch, the
pride of Cabo San Lucas, gives us a peek at her splendor, as if
she is the star of the show awaiting adulation. The sight of her
makes me gasp.

"Wow! Have you ever seen anything so beautiful?" I ask
Dee, forgetting all about my anxiety. I'm suddenly really glad I
allowed him to talk me into going on this trip. I fumble for my
camera.

This time, when we settle in our room, it truly is paradise—
bright, clean, and cheerful. We have a small balcony that overlooks the ocean, so I slide open the glass doors and step outside
to take in the view. As the warm breeze blows through my hair,
I close my eyes and feel my body melting in the heat, letting go
of its tension—the scent of the sea and the sound of the waves
are heaven. For the first time on this trip, I actually feel safe, as
if this is my sanctuary from machine guns and people speaking
Spanish and me trying to figure out how to fit in. I breathe deep
and just want to sink into the mood. I *need* to sink into the
mood; I've been way too uptight since we got here.

But the phone starts ringing. Our friends Shirley and Duane have been down here for several days now and can't wait to see us.

The four of us meet at the marina where hundreds of fishing boats and yachts are tied to the docks and the smell of dead fish is almost overpowering. Although it's late in the day, the sun is still angry-hot and I'm sweating like a pig, but it's such a relief to see familiar faces. It's been well over ten years since we've gotten together. This is going to be a great vacation, I know that now.

Shirley's straight, strawberry blonde hair is pulled into a ponytail, the fair skin on her nose and cheeks sunburned from three days in Cabo. She has always had a cavalier attitude, as if nothing fazes her, as if she knows something you don't, which she displays with squinting eyes and a sideways smile. Seeing her again brings back lots of great memories. When we were in high school, we used to "borrow" her mom's nasty Pall Mall's and smoke them upstairs in her bedroom while listening to "Day Tripper" by The Beatles and discussing the meaning of life. I thought my world was going to be carefree like that forever. And Shirley once paid me the greatest compliment I think I've ever received. She used something I wrote as the quote beneath her senior picture in the yearbook, something about finding your philosophies and then turning around and helping others find theirs, I think. When she showed it to me, it brought tears to my eyes. I never thought I could say anything that would matter so much to anyone else.

Duane looks the part of the consummate tourist—gray beard, glasses, sunburned skin, and a red, white, and green band on the brim of his straw hat that proudly proclaims "Cabo San Lucas." I wish he'd take off that silly hat; *I* don't want to look like a tourist.

Everyone wants to go fishing tomorrow, so the four of us proceed down the wooden pier to find a boat. As we walk, we pass groups of *Federales* patrolling the marina. They're dressed in camo gear and carrying guns as long as my leg. Why are they everywhere? And who are they supposed to be protecting? It certainly doesn't help my apprehension any.

Every few steps we take, vendors approach us, each with a special deal on everything from jewelry and brightly painted pottery to drugs or the opportunity to photograph a young boy with a large, green iguana wearing a small sombrero and vest, and perched atop the boy's shoulder. This one's smiling that lizard-y sort of smile that seems to say, "Get too close and lose ya nose, buddy. But go ahead, I dare ya."

"Five dollar, cheap," the boy taunts.

"No, gracias," we tell him.

Another vendor sells Shirley a beautiful, looping, silver necklace that soon turns her neck green. This is Mexico, I remind myself; nothing's what it seems.

A bit later, Shirley and I sit on a crumbling cement wall to chat while Dee and Duane fork over the down payment for tomorrow's boat into the hand of one of the *capitáns*. Everyone's excited now. Even me. I've never been deep-sea fishing before.

After a leisurely dinner of red snapper fresh-caught right out of the sea, and the most delicious homemade chips and guacamole I've ever tasted, Dee suggests we go over to Cabo Wabo, Sammy Hagar's club.

"I think Sammy's playing there tonight," he says, sounding all bright and cheery.

"Nah, we're too tired," Shirley groans. "We're going back to the room and go to bed. Besides, we have to get up at five in the morning if we're going fishing."

"Well, Pat, why don't you and I go then?" Dee asks.

How come he's so full of energy all of a sudden? Five in the morning sounds like torture after the long day we've already had. Besides, seeing some rock star isn't my number one priority. And according to Dee, there will be more shows later on in the week, so why do we need to rush right over there at this time of night?

"It's already ten o'clock, I'm sure it's too late to get in now," I tell him. "The show's probably already started."

"Well, let's just walk by. Maybe we can hear it from the sidewalk."

"What fun would that be? It'll just make me wish I was inside."

"Let's just go walk by." Dee reaches for my hand.

I want to say, "Can't we just go back to our room?" but I don't want to disappoint him; he's worked hard on planning this trip and he seems so happy right now.

Saying goodnight to our friends, we walk down the uneven sidewalks and narrow, primitive streets to Cabo Wabo. Most of the vendors have gone home for the evening, their tiny crevices of shops crammed side-by-side, some with brightly colored, cheesy decorations hanging above the peeling paint of the doorways. You have to watch where you step because there are broken beer bottles and trash all over the sidewalks. And Dee is walking so fast, I'm having a tough time keeping up.

Only the main streets are paved and the dust settles everywhere making even my teeth feel gritty. Once again, locals offering everything from drugs to ladies to timeshares approach us on every block.

"I can't believe that guy just asked me if I wanted a lady while I'm with you," Dee says with a little grin on his face.

I frown, pretending I'm offended. Then I realize how tired I am all over again.

We walk around the corner and in the middle of the block is the Cabo Wabo building, trying to look like it belongs here, yet standing out larger than I would have expected in this small town. Made of beige stucco, it sits farther back from the street than most buildings, the bright colors of its logo swinging on a wooden plank at the edge of the sidewalk alongside what appear to be ancient gears from the bowels of a ship. The midsection of the building rises in what looks to me like an enormous phallus. Oh, but I guess it's supposed to be a lighthouse. CABO WABO is aglow in neon letters, with one or two sections burned out.

The place is hopping. People stagger in and out, laughing, singing, and shouting. Security guards are in position on either side of the main wrought-iron gates, which stand wide open below the large, rounded entryway. Loud music gushes from the roof and from the doors. The atmosphere is lit like the neon signs. A video of a rock concert flashes on an outside wall like a small version of a drive-in movie while a smell of musty brine drifts on the breeze. Dee and I stand motionless on the edge of the sidewalk taking in the scene. With the setting of the sun, I swear the temperature has risen 30 degrees. Sweat is still pouring off me and at this point, I feel like I'm about to pass out. What are we supposed to do now? I look down at my feet as if to convince myself who and where I am—the blue sandals I'd bought for our vacation are standing on cobblestones in Mexico, but my eyes and ears are witnessing a full-blown rock concert on a screen like in America. It all feels so strange, like a collision between two worlds and neither side is being integrated into the other. *Nothing's what it seems*, I remind myself again. I have no idea how deeply that assessment is about to become forever etched in me before my feet ever touch American soil again.

A handsome young man in khaki shorts and a T-shirt slides up beside us, fans out his stash of tickets, and asks if we want to go to the show.

"How much?" I ask.

"Thirty dollar a piece."

But Dee's not so sure it's a good idea. He walks over to the front gates and says something to the security guards, then waves me over.

"We can get in for $20 each; come on."

He pays admission and the men at the gate wrap wristbands around our arms. We're in.

This place is like nothing I expected. It's a bar with the baddest attitude I have ever seen. The atmosphere overloads my senses. I see ... I hear ... I smell ... I taste ... I feel ... What do I focus on first?

There's an outdoor bar where people are sitting at rough-hewn, log chairs and tables with umbrellas. More people are leaning on the bar or congregating in small groups. This room has no roof. Walls are painted with crazy colors and crawling, dripping shapes as if done by some stoned, eccentric, professional artist. The bar boasts the biggest selection of tequilas I've ever seen. Cabo Wabo tequila however, is the main attraction, sitting in a small alcove like a shrine above the other bottles of liquor.

There are so many people milling about, it's difficult to squeeze through them to get to where the real action is, but somehow we manage. I'm holding Dee's hand so we don't get separated. The music grows louder with each step. And louder. Like passing through a stone castle entry with large, oak, tequila barrels stacked on each side, we enter the main bar, which is dark. People are crowded together facing a small stage along one wall. The room is painted with more acid-trippy affectations and rock and roll memorabilia.

At first, Dee and I just stand there in the doorway, taking it all in. There's a man in the spotlight onstage and he's singing his heart out. He's wearing red sunglasses, yellow print shorts, and a colorful T-shirt that proclaims "Cabo Wabo," and he has a tattoo of a cartoon bird on his right arm, just below the sleeve of his shirt. He's screaming into the microphone like a rock and roller who knows what he's doing and tossing his hair, which falls past his shoulders in corkscrew unkempt curls. The vibe in the air is shining, quivering like a mountain ready to explode. The drummer is mostly hidden behind the cymbals and drums and there's another guitar player, a handsome and slender black man, wearing a funny felt hat with bells, while a bleached-blonde, middle-aged keyboard player stands off to one side. The bass player is dressed in a black, glittery, Harley-Davidson T-shirt. She has thick, dark hair down to her butt.

Colored lights spray across the room as the crowd, a few steps below us, moves like a rolling ocean current. I'm not sure if I want to jump in or not; the ocean can soothe your soul but you can also drown in it.

When the song's over, the singer onstage starts chatting with the audience as if he has all the time in the world to finish the show. Maybe he does. This is Mexico. People aren't in a hurry down here; it's too hot. He's clearly in command—confident and cool. The long, shaggy goatee on his chin bounces as he talks. I find this rather amusing. I don't think I've ever seen anybody with a goatee like that before.

"I fuckin' *love* you guys," he coos. "I built this place for you, so you have a place where you can come and have a good time." He tells the audience he would do all his shows for free if they'd let him. He's working on that, he says.

I expect that since he's an entertainer, he's going to act like he's better than everyone else, but this guy's telling the crowd about how his wife doesn't always want to have sex when he does and that his mother loves to grow tomatoes in her little garden. I've never heard anything like it. I'm becoming even more intrigued.

Flashing perfect, white teeth with a huge grin, he then reaches out and shakes hands with people in the audience, takes a swig off his beer, then hands it to someone in the front row. He scribbles his name on everything they offer—photographs, album covers, hats, shirts, and bare breasts. Someone in the crowd tosses him a T-shirt and he takes off the one he's wearing and puts on the new one. He tells story after story; whether it's BS or not, I don't know, but everyone seems to love it. Then he takes a big swallow of straight tequila from the bright, blue bottle chilling in the bucket onstage. Tequila runs out of his mouth, down his chin, and spills all over the front of his shirt. Drenched in sweat and tequila, he reaches for a bottle of water and pours it over his head. Then, with his hair dripping wet and grinning like a naughty kid, he throws the water all over the people in the audience.

"There's only one rule here," he tells the adoring crowd. *"There ain't no fuckin' rules!"*

The audience erupts in cheers and lifts their drinks in a toast to their master—Sammy Hagar.

This isn't a concert, it's the biggest party I've ever seen. And though I'm on the sidelines, its magnetism is potent. My labels of "respectable Catholic girl" and "responsible mom" do their best to rein me in: Your world consists of propping the shampoo bottle upside down to get every last drop, timing the bills to reach the checking account after Dee deposits his paycheck, and setting a good example for your kids. *You don't belong here.*

But something else whispers from the depths of my being, "Oh, but I *like* it!"

Sammy puts his game face back on and becomes the rock star again; he cues up the next song and the room explodes. I can hardly believe the words that are coming out of his mouth, and he doesn't even hesitate or make any apologies—he's singing about pussy and smoking pot and getting blowjobs. But he also sings about God, love, his search for truth, and about never letting go of your dreams. How can anyone be so self-assured as to say things like that? I guess if you're rich, you can get away with anything. Or maybe he's just being himself. Either way, it makes me feel kind of empowered—there's no one here judging him and maybe there's no one here judging *me* either.

The band is so *on*: tight, professional, loud, pulsating energy, bursting into flames. I didn't expect such rock and roll expertise in the heart of Mexico. It's that paradox again.

A nearly tangible energy surges from the stage; there is nowhere you can go to escape it. The sound scoops me up and my body suddenly seems to have a mind of its own, as if it understands something beneath the music, craves it, and begins to move without the consent of my brain. This is what it must be like to do something you know is illegal but it feels so fine, you just can't stop yourself. And no one cares. I think my mouth must be hanging open. I have never before seen anything so raw, so honest, so electrifying. I look over at Dee as if to say, "Can you believe this?" and he's smiling the biggest smile I have ever seen on him, bobbing his head to the beat, his eyes shining.

"*Yeah!*" He shouts above the din and gives me a high five.

I feel warm, even on the inside.

When the concert ends and the crowd thins, we stay to have a few drinks and dance to the music of the house band. Tired? Who's tired? I can sleep when I'm dead! I can't remember a time I have ever had this much fun.

In the morning, when the alarm clock goes off at 5:00, neither of us hears it. By the time we wake up, we've already missed the boat.

Several days later, Dee and Duane charter another fishing boat for the day while Shirley and I go shopping. Shirley wants to purchase souvenirs to take home. As we walk up and down the narrow dirt streets and in and out of shops that line every nook and cranny, the sweltering heat reflecting off the sidewalks, combined with the high humidity, make it hard to want to move at all. It's not like the air-conditioned malls we're used to in America. And nothing in any of the shops has a price tag—it's what they can get out of you.

"Want to go into Cabo Wabo and have a drink?" I suggest, since it's only a few doors down, and I'm so hot and thirsty I can hardly stand it.

"Okay," Shirley agrees, explaining that her ankles are swelling from the heat and her stomach is angry from drinking the water.

There's no band onstage during the day, and there's a rope across the performance room of the building. We find a table in the outer bar, underneath a large umbrella. The waiter brings ice-cold margaritas with slices of fresh lime perched on the salted rims. A handful of people sit at other wooden tables while televisions mounted high up on the walls play a live football game in English. Speakers everywhere pump out rock music. In one corner, two hungover-looking gringos lean over a pool table, setting up the next shot.

Although at this time of day, the noise and party-like atmosphere are as subdued as the two hung-over gringos, I sense something here, something I've never felt in any structure, except perhaps an ancient stone church I'd attended as a child. There is spirit here, like the warm anticipation of seeing a favorite, long-lost relative. It floats down from the roofless room, slides like silk out of the walls, and drips like invisible honey mist from the dark, green umbrella into my soul, a sort of otherworldly peace amidst the clamor. Like a secret beneath a Mardi gras mask, it feels reminiscent of John Lennon's song "Imagine." I inhale of it deeply, as if taking intoxicating smoke into my lungs. I desperately need to cling to its presence just one moment more. A childlike smile comes to my lips.

"Oh, man," I tell Shirley. "I just *love* this place. I don't know why; it's just a bar!"

She peers at me from over her margarita glass, licking the salt from her lips.

"This is so weird," I continue. "I feel like I'm home, like I'm part of the walls or something; I feel like I could stay here forever."

Shirley's not impressed. "Yeah, well, whatever. Just finish your drink and let's get going."

But I want to sit here and savor the delicious, light green, frozen concoction in front of me. Most of all, I want to bask in this feeling I can't name. Something about this place is real and right in a way that's philosophical, as if my soul has slipped into a juxtaposition of the sacred and the physical. Even the walls scream with unabashed lucidity, "Be yourself. *Just fucking do it!* Let go of the feeling that it's wrong or that any part of you is wrong. There's a reason you're here . . . ."

CHAPTER 5

Reborn

Ouf!
Let me get out; I must have air.
It's incredible!
Marvelous!
It has so upset and bewildered me that when I wanted to put on my hat,
I couldn't find my head.
—Jean Francois Le Sueur in reference to Beethoven's Symphony No. 5

October 11, 2003

Dee slips out of bed in the darkness causing the lightweight, Aztec-patterned bedspread to fall to the floor.

I open one eye and look at the clock. It's 3 A.M. "What are you doing?"

"I'm going to Cabo Wabo to get in line for tickets to the show tonight. They go on sale at eight." He tugs on his beige, nylon shorts and scratches his beard.

Shirley and Duane went home yesterday, so I don't want Dee to be all alone. "You want me to go with you?"

"Go back to sleep; I'll take care of it."

Grabbing his rumpled shirt off the back of the chair, he heads for the door.

I allow myself to fall back to sleep, lulled by the sound of the ocean waves rising and falling against the beach accompanied by the sound of my thoughts. *It's so cool that Dee and I have something new in common after all these years. I love it.*

It's just a regular Cabo evening—scorching and humid, and tonight I'm wearing the new tank top I bought at Target for this trip. It's faded orange, with the outline of hibiscus flowers across the chest. I don't wear stuff like this at home; it never gets hot enough, plus I'm really too fat for it, but nobody here knows me anyway. In any case, the top doesn't look too bad on me and that makes me feel kind of special.

As Dee and I walk into Cabo Wabo, I'm looking forward to getting to see the whole show this time. I'm not aware that my life is about to change forever.

This is *the* concert. The moment in time that blows me to pieces and reassembles me in some sort of divine revelation.

After the show, as Dee and I leave the building and make our way down the dirt road to our rented car, he puts his arm around my shoulder.

I'm singing the song I just heard Sammy sing about dreams, or what I can remember of it, and I try again to explain that something mysterious and wonderful has just happened. I've never felt like this before—*alive!* And bursting at the seams.

"Something really *is* different about you." Dee's voice has a high pitch to it and his eyes are intent upon my face. He never looks at me like this, like he can't figure me out and he's not sure if he likes it or not, but he finds it rather amusing either way.

I feel a new passion stir inside of me as I look at my husband, and at the dusty atmosphere of tolerance in the small town of Cabo with its dank ocean scents, chickens with dried dirt caked on their feathers as they dart across the street in front of us, flapping their useless wings. It's as if only hours ago, everything was in shades of gray and now it's sizzling with color.

The evening and the tequila must have made me crazy. I feel utterly present in the moment and it is *magnificent*. I suddenly remember the reasons I fell in love with Dee twenty years ago. It's as if all those years are now reinforced in a new and profound manner, a soul-deep level of love, deeper than I ever thought possible—absolute, free, and full of joy. My body starts popping all over, exploding like internal fireworks, and dripping with a desire even stronger than when I'd first slept with him.

Before Dee has the door to our room unlocked, I've taken off my top and my bra and dropped them to the floor. The realization that I'm standing right out in the open—in public, completely naked from the waist up, drives me further into this burning frenzy. *This is not me! I LOVE it!* I grab Dee's hand and put it on my bare breast. I'm going to do him right here in the hall.

"Whoa!" He laughs and looks in both directions to make sure no one is coming. But I don't care. I'm already unzipping my shorts and sliding them down, then reaching for him as we fall into the room. The white stone walls, with bright blue, yellow, and orange waves painted on them, blend into the coverlet on the bed, as it slips like a trance into the sliding glass doors, opening to the sea, *becoming* the sea. I am swept into the essence of its power, its freedom, its pleasure. And I'm madly in love with my husband, unexpectedly transformed into a raging vortex of pure, uninhibited sex for the first time in my life.

The door is still wide open and we are barely inside the room but I'm all over him, sucking his tongue and his bottom lip, biting his neck and his left nipple. His skin tastes salty from sweat. I must have more. Now. I pull down his shorts, desperately needing to touch every inch of him. *Oh God, hurry up!* Pesos fall out of his pockets and make a ringing sound as they bounce across the floor, spinning like tops before coming to rest on the red, hand-woven Mexican rug.

I'm shaking all over and breathing hard as we fall to the floor like one, great toppling lodge pole pine. He tries to close the door, but I won't let him. It's not important—who cares? This is what's important—this—us—right now. If anybody wants to watch, let them.

The slate tile is cool and smooth against my back and the rug burns my butt and my elbows, but its tiny discomfort only fuels my excitement. We make love on every horizontal and vertical surface available—the floor, the end-tables, chairs, bathtub, the kitchen counter, the bed, against the wall, the mirror, the door. I need it all. I need everything he can do to me and I can do to myself and we can do together. And it's still not enough, although everything we do, I explode like it's the first time all over again. I'm dizzy with this feeling—higher than high. It's as if I've become intimately awakened to a psychedelic and spiritual realm of my body, a part of me I never knew existed. Is it possible other people have sex like this all the time? *Married* people? Why haven't I ever felt like this before? It reminds me of that song "Crush" by the Dave Matthews Band—this feels like that. Suddenly the little indent on Dee's lower back is the sexiest thing I have ever seen; I *must* have that too.

The large rug leads to the sliding door, which opens to a balcony overlooking the sea. And we roll all sweaty and sticky out the door and onto the balcony, never missing a beat.

Out here, the stars seem so close, I just know that if I were to stretch my arm out far enough, I could reach right up and pluck one from the sky and bring it into my heart. This thought makes the night seem even more magical; and combined with this profound connection with my husband, and the feeling of the warm Pacific breeze moving over my naked body, I'm experiencing a new form of heaven. It's so amazing, I can't contain myself. I close my eyes, my head falls back, and I begin to scream from somewhere deep in my soul.

I've never been loud during sex before—we have kids—*what if they heard me?* The ocean waves crash against the shore in intense bursts that seem to echo the sounds coming out of me.

"Jesus," Dee says. "I've never seen you like this." But he's not complaining.

I'm intoxicated with love, with life—an innocent initiate of a mighty power that has combined these things into something wonderful and all-encompassing that I've been starved of forever. And yet this feeling isn't due to a sense of lack so much as the result of overflowing emotion; it's as if all the frustrations of the world are being released through me, and those frustrations are being replaced with unspeakable and limitless joy almost faster than they can be released. Never before have I understood so profoundly what the physical sensations of the body have to do with love.

I used to think that sex, and my life, were things I had to endure in order to please others. So I repressed my sexuality as I repressed living life, as I repressed my dreams. It didn't occur to me until this very instant how much those ideas I had accepted as truths and my lack of confidence intertwined.

Now I see how beautiful it all is—my woman body, Dee's man body, and the incredible joy I'm feeling right now. How did something so divine get so screwed up?

I look over at Dee. His eyes are closed. Then his mouth drops open, and he begins to moan—a guttural animal sound, like that of a great beast in a dark forest.

My mind begins to churn out a million foreign thoughts. It feels as if I've just discovered that the sun rises in the south, when all along I believed it rose in the east. Is it possible that the way I feel right now is the result of that mystical moment I had in Sammy's bar a few hours ago? It's as if some spiritual tentacle, the pulse of something beyond the music has entered me and now connects me to its beat and the rock and roll of sex. But that experience wasn't just about sex. Maybe this great sex is a means to get my attention, a sort of code to unlock the door for the recognition of my *total* self because that out-of-body experience revealed to me what true joy is—the acceptance that I am already perfect the way I am, not better or worse than anyone else.

And now as I lie beside my husband on the balcony, our bodies heaving, the warm magic of the night also touches my mind and spirit, and it occurs to me that what I'm doing right now, without realizing it, is celebrating *all* of me. *This is the way life is supposed to be.* I'm happy—no, overjoyed; Dee's happy—his eyes are still closed and there's a slight smile on his lips.

Damn; this is huge. Where is all this profound insight coming from?

The next morning when I open my eyes, the first things I see are the pesos lying on the floor along with guitar picks and plastic wristbands from the concert. In my haze, I wonder, *did this really happen?*

As if I have no choice but to respond once again to my body, I'm out of bed and dancing. I twirl around the room with my arms outstretched. I am a 6-year-old in a field of daisies.

"Dee, I love you *so* much." I run back into the bedroom to squeeze him. "Oh my God, and I love me! I love my life!"

Of course, none of this makes any sense. I went to a concert yesterday, a respectable wife and mom and now I'm a whore in the bedroom and an innocent child in the living room? I must have had too much to drink last night. But if that's true, how come I'm dancing and not puking?

All the while I pack my bags to get ready to go home, I can't stop thinking about my amazing transformation. And when the attendants pass out snacks on the plane, thinking about whether I want soda or peanuts feels like such a waste of energy. Even if I live to be 100 years old, I don't think there would be enough time to process what has happened.

The airplane's seatbelt feels like it's trying to bring me back down to my known sense of reality—that I'm being restrained—in more ways than one, so I force myself to look out the window to take my mind off of it. Everything looks so different from up here; you can see things you'd never be able to see on the ground, like dry, sandy riverbeds that stretch for miles, and plots of land that look like patchwork quilts. It seems impossible that I'm floating in this world that only birds used to know, like I'm witnessing one of the secrets of creation. It also seems impossible that I had such a bizarre experience yesterday and now I feel like I've been baptized into a world of joy.

But how could a spiritual encounter take place during a rock concert? Weren't things like that supposed to happen through religious rituals? And yet, I've seen glimpses of God in unexpected places before—like the scent of the pine trees after a summer rain, or when I first looked into the cloudy blue eyes of my newborn babies and held their little wet bodies in my arms and I just couldn't get over the fact that that tiny life came from me—so maybe this isn't that much different.

The clouds look like dollops of whipped cream and the blue sky above them appears to go on forever, like my thoughts. Maybe this extraordinary event has been incubating in my soul since I was a kid. Back then, although I tried really hard, I didn't feel God's presence in Catholicism so, very gingerly, I started peering over the fence to see what else was out there. When I was 11, I stumbled upon Native American philosophy at the public library. The books had pictures of feathers on them, and paintings of colorful shields, the sun, and moon. They contained stories of totems and lessons from the buffalo and eagle, stories of truth and wisdom gleaned from nature.

Up until that point, everything I read had been conveniently censored—picture books and stories that told me what to think. I wasn't used to provocative material. I wasn't sure I *should* be reading that stuff. I kept reading. I couldn't stop myself. And as I did, something familiar emerged from between the lines on those mothy-yellow pages and whispered into my heart, "*Yesss* . . . ." It rose up like the forbidden serpent and bounced off the thick, dark, wooden bookshelves and the aisles of all those books hissing like a wicked pleasure: "*Ssssssssin.*"

What I'd been taught in Catholic school didn't touch on ideas like that. But a voice from within those Native American books hinted that their teachings just might offer insight into the spiritual questions my religion hadn't been able to answer for me, questions I wasn't quite sure how to articulate. For one thing, they didn't tell me I was a worthless sinner; they said that life is a circle, and we are the same as the animals, the plants, the wind, the oceans, the rivers and streams, the heavens, the earth—they are our brothers, our sisters, our mothers and fathers and we must respect each of these things and care for them. It all made sense.

In addition to that, my dad worked with some really nice people, but they were atheists. I couldn't understand how such wonderful people were doomed to hell after they died just because they didn't believe in God. And what about the isolated tribes in New Guinea? How was it fair that they were damned to suffer for eternity just because they had the misfortune of being born in a place that had never heard of Jesus?

Nobody I knew seemed to have an answer to these questions that would satisfy me. All they did was parrot what somebody else had said. And I couldn't figure out how there could be so many different theories, such as the Native American teachings in those books, and every one of them was simply *wrong*. Who decided these things anyway? That A was right and B was wrong? What if they were *all* right? What if they were *all* wrong?

My parents were hardworking, honest people who believed in God, went to church faithfully, and lived by the Ten Commandments and the laws of the Church. They believed in the saints; they quoted the Bible. I wondered about things. And yet, I worried that God would send me to hell for looking in other directions for spiritual gratification, so I kept one foot in the Catholic faith and stepped out with the other—but only with my big toe. Catholicism did teach me to be a good person, however, but for the wrong reasons—out of fear of God punishing me, not out of love and acceptance—which is the way I think it *should* be.

Now I feel like I'm being pulled into a new understanding of what God is, not only by one big toe, but by my entire being. Even the uninhibited sex I just had with Dee seemed somehow connected to God, as if it were an extension of the same ecstasy I felt during the concert, the ecstasy that can only come from a personal relationship with something divine. It was comprised of nothing but pure joy and universal love. At that moment, I recognized within myself a sound I'd been longing to hear, a taste my tongue could not forget for a thousand years, a touch that knew every inch of me, a love incited and ultimately absorbed back into itself by something supernatural. And I needed to absorb it with every part of me—open my ears, my mouth, my legs to take it in, surrendering to the great wonder unleashed inside of me and follow its physical manifestation to its depths where it bridged into the realm of spirit.

Where is all this coming from, really? I don't have thoughts like this! This is way too heavy to be coming from my housewife-encrusted brain.

But the thoughts keep pouring out.

I look around at all the people on the plane tucked into their assigned seats and I wonder how many of them have ever experienced anything like this. None, I'll bet. Maybe if I think about it long enough and hard enough, I can find a reasonable explanation or at least a poetic explanation. I'll take either.

Instead of worrying about how the tiny space is making my knees ache, I lean my head back on the seat and allow my mind to dive in even deeper. It's been starved for philosophical meandering for decades anyway, and now it's like an escaping prisoner....

Something intangible came to me last night. Not something Sammy caused or was aware of, but something else. It was as if a force beyond human beings had a hand in this, some sort of positive light or higher power. Something used him to speak to me, and I understood its message on a fundamental level. But what? And why? There's no reason this should have happened to *me*. I'm not a fan of Sammy's; I barely even know who he is. Not only that, but nobody goes to rock concerts looking for spiritual encounters. They go for the music and, for some reason, I just got more. I trusted it instinctively, allowed it to lift me wherever it wanted to take me, above the physical, through Sammy, through all of them in the room, and through the music. But this music was not the mere cranking out of tunes by musicians, it was something beyond notes, beats, and lyrics, even beyond a connection to the performance of it.

John Lennon once said,

> When the real music comes to me—"the music of the spheres, the music that surpasseth understanding"—that has nothing to do with me, 'cause I'm just the channel. The only joy for me is for it to be given to me, and to transcribe it like a medium.... Those moments are what I live for.

He knew. He understood.

As I watch the simulation on the video screen of the plane crossing the states back to Colorado, I wonder how it's possible that I suddenly know all this. I don't know; I just do. The music created an opening inside of me, and when it did, the force that came through that opening entered a place where rudimentary feelings dwell—sex, emotion, spirituality—dissolving mortal limitations. It was as if something reached its hand down my throat, into the deepest part of me, and pulled my soul out— soft, wet, and still steaming. And then it took me inside of it, beginning with an audible wave that reverberated throughout my body, mind, and spirit, merging with the beating of my heart, and *revealing* me. It provided a sanctuary where there was no reservation or concern about consequences, nothing but the simple act of living life for its own sake without the attachment of thought.

I feel like I'm sinking into a part of my mind I didn't know I had. I'm not even the least bit distracted by the fact that it's starting to get cold on the plane and my tank top and shorts are no longer appropriate traveling attire.

Before long, I feel the wheels of the plane touch the runway; we're almost home. I'll have to continue my self-interrogation later.

When we get to the car, it's a relief to plant myself in the passenger seat, crank up the heat, and let Dee take us the final hour's drive home. I swear it's 30 degrees out.

As we drive, the sun is setting and the air grows even colder. I dig out my heavy green jacket from the bottom of my suitcase as Dee unwraps one of Sammy's CDs that he'd bought at Cabo Wabo and inserts it into the CD player.

Watching the miles roll by out the window, I notice that everything is dry and shriveled up, bracing itself for winter. Road signs are in English again, passing cars all have Colorado plates, and the terrain is flat with the guardianship of the Rocky Mountains now slipping into a deep, purple haze to the west. The air smells clean, with the noticeable absence of the scent of the sea.

It's all familiar again, but not—it's all different, as if I'd stepped sideways into another definition of reality and now nothing is the same.

Rounding the turn onto the next long stretch of highway, Dee points to something in the sky.

"Look at that huge eagle," he says. "That's really cool."

"Yup, I see it."

Right then, a song about flying eagles blasts out of the speakers.

CHAPTER 6

Awakening the Sleeping Giant

To reach the top of the highest peak, you must first believe that you can.
—Source Unknown

January, 2004

My entire world has changed. I've lost 30 pounds in three months and I haven't done anything different. I never thought I'd look like this again. I figured I was doomed to rolls and flab and a saggy butt. And now that I've been given a new lease on a better body, I've decided to celebrate it. I'm stepping out of my socially appointed label of "middle-aged woman." I'm not a label. I'm much more. I am me. So I've been buying tight jeans and form-fitting tops, and lingerie with lace and strings—and oh my gosh, I feel sexy. I'm also celebrating *that* part of me—sex—and exploring new things in that realm too, things I've never done before, *and it feels so fine!* Dee probably thinks he's died and gone to heaven. He has a little spring in his step lately.

Neither of us can figure out what's gotten in to me. It's amazing when you realize there's a difference between merely getting through each day and *really living!* Where has this feeling been hiding all my life? I feel so, and I hate to use this word, but—beautiful. My whole life, I've never felt beautiful.

Other people are noticing the difference too. Last Thursday at the grocery store the clerk told me, "I love your new look," as she rang me up. She's never remarked about my appearance before.

Even my neighbor went out of her way to tell me, "When I saw you walking down the street the other day, I didn't recognize you, Pat. I thought you were somebody new who just moved in!"

I *am* somebody new. I feel like there's sunshine bursting out my pores. And it seems like everywhere I go, people notice it. Sometimes they even ask me what my secret is. I simply tell them, "Being happy."

Happy? What is "happy?" I don't think I've ever really known what that means. In my life, I've felt relieved, comfortable, secure, and pleased, but never really happy. And I guess I never even allowed myself to consider that I *wasn't* happy. Although I knew deep down that something was missing, I filled up the holes with pleasing my family. Not that that was a bad thing, but I think I must have lost part of me in the process. I just never knew it.

And now I'm so full of emotion, I can hardly contain myself. It hurts so fine that I have to get it *out* of me—no, hold onto it—oh, which one? Both. God, I'm on fire!

This morning I can't get Dee and the boys off to work and school fast enough for me to be able to sit down at the kitchen table so I can write all this down.

I've been writing almost as long as I can remember. I can't look at a mountain and not wonder what it would feel like to be a mountain through all the seasons and years it's stood there. I see a mown cornfield at dusk, the shadows of its eight-inch stalks making a pattern on the crisp, shallow snow and it moves me, creates emotion in me that's hard to explain, yet screams for release. So I write about it. I have to. Sometimes I show my poems and musings to my friends or my mom, but that's about it.

And today, I really shouldn't take the time to write; I need to get started on my annual "post-holiday" reorganization of the basement. I still have all the Christmas stuff to put away and I'm getting tired of tripping over all the boxes that are standing like redwood trees all over the family room. There's so much stuff to sort through, it's going to take me forever. I'll just give myself a few minutes of writing time while I have some coffee and wake up—until say . . . nine o'clock—then I'll get to tackling the basement stuff.

I push aside the stained floral placemats and salt and pepper shakers and brush the crumbs off the table from the boys' breakfast cereal, then I open my notebook to the next blank page. My hand is having a tough time keeping up with what's pouring out of my heart:

> Maybe I'm lying to myself and refusing to see reality, but does it really matter? In the meantime, can't I ride this high for as long and as far as it takes me? And listening to the music transports me back to the warmth and belonging, being my true self, letting go of all the bullshit and loving Dee. Is there something wrong with that? I'm dying to understand what happened and how, so that I can get this back after it leaves me. For all the ridiculous wording here, for all the childish appearance of it all, that's great, right—good vibes, good sounds, cool rock stars. A good time was had by all. So why am I so changed, so deeply affected?

Maybe it will always be with me now forever. Maybe I need to quit thinking that it will go away. And that's the core of it, right? Quit thinking negatively. Instead of telling myself I'm being "realistic" not to get my hopes up and risk getting hurt, perhaps I need to *get* my hopes up, think positively, and if it doesn't come to fruition, just shrug and say I tried. It all sounds so nice now and so easy. Will it last? I'm going to try to make it last. Oh please, Lord, help me make it last. My life is so much more fun.

Can this really be me? I'm infused with an energy I've never known before. I feel like I have a purpose, even though I don't know what it is. Maybe it was just the tequila I had that night, or the combination of what I perceived as the most awesome music I've ever heard *and* the tequila. But I've been to more rock concerts than I can count, and nothing like this has ever happened to me.

When I look up at the clock above the fireplace, I see that it's well past one. I didn't even notice how fast the time has gone. And I probably still wouldn't have noticed, except the words are getting all jumbled in my head and my brain is starting to fade—I have to get something to eat.

Okay, I tell myself, after I finish my lunch, I'll get to the basement stuff. I've been writing long enough.

Fixing myself a peanut butter sandwich, I grab a can of Diet Pepsi and sit back down at the table. But instead of finding a stopping place, my thoughts keep on going—I am so frigging *happy!*

I wonder if the town of Cabo San Lucas had something to do with my magical transformation. While I was there, specifically in Cabo Wabo, I felt I could be the person I was meant to be. I could do anything I wanted, say anything I wanted, dress however I wanted, and there were no judgments against me. No one cared. In that environment, I felt uninhibited and free—an almost tangible feeling that heaven is here and now in one's state of mind. A dream? Perhaps, yet somehow I feel sure that it's now within my reach.

By this time, I'm writing again. I can't seem to stop myself. This is the stuff that's important, not the basement—who cares if I have to trip over boxes for one more day?

Each time I think about the Cabo experience, more is revealed to me—as if that moment contained little seeds that were planted inside me and are now growing roots in every direction at an exponential rate and without any effort on my part. *If I can just hurry up and write them down before they escape me,* the kinds of deep thoughts I haven't allowed myself in decades—about God and relationships and why there's so much anger and misunderstanding between people—and why does money rule the world? Because Dee and I fight about that all the time. He says, "That's the way it is," and I say, "That's not the way it *should* be. *People* should come first."

And then there's the interconnectedness of all things, people, and worlds that I saw that night. When I try to describe it, its meaning goes in a hundred different directions. And yet, they all tie into one another, like how my yearning for more out of life led me to Native American philosophy as a kid. The messages felt so right, I just *had* to know more. That eventually led to my taking up tae kwon do as an adult and then studying philosophy. I was like a starved shark in a school of minnows—devouring everything in sight and never feeling satisfied.

And now Cabo and a rock concert? If something like this can happen through a rock concert, it can happen anywhere, right? The possibilities are endless! I believe this because when I think back on it, over the years, I've been getting the same message from a lot of different sources, so it must be right. One of my all-time favorite books is *The Gospel According to Zen,* by Robert Sohl and Audrey Carr, because it demonstrates how truth is truth in any form. And that's how I've always recognized truth—when it comes at me in different forms and feels warm in my heart. Like now, all of this is taking me down the same path I've been on so many times before—a desire for truth and meaning in my life—so I know I must be onto something.

And I no longer doubt that God exists. I felt Him/Her/ It with every cell in my body and mind that night. And what amazes me is that I don't feel like I need to convince anyone else about this either because it's *my* reality. It doesn't matter if anyone believes me. I know what I saw. I know what I felt. Under similar circumstances, someone else might experience something completely different, and that's how it should be. We all have to find our own way.

Before I know it, my sons are home from school. *Did I just lose an entire day?* Oh man, I haven't even brushed my teeth or changed into my clothes. I haven't gotten anything done and I don't have dinner planned yet either. This isn't like me. I usually make myself work hard every day—that way I feel like I've earned the right to stay home with my kids and I'm not taking advantage of the situation. But Dee would rather I was out there earning a paycheck and he reminds me of this constantly, so I bust my butt everyday to keep busy, and I find creative ways to save money, like cutting the drier sheets in half and shopping at the thrift store. And we're doing okay. We don't have a lot, but we get by. The best part is—we have some really great kids.

Michael, the youngest, walks in the front door and immediately heads upstairs to his room. He's like the cartoon character, the Tasmanian devil—spinning around and breaking off little chunks of whatever he happens to bump against on his way by. He must be anxious to get his homework done. Yeah, right. He probably bought some new video game he doesn't want me to know about.

"Hi Mom!" he calls over his shoulder.

"Hi! How was your day?"

Too late, he's already out of earshot. His normal response would be "Daylike!" I swear he needs to be a comedian some-day. Sometimes he says things that are so quick-witted and off-the-wall that it shocks me, and then he has me doubled over because I'm laughing so hard. I wish I could be more like that. I can't think that fast. I have to process things first.

John, our middle son, comes into the kitchen and drops his backpack onto the kitchen chair with a heavy thud. "Hey Mom, did you—*are you still in your jammies?*"

"Yeah, I was writing all day and the time just flew by."

"O-kay. Did I hear you listening to Alice in Chains yes-terday?" He sounds impressed. This isn't like John—to be impressed with his mom. And it's not like him to go out of his way to talk to me either, other than to find out what we're hav-ing for dinner. It's a teenager thing—interacting with parents isn't cool.

"Yeah, I guess so." I give him a hug. He still lets me hug him though, so I take all I can get.

"Wait'll my friends hear that my mom listens to Alice in Chains. They're gonna think that's awesome! You wanna hear some more cool music?" he asks, unzipping his backpack.

He's really talking to me! I'm so shocked that I skip right over it as if it's not happening, and start right in with the "mom stuff." I can't help it. I've been doing this for so long now, it's become involuntary. "Don't you think you should practice your viola before you start listening to music? Your lesson's tomor-row."

"I know, but you have to hear this." He puts the CD on and cranks up the volume. "Well?" He's standing in the middle of the living room, his eyes searching my face for even the slightest hint of approval. It's then that I realize he's already much taller than his older brother and showing signs of inheriting Dee's build and stance. How come I never noticed it before? But he still has that beautiful face—innocent and calm, with eyes that instantly make you feel at ease, reflecting a gentle soul with the power to change the world if he chooses.

Only months ago I would have said, "Turn that down. It's nothing but noise. How can you listen to that crap?" Then I would have cringed, recognizing that I was sounding exactly like my mother. Instead, the hard-driving beat is like a sword to my heart. It cuts me to the quick and my soul bleeds something that feels so amazing, it surprises me. "Yeah, I like it a lot. Who is it?"

"Wow, you *do?* I can't believe it! Metallica." He scrunches up his face and pretends to play guitar while he hums along with the melody. Then he grins and adjusts his T-shirt, "WEEREZ," after the band Weezer. It's the same shirt his big brother David has.

As Metallica's music plays, its throbbing, prominent bass, sledgehammer drums, and dark chords are saying something we haven't been able to say to one another—something necessary and sacred. Is it just the music? No, it's more than that. It's dissolving the barriers between us. Why has Metallica's music never sounded like this to me before? What's different? The music hasn't changed. *I've* changed. I seem to be changing in a lot of ways. Wow, I wonder what *really* happened to me in Cabo? It's like I'm a totally different person, and by the way John's looking at me, I think he feels it too.

I sit down next to him on the floor, and we're perusing all his CDs as if we're peers who have just met and are delighted to discover that we have so much in common. It's so exciting that I forget all about what to fix for dinner, or that there's the basement stuff to tend to, because now my son and I are actually *talking*—about life and things that matter to him. I didn't know how politically-minded my own son was until now. Here, clearly, is a young man with his own opinion, a young man whose intelligence I'd overlooked because I'd been too busy trying to figure out how I was going to feed a family of five on one salary or afford to take the dog to the vet.

It's tough being a teenager, I know, but it's also tough being a parent to teenagers—they're trying to establish their identities, you're trying to guide them so they don't fall too hard on their faces when they do the same stupid stuff you did when you were that age. And now none of that matters. We're equal.

A heaviness sneaks into me. How do I go from "mom" to "friend"? Especially since I want to reach out and grab hold of his childhood, his need for me—my need to be needed—and hang onto it just a little while longer. It's been my job for over twenty years now; it's who I am—his mom, David's mom, Michael's mom. Why didn't I get down on the floor and color in coloring books with him more often when he was little? Why didn't I drop what I was doing, go out into the backyard, and throw the baseball with him instead of making sure I had all the ironing done and dinner on the table at six every night?

As the music surrounds and engulfs us, I sense something powerful brewing. It's something even more important than the fact that my son and I are discovering how much we really like each other; this feels like it's something that's about to affect the entire planet. I can almost see it, as if it's a vaporous and swirling apparition. And I swear it's whispering these thoughts into my mind because when I consider the sheer immensity of it all, I notice that my skin feels charged like the atmosphere before a thunderstorm hits.

Yep, something big is definitely coming.

CHAPTER 7

Baja Rock (Trans)Formations

All the music I write is a search for myself.
—Bruce Hornsby

January, 2004

It's going to make me sound like a groupie, I'm sure. But I *have* to tell Sammy Hagar—THE Sammy Hagar—famous rock star, big hair, big lights, big world—about what's happening to me. Whether or not he cares, whether or not he hears, I still *have* to tell him. So I sit down at my small, wooden desk, the one that's crammed into the corner of the bedroom, and with pen in hand, I scribble into my spiral notebook: "Dear Sammy, you changed my life. You showed me a joy I didn't know was possible to feel in this lifetime . . . ."

I try to talk myself out of it for the hundredth time. This is stupid. He's not going to care what I say. I'm one in a million fans all over the world. Am I really even *considering* doing this? He's a big star—how can I just expose my soul to someone who has the power to crush me? It'd be like in the pirate movies— voluntarily walking the plank, jumping off the end into the dark swirling waters below, and naively *believing I'm going to survive!*

"You're just a common housewife—grow the hell up, woman," I scold myself.

I shove the letter back into the desk drawer. I'm such an idiot; I don't write letters to celebrities.

Then while I'm shopping, I come across a DVD of one of Sammy's concerts. In the video, Sammy says that his club in Cabo is a place where people can relax and just be themselves. He says he'd be honored if someone had the best time of their life because of his music, something they'd never forget. The way he says it makes me think, *how strange that I came across this video at the exact time I was thinking about telling him this very thing.* And as I'm thinking this, something warm and comforting seems to come over me, as if to say, "Do it."

I wonder if my stumbling upon this video is a sign that I should send him my letter. Nah, it's just a coincidence. I'm always looking too deep into things. At least that's what Dee would say. Either way, it's a bit odd and maybe I should listen to what my heart is telling me—maybe Sammy *would* want to hear about my experience. Maybe he'd get off on it.

I pull up the file on my computer. After reading what I've written, it doesn't seem like I'll ever be able to make it sound right. How does one write a letter to a rock star? Dear Sir? Dear Mister? Dear "I'm-not-worthy-to-address-you-but-here-goes-anyway," reminiscent of *Wayne's World*? I'd also been writing a poem about all of this—for me, that is—when something told me that Sammy might like it too, so now it's become an even bigger project. My poem has to be memorable. It has to be fantastic. How can I write something fantastic? Oh, how do I get myself into these impossible circumstances? I guess it's because being such a sensitive person, I feel things deeply and passionately. And when I embrace that passion, it consumes me to the point where I sometimes lose myself in it—like I've been doing with my writing lately. Whether this is a good thing or not remains to be seen. I guess it's a good thing if you're an artist, but maybe not such a good thing if you're a wife and mom trying to function on a daily basis. Occasionally, though, it's necessary for someone to pull me out of my self-imposed prison of trying to grasp ideals and spiritual sanctions that always seem beyond my reach. I'll never give up on my own. It's like a stand-off between God and me.

Anyway, there's no rush. I have all the time in the world to finish my letter—to get it right.

Months pass. When I come into the kitchen first thing in the morning, I notice two bowls with dried ice-cream in them and several cups sitting in the sink. Why can't they just rinse them and put them in the dishwasher? My kids are plenty old enough to do that. I sigh. Maybe I should turn around and go right back upstairs to bed.

Get your letter out today, comes a thought.

Ah, I'm still half asleep, so I ignore it.

A few hours later, I return to the computer to continue working on my letter and my poem for Sammy. I'm typing away when another thought comes: It needs to go in the mail *today*. It can't wait until tomorrow.

No, I still have a lot of work to do on it.

I suddenly feel nervous and my heart is beating fast. What is there to be nervous about? Something is pushing me—hurry up, hurry up. I'm almost afraid to disregard it. I don't understand where any of this comes from, so I probably shouldn't piss it off.

Okay, okay.

All morning I attempt to finish what I want to say, because of my personal deadline. When I get to the point where I don't feel I can improve it—today at least—and my mind is reeling with too many words, I look over the poem one last time. It's just going to have to be good enough. I can't think anymore.

Baja Rock (trans)Formations

*The sea
pounds her rocks,
licks white
sand, sprays veils into the sky
as she arches, relinquishing fragments of herself
like an afterthought
until she is no more.*

*The inside world is dust and cobblestones,
walls without ceilings oozing sweat,
blue
tongues, naked breasts,
neon lights
and yellow, green, red
zebra-striped darkness.*

*I don't expect to find thunder here,
or music—a hard
muscle, a gloved boxer;
but its vulgar-sweetness
swallows me warm;
my eyes can't resist
intoxication.*

*Three-piece suits lean on the back bar
and wag starched fingers:
"Don't drink this poison!" Too late.
It connects
with a left hook,
knocks the wind out of me;
hurts so fine—*

The man in blonde curls
detonates the guitar like fireworks;
his words deliciously reckless passion and poetry, white
water bursting the dam.

Self-control slips
through my fingers;
replaced by the colors
of secrets
I never knew were missing. I am

music, voice,
ecstasy, heaven.
higher and higher,
dreaming....

Oh God, am I drunk!
Reality beyond dimension
bears my soul and forever
begins.

My hands are shaking as I drop the envelope in the outgoing mail slot at the post office. Why am I reacting like this? It feels like I'm about to interview for the job of a lifetime—that's how nervous I am. But it doesn't make sense. I'm just mailing a letter to a person I don't even know, something he may never see, so what's the big deal?

I'm vacuuming the living room. I don't mind this job too much; at least I'm moving and getting a bit of exercise. There are worse household chores, like cleaning the bathroom. As I work, out of nowhere, something touches me—a voiceless voice, the air suddenly swollen and thick as if someone's in the room with me, kind of like how you can feel when someone's staring at you from across the room. I turn around to see who snuck up on me, but no one's there. It must be my imagination. Back to work. I swear the couch gets heavier every time I try to move it. And then . . . a voice whispers in my ear, only it isn't actually a sound, but a feeling with the hint of some kind of music in the background—something familiar that I've never heard before—sort of Middle Eastern, maybe? But I don't listen to music like that.

I turn off the vacuum. What's going on? Nothing seems out of place. My dog is outside basking in the sunshine. The boys left for school hours ago and Dee told me this morning that he was going to Denver for a meeting; he wouldn't be home until late. That's probably a good thing because if Dee were to walk in right now, he probably wouldn't even listen to my story. He'd tell me I was imagining things, make a circle next to his face with his index finger, the sign for "cuckoo," and roll his eyes. He might even half-convince me that I *am* crazy. He does that sometimes and since I'm so open minded, I start to believe it. That's even harder on me because I don't know if he has a valid point or if I should trust my gut. Then he'd tell me I should be out looking for a job instead of making up goofy tales because obviously I have too much time on my hands.

But I'm not making this up, *I don't think.*

As I stand here waiting to see if anything more is going to happen, my whole body suddenly feels warm, as if hot syrup is being poured into my brain and flowing slowly down, circulating through my veins and moving down to my feet. Then it's gone. I wait for a few minutes to see if it's going to happen again but nothing more comes, so I switch the vacuum back on and finish my job.

That was odd, I tell myself. But no, I'm just being silly.

A little while later, while I'm taking a shower, that odd feeling comes again, like a heavy, wool blanket covering the whole room. It's really strong.

My mind begins to argue with itself.

"This feeling you keep getting is trying to tell you something—Sammy's reading your letter and he is deeply moved. He's going to answer you," the intuitive side of me says.

But the other part of my mind is an expert at playing devil's advocate. "That's preposterous. You can't expect anything from sending that letter. You'd be a fool to. You're not special. He's a superstar. Just because something is important to you doesn't mean it means anything to anyone else. You need to get a life."

"I feel like I know him . . . ."

"Yeah well, so do a lot of people. It's just his personality. Sheesh, you're so stupid sometimes."

"Believe me, I hear you loud and clear, but the experience I had in Cabo keeps nagging me like a little kid tugging on her momma's sleeve. Did I just imagine it? Fuck no! I felt it with every fiber of my being, every cell."

"So then, just 'cause you felt it doesn't mean it has any significance."

"Then how else can I explain this change in me? And why did I feel compelled to reach out and tell my story to the person it came through, risking no acknowledgment, ridicule, or whatever? It's not that I *wanted* to do it. I *had* to. Like I had no choice."

This thought makes me uncomfortable, so I stand under the running water and let its warmth flow over my head and down my back for a few minutes. There's something really weird happening here and I'm not so sure it's just about Sammy Hagar; it feels like it's bigger than him.

A few minutes later, when I'm slipping into my jeans, that voiceless voice comes back. It's not a hunch, it's a knowing, a certainty. I decide that if I don't pay it any attention, maybe it'll quit. Not that that's ever really worked for me before, but I don't

know what else to do. Why has my brain taken up something so
ludicrous all of a sudden?

When I go back downstairs, I notice there's a whole pile of
Dee's shirts that need to be ironed, so I think I'll get started on
them. And I'll call my friend Liz while I work on them because
talking to someone while ironing makes the job easier to bear.
She and her husband and kids used to live down the street but
they moved to another town a few years ago, so I rarely talk to
her anymore and I miss her. Besides, it'll help take my mind off
all this nonsense.

She doesn't even give me the chance to say hello. When
she hears my voice, Liz asks, "Pat, did you send your poem to
Sammy?" She sounds panicked.

I expected to hear the usual "How have you been?" kind
of stuff, but since she's jumped right in with this, it completely
throws me off.

"What? Yeah, but that's a long story . . . ."

She interrupts me. "Well, the strangest thing happened.
The other night I was getting ready for bed and the TV was
on in the bedroom. All of a sudden, Sammy Hagar came on. I
told my husband, 'Come 'ere. It's Sammy Hagar,' and he came
running in to see. Then the same thing happened a couple days
later. I turned on the TV in the afternoon and they were showing the same concert at the exact same moment in the show
that I saw the first time. And during both shows, Sammy was
singing this song that was something about going higher and
something about dreams. It was really weird." She sounds kind
of apprehensive, as if she's almost afraid to tell me this because
she doesn't want me to think she's crazy. And she must have
recognized Sammy from the pictures I showed her from our
trip to Cabo because it's not like Liz to listen to rock music; she
doesn't even like it.

"Really? That's what he was singing when I had my uh . . . *Really?* Did I ever tell you about that song?" I ask, positioning Dee's blue shirt on the ironing board and smoothing it out with my hand. This isn't your typical housewife conversation about how the kids are having trouble in school or that we're finding new gray hairs on our heads, so I'm kind of surprised.

Several months ago, when I shared with her about my mystical experience, I know I didn't mention what Sammy was singing when it happened. It wouldn't have done me any good; she wouldn't have been familiar with the song anyway. *I* wasn't even familiar with it before I went to Cabo last year.

"No, but God or something was telling me to tell you to hurry up and get that poem to him," she says. "I even put a note by my phone to remind me to tell you this as soon as possible. It felt really important. So what about the song?"

That's odd. It felt important to me too. Liz and I haven't talked for at least four months. How could we both have had the same feeling of urgency over a mere letter to a rock star at the same time? I stop what I'm doing and lift up the iron. My mind is jumping all over the place—she's humoring me; no, she's telling the truth. She has no reason to humor me. But something about her attitude worries me, maybe because she seems so nervous and I've never known her to act like this. Or maybe it's just that nothing like this has ever happened to her before and she doesn't know how to deal with it. I sure know that feeling. But why would this happen to her in the first place? And through Sammy? She's not into mystical stuff. She's the picture of the perfect Catholic woman: neat as a pin and never stepping out of line.

I explain to her that that's the same song Sammy was singing when I had my out-of-body experience, then I ask, "So why did seeing concerts on TV make you think you needed to tell me to hurry up and mail my poem to Sammy? It was just a TV show."

"Because, Pat, it was so strange and it happened twice—he was singing the exact same words *both times*—and I just knew that's what I was supposed to do." Now she sounds like she's out of breath.

I decide to make light of it—she's humoring me. I even put a smile on my face when I say it, "You're just saying all this to make me feel good, aren't you?"

"Oh no! I had the note by the phone to call you. I thought 'I need to tell Pat to send him that poem. Something from him is telling me to tell her.'"

Something from him? The smile melts off my face and I feel kind of creepy all of a sudden, but maybe only because of the other stuff that's been happening recently. There seem to be so many unexplained incidents and although I don't quite know what to make of them, it sort of feels like they're coming from something not-of-this-world.

I step back from the ironing board and rub my hands over my arms because now I feel chilled. Then I wonder, *what is happening to my friend?* Maybe I shouldn't have told her about my mystical experience; maybe my telling her about it has somehow brought its supernatural influence upon her. I feel like I should protect her somehow, but I don't have the slightest idea how to go about it or what it is I'd be protecting her from. I'm not even sure this is anything bad. It's just weird. And now that I think about it, maybe it has something to do with my newfound relationship with my son too. Maybe all of this really is magic and it's somehow spilling over onto others simply because they're aware of my story. Guilt by association, or maybe by information.

In any case, I'm beginning to think that what happened with Liz just now and with John the other day weren't accidents.

I try to return to my ironing as if nothing unusual has just taken place, but I feel like I'm peering into a veiled world I can't explain, as if there's an invisible spirit in the room with me. And yet, that rational part of me still haunts me—do revelations really come via rock stars to stay-at-home moms containing messages for their friends? Of course not! Only a complete moron would even entertain such a notion.

But I'm shaking so hard, I have to sit down.

CHAPTER 8

Psychic Experiences

*All psychic awareness is ultimately meant to guide you back
to that truth. It's your soul, the voice of your true self. And the
more you listen to it, the more you heal.*
—Sonia Choquette

February, 2004

It must be a full moon tonight. It feels like all the liquid in my
body is boiling and I just want to climb out of my skin.

I think astrology is pretty accurate sometimes, at least in
my case—my moods are ruled by the moon. It's my planet. If
Dee and I get into a big fight, it's always when the moon is full.
But I'm also overflowing with passion and we have more sex
and better sex then too. And I tend to get outrageously senti-
mental. The sight of a dead squirrel on the side of the road can
bring me to tears and make me spend hours wondering what it
would feel like to be a squirrel. The ones in my backyard always
look like they're having so much fun.

Since I feel so wonky and can't seem to get anything done
except running around in circles fretting over nothing, I decide
to try meditating. Maybe it will help me calm down.

When I finish, I'm lying on my back on the bedroom carpet, wedged in between the side of the bed and the bathroom door. My eyes are closed. It's time to come back to reality. I have no thoughts, no thoughts, no . . . and then I see what looks like an "SH" or a "CH," along with the numbers 0142. The "C" and the "S" are kind of combined like they're one letter. It's as if someone took a thick black marker and printed all this in the center of a 4 x 6 white note card. Maybe it's some kind of chemical formula. Then I see "betty delores," the words lined up one above the other on what looks like another white note card. Is this supposed to mean something? I don't know anyone named Betty or Delores. I think something is happening to me that maybe doesn't happen to most people, but it doesn't feel harmful or wrong, just *different*. I sit up and try to figure it out, but my mind feels the way it does when my alarm clock goes off before I'm ready to wake up in the morning. Nothing clicks.

I've been meditating for decades and nothing like this has happened to me before, or . . . wait a minute. Has it? When my mind comes back around, I think I remember something similar happening a long time ago. I may have written it down.

I have to know right now, so in my frantic search, I unearth notebooks from the nightstand, the desk drawer, the closet, and from under the bed, then I sit with them piled up around me and start looking through them. I finally find it. It has a large number "1" circled in silver marker on the cover. About fifteen years ago, when I was studying tae kwon do, I learned so many amazing things about life and my spirit that I never wanted to forget them, so I bought these notebooks and started writing things down.

I had taken up martial arts as a means of searching for my concept of God and self because Zen was a by-product of the training. Since I hadn't been able to find my truths through my religion, and there was no one to teach me about Native

American philosophy, I figured Zen's ancient philosophies and paradoxical tenets might reveal these things to me. Zen was mysterious, and so different from Christianity. But the basic principles of tae kwon do made sense to me too—that body, mind, and spirit must be in balance in order for a person to be whole. And the grueling, physical training of tae kwon do was fulfilling—it gave me something I couldn't get from cooking pot roast—self confidence, and a body as solid as a tree trunk.

I'd gotten as far as deputy black belt when we moved to another town and I didn't continue with it.

Although tae kwon do taught me a lot about my mind and spirit, I was no closer to understanding Zen. Or God. My *sa bum nim* [master] used to tell me that Zen wasn't something to be explained. It just *was*, because Zen turned into a concept was no longer Zen. There were so many airy statements like that and it only confused me more. I had an image in my mind that Zen was a little bald monk who kept peeking at me from behind a tree as I walked down a path through the forest of life. Every now and then, I'd catch a glimpse of his round head and brown robe out of the corner of my eye and as soon as I'd turn around to get a good look at him, he'd duck behind a tree again. And he was always smiling at me. It confounded the hell out of me.

Why was it such a big secret? Why didn't some learned author just take the time to spell it out? Of course I didn't realize until years later, that that's the whole paradox of Zen—no one can *tell* you anything—you have to find your own answers because each person's spiritual needs are different.

My master was also the one who taught me how to meditate. "Do not expect anything from *mook yum* [meditation]," he cautioned in his thick Korean accent, his eyes burrowing into my soul. He had these eyes that were so black, you couldn't see the pupils. And they were intense. *He* was intense—a seventh-degree black belt, tae kwon do champion in Korea, and one of the top *sul sa do* [weapons] masters in the United States. So when someone like him gives you a look like that, with that kind of warning attached, you know better than to defy it.

I open the notebook with the number "1" on the front and skim the text—page after page of philosophical stories, frustrations, accomplishments, but something catches my eye. It says that after three years of meditating and never noticing anything unusual about any of my sessions, one day a strange thing happened. As I sat there with my eyes closed and concentrating on my breathing, my mind was simply floating, when all of a sudden, I drifted up into an incredible light. I felt joy and heard singing. I didn't see God, but I knew He was with me. The entire place was celebrating, as if I'd done something wonderful. Then I saw reddish-orange clouds or fog in the distance and within this, a naked man was dancing. He was holding three eagle feathers in his hand. I couldn't see his face but I saw that he had long, curly hair down to the middle of his back. Someone once told me that we all have a spirit guide, so I wondered if this man was mine and I asked him this out loud. As I watched, the word YES silently drifted down from the sky, and then I felt bolts of light, in red, yellow, blue, orange, green, and purple, coursing through my body and circulating through all my blood vessels—energy, light, or both. I remember opening my eyes afterward, and the room around me seemed so normal, as if nothing out of the ordinary had taken place, but something felt different about the world right then, although I couldn't have said what it was. The vision seemed important though—it intrigued and upset me, that's why I wrote it down. Then I went on my merry way and forgot all about it.

As I look at my handwriting on the page, something stirs in me—something I know but can't remember. This makes me squirm. Or maybe it's just that the floor is getting too hard to sit on. I get up and move to the bed, accidentally putting a permanent crease in that page in my notebook.

The next entries are all about self-defense techniques, and there are stick-people diagrams. I'm such a doofus. A few pages further, it says that about a year after seeing that man, I had another strange meditation—my eyelids started to twitch and I felt myself going deeper and deeper and deeper. Everything was black and spinning. I felt cradled by a velvety-soft and warm substance like inside a womb and I had the sense that I was moving downward or inward perhaps. I remember this. I remember being afraid to totally let go. What if I didn't come back out? I even remember telling my mom about it afterward and she said, "Be careful, Honey," but she wouldn't tell me what she was so concerned about. Maybe she thought the devil was going to get me for falling into the dark like that. But none of it felt threatening or evil.

My notebook goes on to say that I then saw a huge stone tower. It was light tan and round with a rather chiseled-look about it. I knew that this tower was part of me. Millions of black birds flew out of it and I told myself to let them all come out. Then I was hovering above the tower, and near its base I saw tall grasses waving in the breeze. I could feel warm air on my body and there were two children, a girl and a boy, laughing and running in and out of the grass. Me? And who? All of a sudden, my eyes opened and I was back in my room. I felt like I'd been asleep for hours but a look at the clock told me it had been only nine minutes.

I remember thinking that since my meditation had been so unusual and so vivid, maybe it was supposed to mean something, but I didn't know what. Who believed in stuff like that anyway? Not me. My master had taught me well. Meditation had always been a way for me to relax and clear my mind, that's all. So I blew it off.

Other than my out of body moment at Sammy's concert that time, nothing odd happened to me since those two early meditations (which happened before my Cabo experience), until *this one*, so I forgot all about them.

And now when I look at the entries in my journal, although they're from nine years ago, something about those early experiences is beginning to make sense. Well, sort of. The thought crosses my mind that maybe the man with the eagle feathers was a representation of Sammy, and perhaps Sammy is supposed to be my spirit guide. And is it possible that the tower I saw during meditation all those years ago could have represented the Cabo Wabo building in Mexico? No. I remember that vision as if it happened yesterday. There is no doubt in my mind. It *was* the Cabo Wabo building.

That's ridiculous. I'm not even sure I believe in spirit guides or any of this other mumbo jumbo. Besides, why would I have a premonition of Cabo Wabo? Or Sammy? I push the absurd thoughts away and read further. "There is more," my handwriting says. "*Much* more. Whatever *it* is, I am sure, no, *positive* with my very soul, that I will be transformed forever by it. It is a spiritual growth or enlightenment of some kind. And I know this doesn't make any sense, but it feels like it's connected to nature, specifically the moon, the rocks, and water. And my writing, my poems have something profoundly to do with all this."

It's a strange feeling looking at words I'd written nearly ten years ago. I remember writing them. I even remember the occasions that caused me to write them, but now they feel like they were written by somebody else. And the feelings I'm having right now in response to them—trepidation, shock, understanding, excitement—are so disjointed that my mind decides to have a field day. Could "rocks" represent Land's End in Cabo? Maybe "water" means the two oceans that surround Cabo—the Sea of Cortez on one side and the Pacific Ocean on the other.

And "writing and poems"—did that mean like what I just sent to Sammy and that that's what I'm supposed to do with my life? Writing seems to be pulling me in without much input from me lately, as if something else is directing all this and I'm just along for the ride.

I sound like a total nutcase—a bored housewife with an overactive imagination. On the other hand, I read somewhere that imagination is the bridge between the world of spirit and the physical world. And the Wright brothers didn't fly because they kept their ideas on the ground, now did they? Maybe my mystical experience did open up something in me because the tower—Cabo Wabo—was where it all happened, through the dancing man with long, curly hair—Sammy—although I don't know where the eagle feathers fit in.

I'm so shocked at my own conclusions that I drop my forehead into my hand because I feel light-headed all of a sudden. These kinds of things never happened to me before—stringing ideas together to come up with preposterous notions about rock stars—or anything else for that matter. I'm not sure if this is considered being psychic or what, but I wonder if the spiritual avenues to the mind through martial arts and meditation could have paved the way for my mystical experience in Cabo. It's not likely, maybe, but I guess it's possible. Why else would I have had those premonitions? If they were, in fact, premonitions.

By this time my head is pounding, so I get up and pour myself a glass of water. And yet, I remind myself that it's a full moon tonight—maybe that's what's making me so temperamental. Full moon—my journal entry mentioned something about all of this being connected to the moon. This is getting weirder by the minute, or maybe *I'm* just getting weirder by the minute, but it feels like there's some sort of overlap in time here, as if all these things have happened before and they're happening again—past and present at the same time. *Now why did I have to think of that?*

Even though my rational mind keeps telling me it's all just coincidence, my brain feels like it's about to explode. I don't know what else to do, so I decide to call my friend Nancy to see if she can talk some sense into me. She's a nurse; she's good at being logical. We've been friends for so long that when people meet us, they think we're sisters.

Nancy befriended me in tenth grade when I was again "the new kid." She owned a purebred Morgan horse and she always wore this fluffy, purple coat that made her look regal—to me anyway. She smoked cigarettes and she knew how to inhale. I thought she was the coolest and most feminine girl I'd ever met. I thought that if I hung around her long enough, maybe some of her femininity and grace and coolness would rub off on me.

We've been best friends ever since. And to this day, there has never been anyone who can make me laugh like Nancy. I'm talking about howling to the point where we laugh so hard we cry. Over nothing. Over Buddy Hackett.

"I just wanted to tell you to keep your eyes and ears open and let me know if any of this makes sense to you," I say to her over the phone. I find myself a job to do while we talk—dusting end tables and little league trophies. This could be a long conversation. Then I explain to her about the betty/delores and the SH/CH0142 I've just seen and before I can finish, she's screaming. Her voice is shaking. I hold the phone away from my ear and wince.

"Oh my God! Why are you saying that to me?" She's acting as if I'm playing a cruel trick on her but she's so overly animated at my benign request, it makes me laugh. And yet, there's fear in her voice.

"What's wrong, you goofball?" I'm still laughing at her, downplaying her fear. If I don't buy into it, maybe she'll snap out of it and I won't get caught up in it like I normally tend to because that's what good friends do—fret together when necessary. Well, girls anyway. Man, and I was hoping she'd be the one to calm *me* down. I haven't even gotten to the weird part yet.

She says she just got off the phone with her neighbor and they'd been talking about a woman named Betty *and* a woman named Delores. When I tell her that I think it's just a fluke, she says, "No way. Those aren't common names anymore, and for you to see both of them at the same time I'm talking to my neighbor about people with the same names is just bizarre. What are the chances of that? It's not just coincidence."

"I don't know," I say and keep right on dusting. I mean, come on, is it really *that* big of a deal? Then I ask her what she thinks SH/CH0142 could mean. I explain that it was all in really bold letters as if something wanted to make sure that I saw it. She says she has no idea. That doesn't help me any. I quickly distract myself by picking up the small, ceramic tea set my brother brought me from Singapore years ago, and cleaning the inside of each tiny cup. Then I tell her what happened with Liz, but she doesn't even seem surprised. "And there's more," I say lowering my voice.

I have to sit down now. *This* is the weird part if you ask me.

"What do you mean? Ooo, you're scaring me . . . ."

I let out a long, deep sigh and then start telling her about the journal entries I'd recorded years earlier—about the rocks, the water, my writing, the tower, and the man with long hair.

"I think I remember you telling me about that," she says, then falls silent. After a moment, she finally pipes in, "Maybe since you keep fighting it, this is the Universe's way of proving to you that you *do* have psychic abilities you never had before, and yeah, it was definitely a premonition of Sammy and Cabo." Her voice sounds small and fragile all of a sudden.

"Maybe. Pretty weird, huh?"

"No, not maybe. This is incredible."

All this time, I've been trying really hard to hang onto my feeble "it's just a coincidence" theory, but the improbability of all this being a coincidence is starting to sink in. These sorts of things have been happening to me on a regular basis ever since Cabo, and if Nancy's worried about it, maybe I should be too. She doesn't usually let things get to her like this. Then I say, "Do you think something may have been preparing me for my mystical experience all those years ago?" Even though it already came out of my mouth, I keep reminding myself that it's absurd.

Nancy pauses. I can hear her exhale the way she does when she's smoking. "Could very well be, dude. I hope you wrote it all down."

And that's as far as we get.

I feel anxious and excited for no reason. I'm also starting to "know" a lot of things I didn't before. And all the while, tiny darts of synchronicity are coming at me from all directions. My friend Jill, who is also my neighbor, recommends I read Dan Brown's book, *The DaVinci Code*. After reading it, I follow up on one of the references—*Jesus and the Lost Goddess* by Timothy Freke and Peter Gandy. I'm not even sure why. Upon first glance, I wouldn't even have considered that this book could be related to anything that has been going on in my life. The more I read, however, the more I see little bits of insight, that if I were to look for validation—which I'm not, *I don't think*—it could possibly be considered confirmation that some sort of spiritual force was trying to tell me something.

The book says that we mistakenly believe we understand who we are and what life is all about, when all the while the truth is hidden in the small things, the unexpected things. Just when we're going through the motions of living our lives in a daze, we are presented with something so magnificent and mysterious that we don't know what to do with it.

As I put the book on the nightstand next to my bed and reach over to turn out the light one night, it occurs to me that this sounds an awful lot like my experience at an ordinary rock concert. *What the hell have I tapped into?* It's scaring the crap out of me, but at the same time, maybe I've been blessed with an amazing gift. Lying in the dark and waiting for Dee to come to bed, I suddenly feel so alone, as if I've stumbled onto something inexplicable, huge, and important. If I stomp my foot and scream, "Go away!" will it go away? Do I *want* it to go away? It also feels like whatever it is that's happening to me, it's a clue to the reason for *all* of life and a clue to the God I have always longed to know on a personal basis. Does this mean all the messages and coincidences are coming from God? But why would God choose to speak to me like this? I didn't ask to be psychic. I'm not sure I want to be. I was taught that there was a negative connotation that went along with fortune-telling. And sometimes, as the saying goes, "ignorance is bliss."

And for some reason, the ideas I'm coming up with right now feel really significant too, although I'm not sure why. I keep pushing that notion aside, but it won't stop nagging me—*this is important*—until I finally get out of bed and grab my notebook.

"I feel adrift on a raft, being washed swiftly downstream without oars," I write. "All I can do is hang on because there's no way to steer or slow it down. I'm not used to merely hanging on. I want to be in control, but that doesn't seem possible. Maybe it thinks I need guidance because I'm so cautious and reluctant to change. But the episodes don't go away. Why?"

Sammy's website has been announcing the grand opening of his new club, the Cabo Wabo in Lake Tahoe, for the past few months. We hadn't planned on going. We can't afford it. Besides, when Dee checked, the hotel didn't have any rooms available and tickets to the shows were all sold out anyway.

But we *are* going. Next month. I don't know how it happened. Everything just sort of opened up as if by magic, as if there's a reason we're supposed to be there. Maybe it's that same "magic" that's been happening to me ever since Cabo— all the supernatural stuff, because in a roundabout way, it's also magically bringing Dee and me closer. We've been married for so long, have gotten so wrapped up in our roles of "Dad" and "Mom" and "Financial Provider" and "Household Manager," I think we've been taking one another for granted without even realizing it. But now we're involved in something beyond that and we're talking about it and going to concerts together. And because of it, I think we're starting to see glimpses of the person we were once so in love with before all the responsibilities. Where I can't stop writing about all my extraordinary experiences, Dee is spending hours online, learning all about Sammy and his music. I think he enjoys it more than I do.

"Did you know Sammy's guitar player, Victor Johnson, used to be in a band called the Bus Boys? They were in that movie *48 Hours* with Eddie Murphy," Dee says, showing me the Bus Boys records he bought.

Why is he buying records? Our turntable hasn't worked in years.

Our relationship is taking on a completely new dimension, one I never thought it would take—and maybe, just maybe— it's pulling Dee into a supernatural realm without his even realizing it, a realm he would adamantly deny existed. Because why, all of a sudden, is he doing all these things that are so out of character for him? Is it simply because he loves the music? No, Dee is changing too. For one thing, he's smiling a lot more than he used to. Maybe it's more fallout from my mystical experience, like my relationship with my son John, and what happened with Liz. Whatever it is, it's all good.

I light some incense and sit down for my daily meditation. Closing my eyes, I let myself fall into the wonderful scent and into the rhythm of my breathing. I feel like I'm floating, and then a picture comes into my mind. My first reaction is to try to figure out what it means, but you're not supposed to do that in meditation. You're just supposed to let thoughts flow in and out of your mind—put them in a stream and let them wash away. But this one refuses to wash away.

I see a giant bubble, like a soap bubble where lots of different pastel and transparent colors mingle—moving in and out of one another as the light and the air hit them. But the bubble is thicker than soap and it has a hole in it—a hole that looks like something came out of it and it froze that way—open. I'm trying to climb into the bubble, but it's a bit difficult because the opening is jagged and more conducive to something coming out rather than going in.

Weird.

CHAPTER 9

Other Worlds

. . . sometimes divine revelation simply means adjusting your brain to
hear what your heart already knows.
—Dan Brown

March, 2004

The large envelope inside the mailbox shows a return address of "Redrocker." Dee must have ordered something. He's been buying a lot of Redrocker (Sammy calls himself that) memorabilia on Ebay lately—T-shirts, record albums, and guitar picks.

But the envelope isn't addressed to Dee. It has my name on it. I almost dare not allow myself to think *it's from Sammy*.

But it is. Inside there's an 8 x 10, black and white photo of Sammy looking very serious and quite a bit younger, and autographed in silver marker. A letter drops out from behind the picture and lands on the floor at my feet.

I figure it must be from the person who handles Sammy's mail. It's probably some form letter saying, "Thanks for writing, you little lemming." But it isn't, it's in someone's handwriting and it takes up one side and half the other on a white sheet of paper. My eyes come to rest on the final words, "Peace, Sammy Hagar."

I fall into the nearest chair.

Sammy says he is touched by my experience as much as I am and that he's honored to have been a part of it all. He says my poem is wonderful and asks my permission to put it on his website. He even tells me whom to contact for this.

I have just gotten a personal letter from a celebrity. Maybe those words should be gilded in gold, you know, like an ancient Greek monument, the kind with columns and pillars adorning its marble walls. Rock stars don't write letters to their fans. Rock stars don't say, "I'm honored . . . ." I read it again as if re-reading it will help get it into my head that I have actually received a letter from a real person, not just some commodity promoted by the media as a "rock star." Sammy actually took the time to jot this down freehand. It feels even less real the second time I read it.

I show the paper to John, who's sitting at the kitchen table having an afternoon snack. He's the same son who introduced me to all that new music.

"Wow, that's really cool." He stuffs way too many potato chips in his mouth at once, making his cheeks puff out.

All I know is that here in my own two hands is proof that all those feelings I had a couple months earlier—that Sammy was reading my letter, that he was moved by it, and that he would answer me—had been correct. I don't think it was just a lucky guess on my part and it was definitely more than mere chance because it was all so overwhelming and scary and confusing at the time, and the message kept repeating itself, even through my friend Liz. I still don't know what to think about that.

And now, I feel as if I've been singled out for a reason, as if I've done something great for the first time in my life. So great in fact, that a big star wants to share my accomplishment with the world. And yet, here I am, still standing in my little kitchen, the same person I was yesterday—a suburban housewife.

Dee is already familiar with most of Sammy's music. He's more into collecting swag from Ebay, but I'd rather hear the music, so whenever I can, I buy a CD. There are a lot—over 25 albums available in local music stores, hundreds if you count singles, releases in other countries, live recordings, and compilation CDs. In between making albums with Montrose and HSAS (Hagar, Schon, Aaronson, and Shrieve), Sammy released several solo albums before he became the lead singer for Van Halen from the mid '80s to the mid '90s. He's also released many solo albums since then.

As I'm shopping, I pick up Van Halen's CD, *5150,* the first album the group recorded with Sammy after their previous lead singer, David Lee Roth, left the band. I haven't heard this one yet. Actually, I haven't heard any Van Halen music yet.

When I play the album, there's a song that seems to stand out, so I look up the title. It's called "Love Walks In." I need to remember this one so I can find it again—it's a unique title for a love song and I really like the melody—it's slow and sweeping.

A few weeks later, I buy a used audio tape of Van Halen's album *Right Here, Right Now,* a recording of a live concert in 1993. Plugging the tape into my car stereo, I listen to it as I'm driving home, passing convenience stores, fast food restaurants, and residential neighborhoods. At one point, Sammy introduces that song I like, "Love Walks In," saying, "This song was inspired by Ruth Montgomery. It's about 'Walk-ins.'"

"Walk-ins?" What does he mean by that? And who is Ruth Montgomery? Maybe she's his girlfriend. But why does it sound like Sammy is saying "alien" over and over again? I must not be hearing him right. Anyway, the only reason I care is because I want to learn the words so I can sing along next time—because

I like the song—or maybe it's because the terms "rock star" and "alien" don't fit together in my mind.

As I make the final turn into our neighborhood, I tell myself that I'll listen to *5150* again when I get into the house. It contains the studio version of "Love Walks In." Maybe I'll be able to understand the lyrics without all the fans screaming in the background.

I put *5150* on and proceed to put away the groceries—boxes of cereal, canned vegetables, six gallons of milk, and extra toilet paper. After a few songs, "Love Walks In" comes on. Time to pay closer attention.

I pull out the insert and follow along. The lyrics are about how an alien waited until the timing was right, then somehow caused amazing things to happen, such as introducing him to the concept of love. Oh brother. I thought this was a love song between a man and a woman. What a waste of that beautiful melody. Why would a big rock star write a song like that and perform it in front of millions of people? Wouldn't he be ridiculed for lyrics about aliens?

Sitting down on the floor, I lean my back up against the side of the couch so I can read the words again. Not that it matters. I'm just a little disappointed, that's all. And then it's as if a bolt of lightning suddenly crashes through the roof of my house and pierces my gut, leaving a gaping hole in both my ceiling and in me—*Sammy is describing exactly what happened to me in Cabo the previous year.*

My entire body suddenly feels frozen all over. Even my brain. After a few moments though, it manages to squeeze out "That's absurd."

I read the lyrics again. They *do* seem to validate my feeble attempts to articulate what happened to me. He wrote about questioning his sanity. He wrote about traveling to another world and about how the strange things he encountered there felt familiar, that the experience changed his entire life, and nothing felt the same afterward. All these were words I could have used to describe my experience, but of course, I didn't. It never would have occurred to me.

The line about an alien causing amazing things to happen and opening a door to love—why is this resonating with me? Because that's what happened to me? But I wouldn't have said an alien caused it. Now that I think about it though, it did seem like a superior intelligence had waited until the time was right in my life and opened up a whole new and wonderful world to me. All the events conducive to my experience lined up in the precise manner necessary for it to take place. And when they were aligned, love truly did come walking in. More like pouring in, actually.

My skin suddenly feels prickly all over and kind of clammy even though I know none of this makes sense. I'm being ridiculous; I'm inventing a connection between unrelated things. Why do I do this to myself? Maybe Dee's right—I have too much time on my hands. Besides, it's just a song—

My heart is pounding.

I look more closely at the *5150* CD insert. The back cover has an artist's rendition of a pastel-colored, round object. I assume this is supposed to be the earth. It's cracked open and the members of Van Halen are stepping out of its jagged edges, perhaps to signify that the newly formed Van Halen band is ready to take on the world with their music. As the next thought begins to gel in my mind, my brain instantly rejects what my eyes are proposing—it's the image I saw in meditation about a month ago.

No fucking way.

Oh, yes.

I swallow hard. All the air seems forced out of my lungs by an invisible vice. Silent tears fall from my eyes and soak the front of my shirt before I even feel them coming out.

It's all right there in front of me—that picture of the band and the bubble is stark reality, but not like how I've always perceived reality. It's as if I'm lifting my window shade and looking at the world outside my bedroom in the middle of July. Instead of seeing the sun shining, leafy trees, green grass, and kids running through the sprinklers on their front lawns as I expect to see, the trees are nothing more than gray fingers coated with ice, the neighbor's windows and garage doors are shut up, and everything is white with a blanket of snow. And yet it is July. But the snow and ice are *absolutely* real.

Jesus, I'm losing it. I begin to pant.

This isn't possible.

How could I have seen this?

Think.

Did my experience in Cabo have something to do with this album? The song "Dreams" is on it, the song Sammy was singing when all this started.

Oh please. You've got to stop this right now.

But my whole body is shivering. I've heard it said that when we're exposed to the truth, our bodies let us know, even when our minds refuse to accept it. It's like that animal fight-or-flight instinct, an adrenaline rush.

The truth? What is "the truth" here? What am I supposed to do with all this? *All* this weird stuff? And why does it feel like I'm *supposed* to do something with it? Still holding the CD insert, I walk around in a little circle—around and around and around, as if by doing so, some sense will be restored to my overloaded brain. Oh, quit it, I tell myself. It's not what you think. *But it sure feels like it.* These things don't happen. *But they are happening.* You're just a fan—knock it off! *No, this has something to do with me and there's no way to explain it.*

I don't know how long I pace, but I never even get dizzy.

Whatever this is, it isn't of this conscious world. It's deep, or else I'm crazy. At this point, I'd better not discount that possibility either. Maybe I should see a doctor. Oh yeah, then what would I say? "Doc, I'm experiencing psychic connections to a rock star and aliens." They'd put me on tranquilizers and tie me to the bed. Now calm down. Get a grip. You're not crazy; you're just being pitched back and forth between everyday life and some kind of new perception that's opening up to you. You're smart enough not to let yourself go over the edge.

Breathe.

I know there are words I need to say, but I'm not sure what they are. I force myself to take a few more deep breaths, and when I'm breathing a little easier and my head seems to be clearer, I figure I should give the aliens concept the benefit of the doubt. None of what is happening makes any sense anyway, so what do I have to lose?

My heart is still pounding as I log onto the computer and listen to several recorded interviews in which Sammy says that "Love Walks In" came about because of his personal experiences in his early twenties. He claims that aliens visited him more than once.

"Yeah, he was stoned out of his mind at the time, that's all," my logical side tells me. But Sammy insists he wasn't taking drugs when it happened and that it scared the shit out of him. He says the beings were made of energy. And through all the ridicule he has received because of this story, to this day, Sammy unapologetically maintains his belief.

I look again at the frozen video of Sammy's interview on my screen. How can a person just sit in a chair and calmly give an interview about something like that without flinching? How can he look normal on the outside if he's been in contact with aliens? Why isn't his skin falling off his face or his hair turning green? But what really worries me is that he's making perfect sense. And if he's making perfect sense, *what does that say about me?* Here I go again.

Breathe.

Then I find out that the term "Walk-in" describes a form of alien that has been invited by a human to take over his or her physical body when the person no longer wants to live.

I can't believe I'm actually considering any of this.

Okay, so maybe Sammy wasn't stoned when he claims to have seen aliens . . . yeah, right . . . but then who knows? The energy part of what he said makes sense. If there really are such things as aliens, they must be some form of energy. After all, that's what we are—energy. I believe in angels and spirits, so maybe it's not such a far cry from believing in them to believing in other forms of beings. Maybe aliens are entities similar to angels or spirits or perhaps it's all a matter of personal interpretation. Maybe it doesn't matter what you call any of this because it all stems from some extension of the Holy Spirit anyway, and it's all connected. That could be. A lot of people say they've experienced an abduction and when it happened, they described an intense light. Light is a form of energy that's often associated with God.

Where is this leading me? Do aliens have something to do with God? I have no idea what I'm talking about. There's no logical link here.

I wonder what the world would look like if I knew for sure that there were aliens out there watching me. Would everything look backward, like when you look in the mirror? Would the sky turn yellow? Maybe it's *already* yellow and I just don't see it that way. Or maybe there are people walking around on our planet who aren't from earth and look just like us. It's also possible that we're *all* from some distant planet and we came to earth in the form of human souls at birth.

All of this makes me feel very small and vulnerable. And yet, if aliens do exist, God must have created them. There are so many unexplained things in the universe and in our minds that we are only beginning to gain an understanding. And everyone has a different opinion—the definition of reality varies from philosopher to philosopher and from one person to the next. Lately *my* definition of reality seems to be changing on a daily basis, so who am I to judge Sammy? I'm still not entirely convinced that what happened to Sammy was because of aliens, but according to his descriptions, it was initiated by a spiritual connection with another "realm of being" or consciousness that changed his life. Maybe his experiences did have something to do with me and my awakening in Cabo, but I don't know why they would. And why do I keep getting the feeling that all of this has to do with my writing?

"I think you'd better start paying more attention to these things," Nancy tells me one day. "I hope you're writing them down."

"But they're—they don't make any sense!"

"I know, but if you write them down, maybe someday when you look back on them, they will. It could prove interesting to see where all of this is taking you. These things are just too weird and they've been happening *way* too often. They can't be coincidence. Not this many times."

Oh, Lord help me.

CHAPTER 10

"Come Here" and "Stay Back" in the Same Sentence

Real music is not for wealth, not for honors or even for the joys of the mind but as a path for realization and salvation.
—Ali Akbar Khan

May, 2004

South Lake Tahoe is like a mini-version of Las Vegas discreetly positioned in the heart of a snow-capped mountain range. Majestic pines that produce pinecones the size of footballs surround the lake. The air is crisp, the sky deep blue, and the water is so cold you expect to see icebergs floating there.

As we drive from the airport to our hotel, Dee and I make a vow to come back and bring the boys with us next time. From the back seat, my friend Leann voices her approval. To have Leann with us for the grand opening of Sammy's new club, the Cabo Wabo Lake Tahoe, is a dream come true for me. All this time I've been telling my friends how amazing all of this is and wanting to share it with them. I wanted them to have a mystical experience like I did. And now, *it's going to happen for Leann!* I just know it! I'm so psyched, I haven't slept for the past two nights.

Leann is another of my best friends. Her dark hair and eyes are so striking that you nearly stumble over your own thoughts when you look at her—and she has class. She always dresses to the nines. She's also "Steady Betty" with an equal amount of wild abandon thrown in to keep things interesting. However, I get the impression that she only reveals her carefree side when she's around me.

After the three of us check into our hotel, we take the elevator down to retrieve our bags from the rented car we parked in the garage. As the elevator doors open, Dee spots a tall, slender man with a beautiful woman on his arm. The man has thick, dark hair down to the middle of his back and he's wearing a camouflage-colored cowboy hat with a high crown, a loud shirt, and faded blue jeans. His long legs carry him with great strides and his bodyguards have to rush to keep up. He obviously knows where he's going. He has an air about him that makes you think twice about approaching him and not because there are several men surrounding him. His movements are quick and confident, arrogant almost.

"There's Ted Nugent," Dee says.

"Are you sure?" I've never seen him before and wouldn't recognize him.

"Yeah, that's him. Should we see where he's going?"

"No. I'm not going to invade anyone's privacy."

"*Should* we?" Dee is applying the kind of pressure only he knows how to do. I have to make a split-second decision or the opportunity will be lost forever.

"Let's follow him!" Leann says, her black eyes filling with mischief.

My mind is racing. I'm seeing a celebrity acting as if he's an ordinary person like the rest of us. I'm not used to rubbing shoulders with rock stars. This feels surreal.

"Okay." I feel like I'm allowing myself to be led into the arena like the bull that's been speared by decorative swords.

We follow "Uncle Ted" through the casino arcade with all the lights, buzzers, and bells pinging, down a long, narrow hall, and soon find ourselves in front of Cabo Wabo. Like a store within a store, this Tahoe version is situated in a corner of the lower level, almost like an off-hand comment waiting to be resurrected when more information becomes available. The air smells stagnant, like the scent of cardboard boxes that have been stashed in an attic for years. The front is painted bright red with the Cabo Wabo logo in lights over the doorway. On the wall is a poster announcing the grand opening of the Cabo Wabo Lake Tahoe, the words "The tequila made us do it" superimposed on a photo of a sunset over Lake Tahoe next to Sammy Hagar's face. With all the lights and colors, part of me feels like a kid in a toy store, but the other part—reserved and responsible, holds me in check—always. And combined with just having encountered a famous rock star, I feel incapable of processing any of it.

Ted slides into the new Cabo Wabo and so do we. It's a small establishment with a bar along one side and a stage in the corner large enough to accommodate a three-piece band. There are a handful of tables and chairs. Dee and Leann walk around to look at the gold records on the walls, and I sit down at one of the tables to wait. Glancing in the direction Ted went, I notice that to the left of the bar is a doorway that opens into a restaurant where large, flat-screen TV monitors are playing videos. I can see Ted's camouflage cowboy hat bouncing. He's taking part in an animated conversation with a short man with a mop of unruly blonde curls—Sammy Hagar.

So *this* is the person behind the voice, behind the mystique that changed my life. Although I've seen him on the stage, it occurs to me that he too is a real person, not some larger-than-life product elevated to astronomical proportions by the Powers-That-Be. Where did I get that idiotic notion?

I turn my head, so as not to be rude and stare, although I *want* to. I'm suddenly like a drawing in a coloring book—two-dimensional and waiting to be colored. My heart is pounding. You're an adult, knock it off, I tell myself. Jeez.

A young lady in a tight-fitting shirt and very short shorts approaches me. "Can I help you?" she asks.

"No," I say. "I'm just waiting for my husband."

"Oh. Where's your husband?"

I point to Dee.

"We're not open until tomorrow. You can come back then." She's not exactly *telling* us to leave, but I respect her implication.

"Come on, Dee, we should go." I get up and grab his arm.

We move into the gift shop and buy some T-shirts. As I'm walking out the door, Dee, who is keeping a keen eye on things, suddenly perks up. "Sammy's coming out!"

I turn around, not looking where I'm going, and find myself literally bouncing off Sammy's chest. Just call me Grace.

"Oh, sorry," I mumble. I can't look at him. I feel like the biggest ass in the world. *I just ran into SAMMY HAGAR.* How can I be such a klutz?

I keep staring at the floor and peek up at him out of the corner of my eye.

"No problem." Sammy smiles.

I would have expected him to say something like, "Hey, watch where you're going, dipshit," or push me out of the way, but instead, he seems patient and kind. It makes me relax just a bit so I raise my eyes to his. They're brown. Deep brown. And there's a depth and enthusiasm in them that exudes a fixed happiness, not an outward façade, but something real. His entire face has a rested quality about it, as if it will be damned to exhibit the years of drinking, drugs, and partying, and the many women he's been with in his rock and roll career.

Something inside of me shrinks.

He's looking right into me as if he can read what I'm thinking. And what I'm thinking is, oh my God, he's real. I've touched him. I didn't mean to . . . and he's really short, shorter than me; he'd seemed so much taller on the stage. But then, you often hear people say that about celebrities.

He's dressed in a light blue, long-sleeved shirt with the top two buttons undone, the sleeves rolled up, and white pants. There seems no attempt to tame the wildness of his long, blonde curls; they're like flames of his spirit. Although there's a hint of street-wise awareness about him, there's also a polished demeanor in his rumpled-ness. He seems like some sweet-natured dynamo, a man of guiltless serenity who makes few apologies. On the other hand, he seems so compactly powerful that I don't think I'd want to get on his bad side.

His wife, Kari, floats at his side like a supermodel. She has long legs, flawless skin, and blonde hair in large waves that fall about her shoulders and down her back. Her eyes are like dazzling gems. She's wearing a waist-cut, white jacket trimmed in white fur and she sparkles like fine champagne, the kind we can't afford on Dee's salary.

"Sammy," Dee makes it sound like they're long-lost buds. "Would you sign this T-shirt for me?" He pulls one of his new shirts out of his bag.

"Be glad to." Sammy looks around for something to write with, then finds a ballpoint pen on the podium next to the entrance of his restaurant. "Pull it tight." He well knows how to do this; he's probably written his name on everything imaginable for the past forty years.

Wow, he's actually nice. I thought rock stars were supposed to have bad-ass attitudes and be rude and demanding.

"That's one of his favorite shirts," Kari says smiling.

I'm relieved that she doesn't hesitate to become part of the conversation or try to disguise her intelligence behind her beautiful face, as she explains about the shirt. She must be used to sharing her husband with the world. I'm not sure I could do that. She doesn't seem like she's outside of it though, she seems directly involved. Maybe that's her secret. And being drop-dead gorgeous doesn't hurt any.

Sammy scribbles his name across the front of the shirt and turns to leave when Dee says, "This is the lady who sent you the poems," pointing to me.

Sammy's eyes widen.

I feel like I'm drowning.

"That deserves a hug," he says, and wraps his arms around me. As his hair presses up against my face, I'm surprised at how baby-fine and soft it is. I'm even more surprised that I'm noticing it at all. Then he looks into my eyes, not the condescending expression of a celebrity to a fan; this feels reverent and sincere. "You really have a talent," he says. "You should really do something with that."

Previously I thought that if I ever had the chance to meet him in person, I would pour myself into the feeling, paying close attention to how the energy felt and absorbing every possible detail. Now I don't have any acute feelings. I'm numb, so caught off guard that my brain goes somewhere else—star-struck. Oh, I *hate* that word even more than I hate the word "fan." I've never been anybody's fan before. I don't feel comfortable being associated with a conglomeration over which I have no knowledge or control. And it's another label. I'm not a label.

I immediately become conscious of the faded purple sweater and tired, baggy jeans I'm wearing. They're the perfect accompaniments to my weary mediocrity and my scrambling, sleep-deprived brain. I'm not myself. Or maybe I'm more myself than anything, not trying to be impressive to anyone, my ordinariness suddenly becoming an embarrassment to me.

I would have been content to fade into the background and not make myself known, but Dee has exposed me. I don't know whether to kick him or thank him.

"What?" I hear the voice coming out of me that doesn't belong to me. "I don't know what I could do."

Sammy is serious. "You really touched me with what you wrote. It gave me goose bumps when I read it," he says.

Does he have any idea what he's doing to me right now? That his words are making me feel like I'm not just the insignificant insect I've always believed I was? He holds out his arm, turns it over, and makes a fist. Then he pushes up his sleeve to show me his forearm. "See? I've got goose bumps just thinking about it!"

I find myself staring in disbelief at the bare forearm covered with goose bumps. I've never met a man who openly displayed so much emotion. So, he has a soft heart. He's an artist. Of course. That explains it. I love it when people aren't afraid to show their emotions. It makes me feel like it's okay for me to show mine too, all the while society keeps telling me to cover them up. I want to know more about this but my mind is in a daze. What do I do? What do I say? The whole world is now in fast-forward mode. I force myself to focus. *If you could ask him just one thing, what would it be?* The aliens thing. I have to tell him what happened to me. I must ask him about this. But I can't seem to bring myself to say it. I feel like a fool. How can I ask this of someone I don't even know? No, I have to. It may be my only chance. Speak, woman, open your mouth—*hurry!* "I . . . wanted to talk to you . . . about . . . what you said . . . about the aliens . . . ." I sputter, seeing my chances of speaking with him any further slipping away with each lame syllable.

"There's nothing more to tell." He looks away. I'm being dismissed.

He assumes I know all about this . . . but I don't. Or maybe he thinks I'm mocking him. *Please,* I want to say, *I'm not some weirdo; I just need to know what's going on. This is important. It's huge.* But there's no time and no words to explain this quickly. Besides, the words I've already said mirror the stagnant puddle of insignificance I've slid into and there's nothing further I can do to remedy that fact. My words fall like a heavy weight onto the linoleum floor.

By this time, other people are gathering. Sammy turns to a middle-aged couple next to me and poses with them for a photograph.

How could I have let my one and only chance to ask him something important slip away so easily? *Star-struck*—ugh! I'm so involved in my own thoughts, I don't even notice him walk away, but some sort of wake remains, as if the air in the room is standing open for a few moments before it closes again. And I'm trembling.

There are three concerts this weekend. Besides Ted Nugent, several celebrities perform onstage with Sammy and his band: Jerry Cantrell from Alice in Chains, Bob Weir from The Grateful Dead, Ronnie Montrose, Toby Keith, Neil Schon from Journey, Billy Duffy from The Cult, and guitarist Johnny Hiland. It's nonstop partying and excitement. For me, this is good and bad. When I get excited, I don't sleep. For days. Dee doesn't either, but not because he's excited. He stays up all night gambling. This results in a big fight between us.

"I don't need to sleep," he stammers with watery, bloodshot eyes. "You're not making any sense! I hope for your sake you don't run into Sammy again."

Feeling defeated, I plop myself into the overstuffed chair next to the only window in our room, the one that overlooks beautiful Lake Tahoe, which is shimmering in the sunlight. "All you want to do is gamble," I say.

"All you want to do is wait in line. I told you, I'm not waiting in line all day anymore. That's bullshit!"

"Well, I don't like to gamble, so what else is there for me to do while you're gambling? You might as well take every dollar you have, tear it into tiny bits, and throw it out the window."

"Maybe you should go and be with Sammy, then you'd have to get a job."

Now who's not making sense? "What? That's the dumbest thing I've ever heard," I tell him. "In the first place, I don't want to be with Sammy."

I'm thinking that he's acting like a complete imbecile. I don't even want to stoop so low as to continue to address his statement. Maybe he doesn't realize that whatever it is that's been happening to me, it isn't because of Sammy. It's because of something bigger. I've known this from the start, but I don't think I've told this to Dee. I've purposefully been vague about all the experiences I've been having—aliens, other dimensions of consciousness, and philosophical theories—because I don't want to be the butt of his ridicule. Besides, he'd rather discuss whether the Broncos are going to make it to the Super Bowl. So maybe he's misinterpreting my ambiguity as that of a fan drooling over a rock star and not wanting her husband to know. Oh, how do I get myself into these situations when I'm merely trying to maintain peace? And how do I fix it? How do I stand up for myself and respect my husband's feelings at the same time?

It's so absurd that I start to laugh. Uncontrollably. Dee glares at me. He thinks I'm making fun of him.

But this argument forces me to take stock of our relationship. When all this mystical stuff began, it stirred up our marriage in a lot of ways. It was rather like the dice in a craps game—you shake up the pieces, spill them on the table, and see what new combination of numbers rolls out. Then you have to decide what you're going to do next. It's also forcing us to look at what we've allowed ourselves to become due to our willingness to settle for less than really living—especially me. Now I'm not only seeing our relationship in a new way, I'm seeing myself in a new way. Maybe I could have prevented this fight if I'd just been honest with Dee in the first place and not assumed he would criticize me.

I also think there was a reason this trip came about so effortlessly—I was supposed to meet Sammy face-to-face. I was meant to experience the full impact of this third-party energy between us that seems to have been brought to life through an otherworldly means, because the entire time we were in Tahoe, I felt some kind of energy, something thick like oil in the air, almost like a power surge, as if something that had been hidden for centuries had finally been unleashed. I even noticed it when I walked from our hotel room and down the hall to the elevators, and when we took a drive to the lake.

Maybe this energy was also responsible for the other peculiar things that happened that weekend: my watch stopped, my hair dryer broke, and Dee's camera quit working. He had to buy a new one. Worst of all, I lost the diamond out of the engagement ring Dee gave me twenty years ago. (Months later, a massage therapist told me that she didn't wear a watch when giving a massage because the energy could cause the watch to quit working.)

My friend Leann, however, did not have a mystical experience. She didn't leave her body and she didn't see God. She did tell me that she saw someone who looked like Jesus though—he was one of the stage crew.

This made me feel like I'd failed her in some way. What did I do wrong that I couldn't give her that feeling of joy I wanted to give her so badly? How can one person look at something, or hear something, and be able to relate to it so much, while the next person can look at the same thing and see something completely different? Apparently, you can't *make* somebody feel what you feel either, even if it's for their own good—like giving them joy. And even if you *could* make them feel it, is it possible for anybody to ever *really* know what you're feeling anyway? And why do these kinds of questions occur to me in the first place?

CHAPTER 11

I Am the Stage

Music is your own experience, your thoughts, your wisdom.
If you don't live it, it won't come out your horn.
—Charlie Parker

August, 2004

It's really hard to pull myself back down to reality, but I have to. The boys still need peanut butter and jelly sandwiches every day for school; they need to be hauled to lacrosse practice and music lessons and now the high school has given me a new project—organizing fundraisers so John's orchestra class can take a trip to Germany. *I* want to go to Germany.

In the midst of all this, the legendary rock band Van Halen has announced a reunion tour. They're going to perform across the United States, and they're coming to Denver. For the tour, Van Halen has a unique stage setup. On either side of the main stage there's an opening in the floor where fans can be *inside* the stage and part of the show. It's called the Golden Ring section, with tickets selling for almost $400 per person. Although being inside the stage would be the opportunity of a lifetime, Dee and I simply can't afford that. I'm already having enough trouble trying to figure out how to help thirty-four teenagers finance a trip to Germany.

Leann says she can get us good seats to the show, as the company she works for is affiliated with the venue where Van Halen is going to be performing, so I let her handle it. The seats she ends up getting, however, are not so great. They're in the 23rd row on the side of the auditorium. I was thinking more along the lines of rows one through five.

As hard as I try to envision ahead of time what the concert is going to be like, I can't picture myself sitting in those seats with Leann and her husband. I'm also having dreams about it, and I'm never in the 23rd row. Something feels imminent, like the calm before a storm.

Three days before the show, my son John's friend tells me that the radio station is having a contest for the Golden Ring section at the Van Halen show, and they're qualifying one person every day of the week with the final drawing on Friday. I hadn't heard about that. "They're asking questions and you call in with the answer. If you get it right, you qualify for the drawing," he says.

Some people are lucky in gambling and winning contests, but not me. I realize this sounds cliché, but it's a fact. This time though, something inside me tells me I'm going to win—without a doubt—so I go online and find out facts about the band, ready for any question the radio station might ask.

The next day, they announce the chance to call in and I get right through. "What was the name of the club where Van Halen was first discovered and who was the famous rock star that made it happen?" the DJ asks.

"It was Gene Simmons of Kiss," I tell him, "and it was at the Starwood Club in L.A."

"You're right!"

He takes my name and phone number. I'm the last contestant for the drawing.

Oh my God, it's really happening.

"Are you gonna cry if you don't win?" Michael asks as he comes into the kitchen after school. He must be hungry. He doesn't usually hang around otherwise. But then, teenage boys are always hungry.

"I'm going to. I'm sure of it." I refuse to entertain the notion of anything less.

I've never been a positive thinker. I've always considered it safer to hope for the best but prepare for the worst, that way I wouldn't be too disappointed when things didn't turn out the way I wanted them to. But now, I've never been so sure about anything in my life. It's almost like it's already happened and I just have to go through the motions.

In the morning, I'm up early because they're going to announce the winner between 6:00 and 8:00. I switch on the radio in the living room. Then I watch the clock, doing everything I can think of to help contain my nervousness—dusting, picking up things, straightening pillows on the couch. I'm almost afraid to leave the room, afraid I'll miss the announcement. And then, about ten minutes before eight, they announce my name on the radio. You probably heard me screaming in Poughkeepsie.

So what is this? Serendipity at its finest? Or is it something else? That same "magic" that allowed us to go to Tahoe? Nancy's voice echoes in my mind, *It can't be coincidence. Not this many times . . . .*

Our tickets give us access to the standing-room-only area inside the stage. Dee and I, and about twenty others, are down in a small alcove; the walkway of the main stage is about shoulder level. Stacks of amps and speakers surround us, rigs with colored lights hang overhead, and huge spinning lamps like giant, stuffed olives line the edges of our trench. We are literally inside the stage, a part of it, like props for the show. We have to be careful not to trip on the snakes of cords that are secured to the floor and the ramps with electrical tape.

An opening act performs first, then people sporting laminated access passes scurry in every direction to hook up guitars, drums, and mics and position the stage for Van Halen. Why am I nervous?

Like a sound wave that's vibrating in a low frequency with little variance in its fluctuations, the emotion in the air is almost palpable.

A woman next to me turns to me and asks, "Are you a friend of the band?"

"No," I tell her, wondering why she asked. Do I look like I *should* be?

There are something like 13,000 beaming faces opposite me, crammed in from the front rows to the back and all along each side. Having that many people looking at me makes me uncomfortable. I wonder if they think I'm rich because these spots inside the stage were so expensive. And I feel a little embarrassed to be here, because it's like I'm shouting LOOK AT ME! when I'm sure there are people out there who deserve this more than I do, so I don't make eye contact with anyone.

The noise level grows with each passing minute, rising from a deep hum to that of a great creature waking from its slumber. My need to move is now almost unbearable. Why don't they hurry up?

Suddenly the lights go out and the behemoth takes a deep breath. Through the darkness, I see figures coming onstage. I hear the sound of their feet and feel the give of the wooden boards as the band members walk on the platform, taking their predetermined places like racehorses at the starting gate.

It's as if I've experienced all of this before—many times before. Not as an observer like I am now, but as a participant. I'm deeply inside of it, past the glitz and glamour and the noise, beyond the roadies who set up and tear down the stage, who stand on the sidelines ready to help out if something should go wrong because the show must go on, beyond those who work for minimum wage selling T-shirts and beer to impatient fans eager to return to their seats. I can feel the excitement piercing my skin and the adrenaline that transforms human beings into rock stars pulsing through my body. I can taste their booze in my throat and the lingering drone of hot lights in my muscles. The inside of my nose burns with the stench of the sweat and cigarettes of those who work to build the stage set and run the lighting and the sound system. I can feel the organization of the building venue itself, the coordination of security people, as if I know it personally. I can taste the monotony of backstage food, the frustration of being pursued by an endless army of strangers wanting favors. And I feel the thumping of my heart as the performers take the stage and the audience looks back at me. But I don't feel like me. I feel like I'm caught in a whirlpool between two states of consciousness, not knowing where I'll end up, or really caring. I'm enjoying the spinning.

All of this rises up from the humming of the amps, the black boards of the stage assembly, and from somewhere deep inside of me like a memory. I'm thinking this a bit strange, feeling this way about the situation. It's just a concert. Just a concert I somehow won tickets to and *knew* I was going to win.

Then the beast roars—a gut-busting, victorious recapturing of its scattered prey—one entity formed from the amalgamation of audience and performers. The lights go up and the sound explodes from every cell in every human body in the stadium. It's as if, contained within the instruments and voices of the musicians, a gigantic mouth is placing itself over ours and sucking the very breath out of us, every last ounce of air, and blowing like a hurricane down our throats.

This is the kind of music I love most of all—when it stirs my emotions, when it makes me angry or want to lose control, or when it shocks me—because it forces me to confront the person I am.

I have two sides to me. One's a sweet, little girl who always tries to please everyone, keep her feet on the ground, do the right thing. That's the side I usually allow to dictate what I say and do. The other side's eccentric, moody, and mysterious and sometimes it just wants to say, "If you don't approve of me— tough shit! And if what I'm doing appalls you, so much the better!"

But I don't think these sides of me are *good or bad,* they're just parts I need to acknowledge and accept because they help define who I am. Philosopher Lao Tzu once said that without "short," how would we know what "long" was?

A lot of times my two sides are at war with one another, like they've been since this mystical journey of mine began. One side says, "This is magic," and the other says, "Nah, it's crazy." And of course the more logical side usually rules and maybe that's not always a good thing. I sometimes think that if I allowed myself to tap into that other part of me completely and honestly more often, I could be a really great writer. It reminds me of something author Sue Grafton once said: "We all need to look into the dark side of our nature—that's where the energy is, the passion. People are afraid of that because it holds pieces of us we're busy denying." Oh yeah. Same with music. When a song or a singer's voice is polished and predictable, it feels like I'm being handed a censored book with lots of pictures and easy-to-understand words. I've spent all my life playing it safe and doing the "right thing." I'm sick of it. Give me music with its edges dripping raw juice. I need to feel it dig its claws into my flesh, into my darkness, the feelings I'm afraid of and have kept hidden. That's when I come alive. From the inside out.

The flames of instantaneous energy catch the crowd and now they're out of control. The beast has taken its first breath and is exhaling fire.

Sammy screams into the microphone, "Hello, baaaaaaaaaby!"

Eddie Van Halen on lead guitar, Michael Anthony on bass, Alex Van Halen on drums, and Sammy Hagar on lead vocals and guitar, proceed into the opening song. It seems impossible that these men who are larger than life, known the world over in a realm of fame a part of me cannot grasp, are right here before me, in my town, on this stage. I can reach out and touch any one of them right now if I want, and I become painfully aware of this fact. I've been to hundreds of big-name rock concerts, but I've always been in the back of the auditorium, row QQQ seat 208 or something. I would go to the show, groove to hearing the band perform my favorite song, have a few beers with my friends, then we'd all drive home talking about how great the artists looked or how well they played a certain song. But they were strictly the entertainment of the evening, no matter how much I liked the band. Then it was back to life as usual.

This is different. I'm somehow the audience and the performers at the same time, looking out at all those faces and feeling the immense responsibility of having to make thousands of people happy all at once. Will I be able to pull it off?

From the side of the stage Dee and I are assigned to, we have a full view of "rock god" Eddie Van Halen. He's thin, with toned muscles, but his face is pale and heavily lined, as if he hasn't slept for months, and his hair hangs in straggly strings down past his shoulders. He's naked from the waist up and wearing these funky camo-print carpenter pants, the kind with lots of pockets on the legs. There's so much silver duct tape wrapped around his shoes, you can't even see them. He rarely acknowledges those of us in the pit.

Eddie *is* the guitar. Thick veins pop out in his right arm as he plays and sweat glistens on his bare chest. His fingers dissolve into the strings, transcending instinct. His axe is the face of his soul and he shreds it, whinnies it, weeps it, shrieks it, breathes through its body. I can't take my eyes off him. And yet, the vibe I get is one of deep sorrow. He seems like he's struggling to resurface for the light that used to sustain his soul, something he craves and has lost touch with. Maybe it's the tattoo on his upper arm—two linked hearts with the name of his estranged wife, Valerie, across them—that makes me think this. Either way, he looks so vulnerable and it makes me wish there was something I could do to help him—your typical female I'm-gonna-save-this-man delusion. How can he be so gifted, so famous, and seem so unhappy at the same time? Doesn't he have more money than God? When he opens his mouth to sing, thick bands of saliva stretch from his tongue, as if he desperately needs a drink of water and it looks like his teeth are black and rotted. Why doesn't he save himself? Millions would give anything for one crumb of his talent. I guess having all the talent or money in the world isn't the most important thing, and maybe he hasn't discovered what that most important thing is yet—whatever that means to him. Nevertheless, the genius in him still flows through his veins, and I sense that it carries with it the possibility that all is not lost. It's all up to him.

Eddie's brother, Alex, pounds the drums on a side of the stage I can't see well. He makes them seethe and riot, transforming toms and cymbals into beautiful women vying for his attention.

Bass player Michael doesn't look like a rock star but he has more earrings than most men I know who wear them, and he has tattoos on both arms and legs. He screams in high-pitched vocals, giving it all he has. At one point, he holds up a full-sized bottle of Jack Daniels and chugs nearly half of it. The sound he creates slides inside me from under my ribs and escalates the rhythm into a Picasso of color. He punctuates the phrases with animal abandon, creates feedback like jalapeno spikes off the stage amps and sears it into my flesh, sustaining raw vibration. He gives the impression that if allowed to his own devices, he'd quite possibly unleash a bass monster that would consume the audience. Smashing his fist into his guitar, he makes the sound rise above the rhythm into a throaty solo, intense and growling. Just when I'm sure the monster has every intention of digesting us, he smiles, laughs out loud at our gullibility, and playfully releases us unharmed. Unharmed but not unaffected. Then he takes another swig of Jack Daniels and grins again. Man, he has a beautiful smile.

Dressed in a yellow T-shirt and yellow pants rolled up above the ankles, Sammy notices me in the audience and comes over. He bends down and says something into my face but I can't hear him; the music's too loud. Then he squeezes my hand, gives me a hug, and reaches down and tousles my hair. I feel like the guest of honor. How did he recognize *me* in that huge crowd? How did he remember who I was? I wonder what that woman thinks now, the one who asked me if I was a friend of the band. Something inside of me lights up like a small candle in a dark corner.

The music keeps coming. Fast and furious. Sammy moves to center stage, then rolls onto his back, long blonde curls fanning out around his head, and thrusts his hips. He screams from a place deep in his soul, and I can almost see a red flame swelling from every chord, glancing blows off the walls like some ravenous, holy spirit. The music oozes from him, and unlike Eddie's controlling obsession, Sammy seems to bask in it, radiate it, allowing it to slide from his heart and run with the sweat down his face and onto the stage. Then, without warning, a tiger pounces from behind his smiling eyes and devours the night, licking the last precious drops from his whiskers. He goes out of his way to make a production of this gesture, making sure we get that the song's about oral sex. What a bad boy.

The audience goes berserk with applause.

A heavy-set woman from somewhere up on the side yells out, "Sammy!" and tosses a bunch of suckers onto the stage. When Sammy turns to look at her, she flashes him her naked breasts, which are flopping like two flesh-colored, deflated watermelons.

Sammy goes over and picks up one of the suckers. He unwraps it and puts it in his mouth, then gestures toward the woman saying, "Them are monsters." I'm sure he's seen more than my naive brain can imagine. I don't think I could take it. You must have to be either really resilient or have a lot of self-control to survive in this business, or the constant temptations of excess would eat you alive. How would you hold on to your soul when everyone wants a piece of it and feels entitled to it? And after years of that, how could you keep on digging into your heart to write your music, giving so much of yourself when you don't even know who you are anymore because everyone else has taken so much of you? Maybe that's what happened to Eddie.

Security guards quickly pounce on the woman and haul her out of the stadium, but she's smiling a huge smile—she's accomplished her mission.

Sammy keeps singing and sucking on the candy. Then, as he walks past me in my spot inside the stage, he comes over with the sucker, getting ready to give it to one of the fans. Other people scramble to grab it, but Sammy goes out of his way to make sure I'm the one who gets it.

I pop the sucker into my mouth. *The candy was wet before it touched my tongue . . . .* Okay, I admit it—this is a turn-on. A spark stirs in my soul and between my legs. I shift my stance to take my mind off of it. I'm married. I can't allow myself to succumb to such thoughts . . . I shouldn't . . . *The candy was sticky before I put it in my mouth . . . .* It would be so easy to indulge myself right now, to let myself fall into the sensation that wants to take over my body and the thoughts that want to surface—so wickedly sweet. *Oh why the hell not?* Why do I always have to be the good girl? *His spit is in my mouth. He did it on purpose. He knew what it would do to me . . .* I'm only human—and female, what can I say? Oh God, I'm caving—*what would it feel like to have sex with a rock star*—feel him moving inside me—just once—somebody who's seen it all? Would he take my soul or would I be disappointed because sometimes fantasies are more exciting than reality? I spin the sucker around inside my mouth and wrap my tongue around it. And suddenly it dawns on me what I'm implying by playing with the damn sucker like this. Shit! Why am I letting him do this to me?

"You have to stop this right now," my sensible side says. "You're married. It's not good for you to have thoughts like this."

"Just this once—" the other side makes one, last-ditch effort. "Let yourself live a little!" Then, as always, but with a little more coercion this time, "sensible side" hauls the inappropriate thoughts away like the proverbial hook pulling a bad performer off the stage. The spark then slinks back into the shadows where these kinds of sensations are safe. Well, for the most part. It keeps looking over its shoulder every now and then, checking to see if there's a chance I might change my mind, like, "Not that it would ever happen, but what if I *did* have the chance? Would I actually do it?"

Why do I have to be so goddamned human? And why is life so frigging complicated? I hate this feeling—this loss of self-control. I like it. Oh God, I love it.

Dee is watching me closely. "Ewwwww, he had that in his mouth!" He wrinkles up his nose and frowns.

"I know." *Damn, I feel so good right now.*

Since we're down in this hole inside the stage, the band members swirl around us as if we are the centerpiece decoration and I feel like I'm suspended in time, caught up in the music as I allow it to enter me and roll through me without thoughts or worries—a feeling of wanting to hold on and let go at the same time. I try to absorb every detail of the deluge that encompasses me. I want to soak in the sensation of being in this privileged space, watching it all transpire around me but knowing it will soon end.

No sooner do I completely let go than the show is over in an evaporation of sound. I need more. I want more, but there isn't any more. I walk out of the building, forced to settle for an awareness somewhere between ringing emptiness and enduring excitement while a sticky sucker glues itself to the inside of my pocket.

CHAPTER 12

Tidal Waves

If there is no passion in your life, then have you really lived? Find your passion, whatever it may be. Become it, and let it become you and you will find great things happen FOR you, TO you and BECAUSE of you.
—T. Alan Armstrong

August, 2004

How am I supposed to go on coordinating the car wash fundraiser for the high school and making meatloaf for dinner like I'm just an ordinary mom, when such extraordinary things are happening to me? I feel like I should have a flashing neon sign on my forehead that reads, "Ask me about my mystical experience with Sammy Hagar!"

Nancy says that since I've been back from Cabo, my life sounds a lot like what Dr. Wayne Dyer talks about in *The Power of Intention.* She says he addresses this very thing. I'm not so sure I believe her, but I buy the book anyway.

Dyer writes that when we are on the correct path of what our lives are intended to be, everything falls into place and the people and circumstances we need to help us carry out our life's purpose appear like magic. He describes exactly what has been happening to me, not in esoteric terms but in understandable, practical ways. He says that we can make the voice inside of us reality. We shouldn't worry about how ridiculous something sounds, or how unattainable it seems; if we open ourselves to receive it, it will come.

Finally, somebody knows what I'm talking about! I think I can keep going now—wherever it is I'm going.

The supernatural incidents are starting to feel more and more important for reasons I can't comprehend. As consolation, I tell myself that if something remarkable doesn't happen within the next few years, I will come to the conclusion that I have a *way* too overactive imagination and just drop it all. In the meantime, Dyer is the only person I've come across who seems to understand all of this. And does he really count? I mean, I can't exactly call him and ask for advice. Same with Sammy.

Why couldn't this have happened to me with my next-door neighbor instead of with a celebrity? It would be much easier to talk to my neighbor. I could run right over there after he finished mowing his lawn. He'd be leaning on the mower and admiring his work, his Bob Seger and the Silver Bullet Band concert T-shirt from 1984 soaked with sweat and I could just walk up to him, offer him a cold glass of iced tea, and ask, "How's it goin'? Your grass looks beautiful. I bet you'd like something cold to drink."

He'd smile, thank me, and take the tea. Then he'd guzzle it, and after he finished, I could then say, "I've been having some trouble understanding all the psychic episodes that have happened to me since I met you a few months ago. Do you have a minute? I have some questions for you."

He'd say, "Sure, what do you want to know?" and simply answer my questions right then and there. When I was satisfied, he'd tell me, "If you have any more questions, just let me know."

Then I'd walk back home, carrying his empty glass and smiling to myself because I know he's right there with the answers anytime I need them.

Maybe I should try asking Sammy anyway.

Sitting down in front of my computer, I scooch myself into the worn, black cushion of my Wal-Mart-special desk chair. A wire pokes through the fabric and into my butt. This could be another long process.

As I type, I keep seeing the out-of-body moment I had in Cabo and hearing the song "Love Walks In" and all the other coincidences that won't allow me to ignore them. They're replaying in my mind like a DVD on repeat mode, but much more focused around the edges. Maybe this is confirmation that writing this letter is what I'm supposed to do next, I don't know, but it's a positive feeling, so I just go with it.

I'm busy telling Sammy about the aliens thing, telling him that I don't know what to believe, when the glass candleholder on the corner of my desk suddenly explodes, shooting shards of glass and liquid wax all over my desk and my keyboard. And there are two triangular pieces of glass left spinning like tops on the desk in front of me. I just sit and stare at them for a moment. Ah . . . what just happened? I've had that candleholder for years, burned lots of candles in it. It didn't have any cracks in it and the flame wasn't touching the glass anywhere . . . . I've never even heard of a glass votive exploding like this. If they did, the Consumer Product Safety Commission would have taken them off the market long ago because some manufacturer would have gotten sued or something.

I find my camera and take a picture of it, just in case someday I doubt whether it really happened, because I'm doing that a lot lately—doubting the things I'm seeing and hearing and feeling. Then I sit back and stare at the mess again. Did some kind of spirit do this? Some kind of alien? Was I *not* supposed to tell Sammy about the aliens? Were they excited that I was? Wow, this is creepy. There's nothing I can do but sit here alone with my thoughts. And clean up the glass and melted wax.

A few months go by. I've just gotten home from the post office and dropping off my letter to Sammy. I put a load of clothes in the washing machine, then, picking up junk mail that has attached itself to various horizontal surfaces in my kitchen and dining room, I go to feed it to the shredder. As the machine whirs devouring the papers, my mind is entertaining all sorts of deep, philosophical thoughts, like, *I guess I should take down the valances so I can wash them. They're looking pretty grimy.*

"The unfathomable is now possible," comes a male voice.

What? I hear the words as if someone is standing right next to me talking to me, but there's no one else in the room. Just to make sure, I glance around. Nope. It's just me and the shredder, the dirty valances, and the dining room table.

"The universe is welcoming this with open arms," it comes again.

"Okay, God, the Universe, whatever-you-are, just exactly what does this mean? That there are reasons I don't know about for my sending that letter to Sammy?" I ask aloud because I'm feeling a bit ambivalent about it. I look up at the ceiling, hoping one of God's messengers will appear and explain everything. But the only thing that appears is a rather large cobweb I must have missed while dusting.

At this point God is probably thinking, *Now go away, little girl, this is enough for your small brain right now. We'll be in touch. My people will call your people.*

Since no Great Spirit materializes, or any aliens for that matter, I go upstairs to find my notebook. Nancy says I should keep track of all these wacky things because they might make sense someday. And yet, it would be so easy to write this off as my imagination, which it more than likely is. Um, *isn't* it?

A few weeks later, I'm eating a fortune cookie from the big bag I just bought at the Asian market, and the message inside reads, "The world is always ready to receive talent with open arms." The words sound familiar, so I check my journal to see if I may have recorded something there. Sure enough, there's an entry dated three weeks earlier where I'd written, "The universe is welcoming this with open arms," along with "The unfathomable is now possible." Ah well, it's just a coincidence; fortune cookies are a game. Besides, I'm good at being logical. I've perfected the technique through years of denying my inner feelings. I can remain rational now too.

Days later, I grab another fortune cookie. Again, the message inside reads, "The world is always ready to receive talent with open arms." What is this? Did the cookie-making machine have the hiccups when it made this batch? Maybe they all have the same fortune. There are more than three dozen cookies in the bag, and although I hate to waste food, I have to know, so I dump out the entire bagful onto the kitchen table and start breaking them open one at a time, hoping for some explanation other than anything mystical. Please, please prove to me that I'm not losing my mind, please! But after I've inspected the contents of every single cookie, and eaten far too many of the bland, crunchy bits in the process, I find that none contain that same fortune. I'm left with nothing but a huge mess, more unanswered questions, and a stomach ache. Just what I needed.

As I brush the pile of crumbs off the edge of the table and into the wastebasket, something tells me I should hold on to the message that came to me twice, so after I finish cleaning up cookie dust, I tape the two tiny pieces of paper with my fortune on it onto one of the pages in my notebook.

World, universe, open arms, open arms—is this supposed to mean something to me?

There's a lot of clutter on my desk, and it seems like it's always too much effort to move it every time I want to work. The worst part is that each item has value *right now*, so I can't put any of it away. I need the books about people who have had similar experiences, my journals, coffee cup with a dried-out teabag glued to the inside, and a plate with moldy cheese stuck to it. Not only that, but I can't find my slippers and my feet are cold. All these things seem like a representation of my life—a jumbled heap. How do I sort through them? Why do I feel like I have to? Because I can't get to my computer if I don't. I also can't *not* write. I'm turning into a writing junkie. I would do nothing but ride the train of what comes out of my heart and my hands if you'd let me. I wouldn't eat, sleep, shower, leave the house, exercise—nothing. It's a rather magical relationship really. When I allow myself to step away from my mind, what emerges has a life of its own. I'm merely an outsider whose purpose is to transcribe the story that wants to be told. I'm also learning a lot about myself in the process though, like what I believe and what's important to me, because I have to think really hard to determine what it was that caused me to react the way I did in each situation, so it's kind of like being my own therapist. And I'm gaining a new respect for other people's perspectives, because all this forces me to think about stuff like that, stuff I maybe wouldn't have thought about if I hadn't been writing about it. What's more, I feel myself growing as a person in huge ways because of all this. I never would have considered that one rock concert could have such extensive repercussions.

Today my addiction screams, "You've recorded so many crazy incidents in your journals since Cabo, you should write a book."

"Yeah, right," I tell it. "I don't know how to write a book. And where on earth is this notion coming from?"

"Maybe not from earth," comes another thought.

Just what is *that* supposed to mean? My gaze falls to the mark on my desk left by the hot wax when the votive exploded, and it makes me feel uneasy all over again.

Time will tell, right? I just have to be patient, but I'm squirming in my chair. The enlightened ones say we must be completely present in the now, because all that matters is this moment. We're supposed to perceive each experience as if it's the first time we've experienced it. Beginner's Mind, Zen calls it. Maybe it's easier to do this if you're a monk on a hillside, or some wealthy, 17th century white guy like René Descartes, who formed an entire philosophy about reality by observing burning candles and melting wax. Funny how that particular example just popped into my head. Anyway, maybe Beginner's Mind isn't so easy to implement if you're a middle-aged woman with a million things on your mind, mostly because you're the mom of three teenage boys and having paranormal stuff happen to you at the same time. But I try. Sitting here at my desk and looking down at my spiral notebook as it covers the gouges and dings, I watch the great avalanche of words pouring out of me, but not the ones that contain the technique for being patient and accepting the *now*.

Write a book? I have my hands full just trying to keep track of all this weird stuff. How would I ever find the time to put it together in a meaningful way? It's all happening so fast that I can't even get it all into this pain-in-the-ass notebook that won't let me be.

Giving in, I pick up my pen and begin to write, and as my hand moves across the page, a warmth starts to rise inside of me like taking a sip of hot soup on a rainy evening. I can feel it approach—quietly like water soaking into a paper towel.

I attempt to describe it in my journal: "The feeling is getting stronger. And stronger. I almost feel like crying because of the overwhelming emotion . . . Oh God, I *am* crying." This is no longer a teensy hint of a sensation, it's huge. And it's scaring me. It feels like a jolt that's sucking all the breath out of me, like the moment right before orgasm when there is intense buildup and then it breaks open, releasing everything inside of you—a mental, physical, and spiritual rush, but this time without the pronounced sensation of pleasure. In a matter of seconds, I feel tremendous love, anger, fear, joy, fulfillment, despair, confusion, peace, agony, frustration, and every possible emotion pouring into me all at once. Before I can react, it quickly fades. Then right away, it builds again, like a wave rising and falling, something great bursting at the seams and then regrouping.

I cover my mouth with my hand, I don't even know why, and tears continue to fall, but I don't know what they're for. My breathing comes in rapid, shallow inhalations followed by exhalations that seem forced out my nose like snorts, as if my breath is trying to catch up to what I'm feeling. What *am* I feeling? Maybe this is what an anxiety attack feels like, but that doesn't make sense. I wasn't worrying about anything. Besides, I don't have anxiety attacks. I try not to think about it, but I can't help it. I feel like I'm under the influence of an unseen energy, a power beyond human beings. *Beyond human beings?* What then? Spirits? *Aliens?* Don't even go there.

It's forcing my mind to forget about everything I'm doing at the moment and concentrate exclusively on what it's trying to tell me. *What is it trying to tell me?*

And it's speaking to me in feelings because words can't relate its message.

Where did that come from? It's definitely independent of me.

If I smash my toe into the leg of a chair, it hurts and I usually cry out. If one of my kids hugs me for no reason, it makes me smile (or wonder what they've been up to). I'm used to these feelings. I know how to react. This is different. It feels like the warm, sweet breath of someone I love on my face, or maybe a sound I can't actually hear, magnified to the point where it causes me to shudder.

I put the pen down and turn my gaze away from the paper. I can't go on. It's too huge, so I just sit staring off into space while I wait for my mind to quiet down. After a few minutes, the feeling subsides and my hand picks up the pen again. Words pour out. I don't think they're coming from me:

. . . something immense has cracked open and opposites must both be released like magnets + and − for any circuit to be complete, to work at all. But don't swim toward the negative, just note it's necessary to complete the connection. Don't be scared. Trust in God and love and positiveness. It is most powerful. Let yourself sink into the velvety warmth of its light. Allow it to steer you. You can't go wrong. *Wow. Where did that come from? From God? Oh man, I am only a small person.* This is meant to be, you are strong. It is good and it is right. *I am giving myself way too much credit. Time to do housework and quit being so fucking lofty! . . . now quit thinking this is so serious, it is not world changing! Put it in perspective!* It has to do with the music. The key is the music. *Why? Key to what?*

Then it quits. Ever since the experience I had in Cabo San Lucas, it seems like something's been trying to communicate with me and whatever it is, it seems to be getting bolder all the time. First, I got the feeling that someone was in the room with me, giving me the message that Sammy was reading my letter. A few months later, I actually heard words being spoken and then I kept seeing visions of things that made no sense. Not long after that, my candleholder exploded. Now it almost feels like it's literally entering me. At the same time, I'm getting the idea that it's reached a barrier and can't come any further, so now it's my turn, to reach out to *it*. *Where is this idea coming from?* And how do I contact *it?* I'm not sure I want to, or if I should, and yet, the odd part about it, as if all of this isn't odd enough, is that it's only scaring me because I don't know what it is. It doesn't feel evil or negative. It feels like it's a part of me that's trying to surface and I keep squashing it because I don't understand where it's coming from. Maybe it's a surge of energy from another dimension that's trying to take me somewhere or get me to do something. Oh yeah, that's a comforting thought.

Leaning back in my chair, I wait to see what else is going to happen because it feels like I have no other choice than to be its vehicle. Nothing does.

"Okay, well, I don't have time for mystical riddles today," I announce, mostly to convince myself that I really do have my shit together. Then I return to my chores. I have about sixteen different jobs going at once. I don't know why I do this. I start cleaning the bathroom and when I go to take out the trash, I notice there's a big stack of unopened mail on the kitchen counter. I don't want to lose any bills, so I start sorting through that, thinking I'll put the junk mail out with the trash. Then I decide that I need another cup of coffee, but the pot is empty. When I go to make another pot, there's no more coffee in the can, so I have to go to the basement and find another one. When I get downstairs, I can't see because the light bulb at the bottom of the stairs is burned out, so forgetting to bring up the can of coffee, I walk all the way back upstairs to find a bulb. And while I'm standing in front of the linen closet where we keep all the bulbs, I can't remember why I came up here in the first place. Ah well, the sheets need changing. I might as well do that while

I'm thinking about it. I don't understand why I just can't get anything done.

A bit later, I'm emptying the dishwasher and something rises inside me like an ancient superstition. It's that wave again. It moves over me and through me. I stop what I'm doing in an effort to "hear" what it's trying to tell me, not with my ears so much, but with my soul. I figure it must have gained some momentum from the first time, so now I'd better be prepared for a doozie. What else can I do? Run out the front door and down the street fleeing from—*what?* But it just quits, so I go back to emptying the dishwasher. Huh. Good for me. I've managed to stay cool and collected once again. When I think about it, though, I guess life is full of unexplained things, so maybe I should start giving these incidents a bit more credence and stop telling myself it's all just my imagination because all that does is make me sweep it under the rug and nothing gets solved that way.

Six days later it comes back, so I decide it's time I asked for God's protection—formally, that is, even though a very big part of me thinks that God is really the ringmaster in all this. I sit down at the kitchen table, position my elbows on the table in front of me, and sink my head into my hands. I can hear the clock ticking on the wall. "Dear God, please help me. What are you doing to me? Or what am I doing to myself?" As I utter these words, it occurs to me that maybe all of this isn't as scary as I've been making it out to be, because this otherworldly force seems to be taking me inside myself—beyond the obedience, fear, and inferiority, to the root of my soul and the real person I am and it's teaching me to believe in myself.

It also makes me think about this book I've been reading called *The Journey* by Brandon Bays. She had a mystical journey that changed her life too. She says that once you've had an awakening like this, its source won't leave you alone until you fall so in love with it that you just can't tear yourself away. I'd say that pretty well sums up what's been happening to me. Maybe that's why I feel such a constant pull in both directions; I'm fighting against believing in a concept I love more than I care to admit to myself. And maybe that concept is God. Or myself.

CHAPTER 13

A Goddess Introduces Herself

It's not what you look at that matters, it's what you see.
—Henry David Thoreau

October, 2004

Since last year's trip to Cabo was so amazing, Dee and I just *had* to come back.

Tonight we return to our hotel room and fall into bed. It's late, or it's early, however you want to look at it. We've had a fun day playing in the sun and a fun night of dancing. So in these wee hours, I sorely need my rest.

Haaaaaaaaaaaa . . . . comes a soft touch slithering into my sleep.

My eyes open wide in the darkness. It doesn't seem like I've been asleep for more than a few minutes.

Haaaaaaaaaaaaa . . . . it comes again. It's not really a sound. It's more of a suggestion coming into my mind—but generated by somebody else. Emotions form in me that don't translate into English. I sit up and strain my ears. All is quiet except for Dee's snoring.

I get out of bed and walk across the smooth, ceramic tiles to the sliding glass door. I can hardly see. I'm not frightened. I'm not feeling anything at all. Pulling back the heavy drapes, I step out onto the balcony where the scent of the ocean is so strong, it surprises me. The air is cold. Darkness bathes all of Cabo as long fingers of coconut palms dance in a slight breeze, and the only sound is that of the Sea of Cortez washing against the sand of Medano Beach five stories below. It's soothing, but I know I haven't been called out here to appreciate the water.

My eyes are drawn to the majestic structure of stone that protrudes out into the Pacific Ocean—Land's End. I swear the rocks are glowing. They're radiating a purplish, light blue. Or maybe it's just the light of the moon reflecting off the rocks. I look for it, but I don't see it. No, the rocks are absolutely glowing and a vibration so low I can barely detect it seems to radiate from them. There is spirit here, something noble and unmistakably female—as if the rocky peninsula were a sleeping goddess that fell off some fiery meteor in another lifetime. And she's been lying here ever since, extending her great arm to the sea, waiting for me to remember my name, the name she gave me thousands of years ago. I sense her smile because she knows I have heard her at last, as if she has spent her entire life searching for me like a loving parent calling a child home. Or perhaps I've spent my entire life searching for *her.*

I must be dreaming. Where else would these thoughts be coming from? I've just been awakened from a dead sleep, my brain couldn't possibly have come up with such heavy stuff on such short notice.

A few strands of my hair blow in front of my face as I scan the horizon and the rocks for an explanation. There is none. I grab hold of the railing to steady myself so I can get a better look. The rocks are definitely glowing. And it feels like there are invisible rays of energy coming from them, and being absorbed into my skin. It's not a physical sensation though. It's more like an emotion. I frown, suddenly aware of the scent of the hot-pink flowers in the box that hangs on the railing. They smell kind of bitter and sweet at the same time.

Rising from somewhere in my mind, again I "hear" words or a melody coming from Land's End like some hazy, distant sigh. The sound is made of notes I've never heard before and played on instruments I don't recognize, *if they're even instruments at all.* As I listen, I get a sense of letting go of everything that is holding her or me captive to this earth, as if the rocks and me are one entity.

"What do you want?" I whisper to whatever is out there.

The energy seems to extricate itself from the rocks and move toward me, like the spirit of the wind, a gossamer mist, swirling like some cartoonist's idea of a glorious phantom. But it doesn't feel harmful or threatening, it's warm and comforting. It surrounds me and takes something from inside of me—scoops it out—but with love and kindness, the way a mother takes the pain away when she hugs her child who's just fallen off her bicycle. Is this the same energy that came to me in Sammy's bar last year—something familiar that I'd forgotten existed? The spirit that's been trying to communicate with me ever since? It sure feels like it.

It also feels like when you meet someone who feeds your soul. You know it instantly and you can't let them leave before you find out what the message is that their presence is bringing you. And since you don't know them, you're not sure if you should say something or not, but because you may never see them again, if you're going to say something, you'd better do it, before it's too late. Like when I met Sammy. The problem then becomes—what *do* you say? In Zen, they might call this a *koan.* (A riddle without a solution, used to show the inadequacy of logical reasoning.)[1] This thought makes me smile—rock and roll and Zen. What a perfect dichotomy.

I look again at Land's End. *It's just a pile of rocks.* And yet, its spirit seems to hang in the air like a master waiting for her apprentice to remember what to do next. But I can't figure it out. After a while, the cool breeze off the ocean touches my naked body, making me conscious of its sobering reality. Still, I can't seem to pull myself away from the spell that consumes me, so I sit down in the plastic chair on the balcony, draw my legs up, and wrap my arms around myself to keep warm. And then I just sit like in meditation—receptive, calm, waiting. For hours. I don't even feel the time pass, I just notice all of a sudden that it's getting light out and a little warmer. The sun is rising out of the sea in a huge, bright, orange ball, which turns gold, then almost white, as it paints the dark water and the dark sky with splashes of pink and turquoise. And as the sun comes up, I realize that the goddess has somehow slipped away with the night, tiptoed out of my awareness, and gone back to wherever it was she came from.

Did I doze off? Did I dream all this?

The brighter the sun gets, the more it hurts my eyes and makes me realize that I'm sitting, stark naked, right out in the open. I think this is hilarious. It reminds me of the story of the Garden of Eden, where I was taught that after Adam and Eve ate the fruit of knowledge, they suddenly realized they were naked and hid themselves because they were ashamed. Ordinarily, I would have done the same thing for the same reason, but now I'm not. And I'm not ashamed. It feels pretty wonderful really—sitting out here without any pretense, the sun beating down on the parts of me that have never seen sun before. I could get used to this.

I look over at Land's End and she looks somehow different, the way you might perceive a co-worker you had great sex with last night but don't want anyone else in the office to know about.

I've heard it said that when we're meditating, or engaged in some sort of activity where we're not thinking about anything in particular, or when our minds are still on that threshold of twilight, between the waking state and the dream state, that's when we're most open, and most receptive to spiritual contact. So maybe what just happened wasn't a dream. Maybe the intelligence from another dimension that's been trying to contact me for over a year now, really did come to me. And maybe it had something to do with my mystical experience last year.

Either way, this encounter has changed something in me, taken something out of me, put something in. Native Americans believe that all of nature has a voice and if we listen closely enough, we'll be able to hear its song. And that's how I feel right now. I'm not quite sure how to describe it, but I swear, I feel like a song.

CHAPTER 14

Rock and Roll in Your Face

When I play, I make love—it is the same thing.
—Arthur Rubinstein

October, 2004

As Dee and I walk by Cabo Wabo tonight, we notice the line for tickets to the show tomorrow night is already forming, so we rush back to our hotel room, grab the clean white pillows and a blanket off the bed, and fill a plastic bag with bottles of water and tortillas for breakfast. Like brazen thieves, we tiptoe past the concierge desk as we make our way through the lobby, past the statues of one-armed, naked mermen wearing great anguish on their faces while slaying sea serpents, and colossal paintings framed in gaudy gold, and slip out the double front doors. I almost expect someone to stop us and ask just what did we think we were doing leaving the building with the hotel's bedding? But no one does, although their questioning brown eyes seem to burn a hole in me.

We return to the line of bodies camped out on the broken cement and cobblestones and arrange the blanket on the sidewalk. Cockroaches five inches long scurry next to the wall of the building we've leaned our pillows up against. I pull my pillow back a few inches, pretending it doesn't bother me when I really want to jump up and scream like a girl. But what good would it do me anyway?

Sleeping on the streets for concert tickets probably isn't so bad if you're in your twenties, but pushing fifty, it's almost too much. I can't believe I'm actually doing this. Except the club holds about 800 people, and when Sammy plays here, 3,000 show up. Although the managers do their best to find a way to accommodate everyone, they can't seem to determine exactly how to do that. There just isn't enough room, so it's first-come, first-served.

It's dark out now but still hot and humid. In Colorado when the sun goes down, it gets cool even in the summer. Not here. It's going to be a long night. More people line up behind us. Some are locals and some are fans. I watch them set up their couches, sleeping bags, air mattresses, tents, coolers full of beer, booze, and water, and battery-operated CD players. What an eclectic group we are: some are chatty, some are drunk, and some just don't talk to anyone. I'm not sure where I fit in. It's like mixing giraffes with housecats. Red ants so tiny I can hardly see them find their way up my legs and bite me from the knees down and all over my arms. The bites itch and when I scratch them, they bleed.

As the night wears on, the line grows—down the street, around the corner, and up the next street. Dee has deserted me as usual, and is walking around socializing. I finally spot him over by the porta-potties talking with a heavily-tattooed couple. I guess I'm okay by myself. The young couple behind me doesn't speak English, so without anyone to talk to, I lie down and try to sleep, but the cobblestones poke right through the flimsy sheet and into my butt, my shoulders, and my back. I don't know how anyone can possibly sleep under these conditions.

By this time, it must be well past midnight. An older model Ford LTD with one headlight dangling like an eye dislocated from its socket suddenly screeches to a stop in the middle of the block while the driver and passengers exchange words in Spanish with several people waiting in the line. I can't figure out why Sammy's fans would want to fight with local people. That's not cool. We're guests in their country.

Now they're shouting and shaking their fists at one another and I realize the people they're arguing with are not Sammy's fans. But some of the fans are really drunk, so they can't help but get involved anyway. They start hollering back at the people in the car. And they're laughing. They think it's funny. This is the kind of stuff that makes me not want to be a fan.

"Shut up," I mutter. I don't really want them to hear me, but I do. "You're going to get us all hurt. What's the matter with you?" What if the men in the car turn violent, join the locals in line, and lash out at the rest of us?

Little pinpricks of fear rise up on my skin. There's nothing but a long line of fans for a concert here; there's no one with authority to keep things peaceful. Then the smell of beer and dried urine wafts past me on the hot breeze. It's coming from everywhere. The smell of beer doesn't have good memories for me, so all I can do is watch in helpless awe and wish I were anywhere but here. And pray.

Minutes later, the *policía* pull up behind the LTD, which is still parked in the middle of the street. Several people in the car jump out and run, blend in with the folks waiting in line, then disappear into the darkness, but the *policía* manage to nab the driver and one passenger. I feel like I'm watching some kind of action movie as they slam the driver's face into the hood of the car with a sickening thud. Then they pull out their guns and aim them at the heads of the two men. I turn and look the other way. Maybe if I don't see the guns, they won't be real.

My whole body is shaking. It's only a matter of time before ricocheting bullets start slicing into the line of people, I just know it. I can already picture blood spurting all over the cement walls of the buildings we're leaning against and running into the cracks in the sidewalk, people screaming and others going down, then panic and mayhem breaking out. There's nowhere to run and no way to protect ourselves. Oh God, please let them hurry and end this before someone gets hurt.

My heart is beating so fast and hard, it feels like it's going to punch a hole right through my chest. The worst part about it is, I don't know where Dee is. He must have wandered off to talk to more people. Why isn't he putting his arms around me and telling me everything's going to be okay? Are concert tickets really worth putting our lives in danger? And how come nobody else seems concerned? Maybe I've just led a sheltered life and I'm making too big of a deal out of it, but there are guns right out in the open. I'm in a foreign country and there's no one to talk to. Everyone else is either drunk or trying to sleep. Maybe that's why they're not worried. Oh yeah, that makes me feel better— they could be mown down in their sleep or drunken stupors and never even know it . . . . *Where's Dee?*

After a while, I realize shots aren't being fired and I turn back to look. The *policía* now have the men handcuffed and there doesn't appear to be any more resistance.

I take a deep breath. Is it safe yet to breathe? I take another. It seems to be okay. I think. Finally, Dee comes up to me.

"Those idiots!" He's making light of the situation.

I'm so relieved to see him that I fall onto him. "Where have you been?"

"Just over there." He points.

I wish I could take this as casually as he does. This scene has brought back memories I never wanted to think of again. I burrow my face into his chest and the warmth of him makes me feel safe.

It seems like it takes forever, but the *policía* finally throw the men into the patrol car and haul the LTD off the street.

All of this just seems to reinforce my initial feelings of apprehension I had last year when we were here. How can anyone live like this all the time? I have a friend whose son is in the Army and he told me that when he's in Iraq, he can't let his guard down for a second. He even has to sleep with his ears open, ready for anything. I can't imagine living with that kind of stress. This is bad enough. I suddenly feel cold and wrap Dee's arms around me.

"You're the only person I know who can be cold in Cabo," he tells me.

After the commotion dies down, Dee and I return to our blankets and pillows on the sidewalk. The hours crawl by. Across the street, there's a building that looks like the boards are peeling off. "Mexico's most beautiful showgirls!" the sign boasts. The walls are painted with pictures of women with human bodies and fish tails—mermaids. One of the mermaids has green eyes. There's something hauntingly beautiful about her and frightening at the same time. She's seen all of this before and much more than I can imagine, I'm sure. I just wish she'd quit looking at me like that. It makes me nervous all over again.

Once in awhile, men go in and out of the warped, plywood front door at the mermaid place and several young women in stiletto heels and very short skirts come out and wait at the curb, reapplying their makeup. Men in cars come and pick them up.

Finally, a very large, dark-skinned man comes out of the building and secures the padlock across the door. Now all is quiet across the street and I'm forced to focus on the blazing streetlights. They're cruel reminders of the long night. And the frigging things are buzzing.

It feels like months before the sky starts showing any hint of getting light, as if it's been one long, continuous night for the past 48 hours. I haven't slept at all. Not even five minutes. And then roosters begin to crow. It's as if their voices are a feeble attempt to console me—"A new day is here, *Señora!* The darkness is over. You survived! It's party time now!" The sound pierces my head like tiny needles, so I pull my pillow around my head. What are those damn birds so happy about? They're probably going to be on somebody's plate before the day's over. Stupid birds. And why does everything down here feel like such a contradiction? First you think you're safe—oh but wait, no, you're not—the rules have changed, sorry!

Humidity rises with the sun and the sidewalk grows more treacherous by the hour. My back and neck feel like they've been stabbed with dull knives and I didn't think to bring any ibuprofen. My head begins to brew a dull, gray hum. Before long, the scent of cooking onions and peppers comes floating in the air. I picture a cute little Mexican mother wearing an apron and cooking breakfast for her sons, but it's probably just one of the sidewalk vendors. Wherever it's coming from, it makes my stomach growl.

Some people are still partying and some are trying to sleep as a man wanders up and down the line of campers, counting us.

"What number did I say you were?" he asks me.

"Huh?" I roll over and face him. "I don't know," I tell him, but I really want to say, "Just leave me alone, will you?"

"I'm trying to figure out how far back in line I am. They only have a certain number of tickets." He goes back to counting. I go back to feeling sorry for myself. *Oh, when is this going to be over?*

Another man comes from the end of the line. He's carrying a bottle of cheap tequila from which he takes a swig every so often. His sweaty, long hair is stuck to his bristly jowls and his bare belly protrudes over the waistband of his shorts as he stumbles, nearly tripping over his own feet. He stops every now and then, accosting people.

"You wanna see my dick?" he slobbers.

I'm hoping no one will answer him, but of course, someone does.

"Ah, go pass out somewhere," comes a male voice several people ahead of me.

This is all he needs. The drunk man pulls his pants down to his knees, revealing a hairy, beach-ball-sized gut gleaming over his sagging manhood—nothing I'd be advertising if I were him.

"Oh shit." I turn away, feeling a headache growing behind my eyes. "Don't encourage him."

He grins and pulls his pants back up.

Thank God he didn't hear what I said, but he does hear someone else make a remark.

"Okay, I'll do it again." Now he's shouting, "YOU WANNA SEE MY DICK?"

He does it again. Then he goes back to looking for trouble and getting right in some people's faces. Luckily this time, everybody ignores him and he staggers back to where he came from, mumbling, "Stupid motherfuckers."

Please, can't we just be done with all this drama? I want to go home. I want to take a shower and sleep in my soft bed. I want some bacon and eggs and a tall glass of orange juice. I hate how I feel right now. This experience has made me something I'm not—part of the mob, exactly what I didn't want to become. I've been sucked into the belly of the beast, albeit kicking and screaming, but I've been sucked in just the same. I don't think I'm the nice person I was yesterday, but I'm in such a daze, so worn out from lack of sleep and having to fight for every crumb, I can't tell for sure. People are talking to me and I hear my voice answering, but the words aren't making any sense. What if I've accidentally said or done something I shouldn't have just because I'm not in my right mind? I wouldn't even remember it if I did. Maybe I should just apologize to everyone right now before I do something stupid, but I'm sure they'd just think I was crazy. They don't know me anyway. I feel like I too have become a contradiction.

It's about 7:30 now. They're supposed to start handing out tickets at 8:00, and I'm still feeling sorry for myself as I watch carloads of locals pull up in front of Cabo Wabo. Five or six people get out of each car and join their friends in line. Maybe it's my lack of sleep, but I have no idea what's going on. I just feel numb and sticky and I wish those goddamned roosters would shut the hell up already.

Finally, the Cabo Wabo staff starts handing out the tickets. This time the show is free. The cost was spending all night in line. Like starving livestock, the weary crowd packs up their sleeping accoutrements, stuffs them under their arms, and shuffles forward to the men distributing the coveted reward—yellow wristbands. Thank God!

About ten people ahead of us, they run out of tickets. "Sorry," the management people shrug.

What? They're all gone? We weren't that far back in the line, how could they be all gone already? It's more than I can take. The pain in my head and back is now unbearable.

As if this isn't bad enough, Dee and I got into a car accident on our way out to dinner the day before. A young local couple with a 2-year-old baby, all riding on a scooter, T-boned us on my side of the car. No one was hurt in the wreck, but Dee and I were so shook up, we didn't even notice that no one gave us receipts for the money we forked over to God-knows-whom, or copies of the accident report. On top of that, the rental car ended up costing us more than $3,000 before we were through, even though we had insurance. Dee also got a parking ticket the same day, and the *policía* almost hauled him off to jail simply because he didn't understand Spanish.

I feel myself crumble. Right there in the courtyard, I sit down on the bricks and weep. I don't even care who sees me. Where did I get the foolish notion that life was fair?

A stranger tries to comfort me. "You can always watch the show from out here in the parking lot—there's a big screen up there." He puts his arm around my shoulder. "It's almost as good as being inside."

"We didn't spend all this money coming to Mexico to see a video," I say, allowing myself to surrender to my gloom.

But that's exactly what we have to settle for.

We do the same thing twice more, camp in line all night long to get tickets for the concerts. On the third night, we're successful. We're finally going to the show.

We go back to our hotel for a shower, a bite to eat, and a few hours of sleep before the concert. It's amazing how a shower can make you feel like a new person.

Once inside Cabo Wabo, Dee and I make our way through the crowds to the stage area, through the throngs of people moving both directions like opposing tides. Suddenly a heavy hand grabs my breast and squeezes. I glare into the faces going the opposite way and each one seems as innocent as the next—they're intent on getting outside or to the restroom or to the bar. I'm furious, with no one face to be furious at. It's like a monster whose venom is slithering within the masses. Apparently, if you're a woman with boobs or a butt, you're fair game because it isn't long before my butt gets pinched. And it happens again and again. The worst part is that there's no one to blame. No one but the great beast known as rock and roll. I guess I have to suck it up and carry on. It doesn't even do me any good to be mad. Nobody cares.

Tonight Dee wants to go one way and I want to go the other.

"See ya!" He waves and becomes absorbed back into the belly of the monster. If he'd known about the breast-grabbing and butt-pinching incidents, I wonder if he'd be leaving me alone. But I haven't been able to tell him yet.

As the show begins, I find myself behind a very tall man. He has thick hair that sticks straight up on top of his head and he's wide. I can hardly see around him. I ask him if he'd mind moving his head to the side for a minute so I can take a picture, but he says, "No. I was here first. I ain't moving," and folds his arms across his chest and plants his feet.

Later in the show, the man in front of me suddenly explodes in a rage. It seems he feels entitled to more standing space than he has. "Goddammit!" He's screaming at the guy behind him who is standing next to me. "Quit fucking sweating on me! You're *gross!* Can't you people just get *off* me?" He shoves his elbow into the ribs of the man behind him, then wipes off his arm like it's filthy. "I can't stand all you people sweating on me!"

"Sorry, man." The guy next to me tucks his arms in tighter to his body in order to make more room.

"Well then, you're in the wrong place, dude," I say, wondering why he even came to the show. Hasn't he ever been to a concert before? It's probably 110 degrees in here, people are crammed in body-to-body, and he doesn't want anyone to sweat on him? Please.

Before long, a woman somehow ends up next to the man in front of me. She didn't come in with him; how he allowed her next to him is beyond me. But I don't really care. I'm enjoying the show—hearing it, that is, since I really can't see much.

All of a sudden, the woman turns around and announces, "When I was here last year, I fucked Mikey!" She means Michael Anthony, Sammy's friend from Van Halen.

Am I supposed to be impressed? She looks to have about as much class as a bucket filled with slimy tadpoles, like the ones my brother and I used to scoop out of the pond near our house when we were kids. If what she's saying is true, Mikey had to have been trashed out of his mind.

"Really?" another woman says, grinning.

The first woman nods. "Oh yeah, baby! Woooo hoooo!" She shrieks, raises her hands in the air, revealing large rings of sweat under her armpits, and shakes her ample ass.

"Wow, that's awesome!" The second woman gives her a high five.

This is not my scene. I'm not a groupie. I don't get into fights with people at concerts, and I'm not used to being around guns and violence. I'm a mom and a wife, a respectable citizen who teaches her kids manners and attends church on Sundays. Well, *most* Sundays. What am I doing here? I wish I could just beam myself back home right now. I want to hug and kiss my kids, drive my car on paved roads with traffic that obeys the law. I want to buy eggs that have been refrigerated, drink water right out of the faucet, and take walks around the block with my neighbors without worrying about getting mugged. And I'm sick of having refried frigging beans with every meal.

I'm so exhausted, I don't even know how we got to the airport and on the plane. But here we are. Pressing my body into the seat cushion, which feels more like a slab of plywood and yet like heaven, I watch out the tiny porthole window as the ground below gets farther and farther away. All the bad stuff is down there on the ground. I can put "survival mode" behind me for a while. A relief such as I've never known before takes over and I notice my hands aren't gripping the armrests for dear life, like they were just moments ago. I didn't even realize I was doing it until I allowed myself to let go.

Dee's sitting in the seat next to me looking completely wiped out. I'm sure I look worse than he does.

All my life, I've always looked for the good in people and tried to overlook their negative qualities. I'm friends with people no one else likes. I've always believed that everyone, no matter how bad they seem, somewhere deep down, has good in them—even my first husband. I blamed his behavior on immaturity. But now, I feel like I can't fully trust anybody anymore. Like everybody's just out for themselves. I've never had a vacation where so many things went wrong.

I know, I'm being dramatic, but I can't help it. I'm dramatic when I'm exhausted. And I'm mad at myself for being so naïve. I'm also a little disappointed that I didn't have another out-of-body experience. Not that I expected to, but I kind of *hoped* to. And yet, there was something about those rocks of Land's End. Maybe *that's* what caused my mystical experience last year, not Sammy, and I just thought it all came from a connection with him.

In any case, I think this trip has made me a little less gullible, a little more mature, and a bit more worldly. Maybe spiritual journeys aren't always gushing with clouds, dreams, otherworldly bliss, and connections to rock stars. Maybe they have to gouge you once in awhile to keep you on your toes. And like Lao Tzu's saying, maybe you have to discover who you're *not* to help you figure out who you *are*.

I scrunch down into the seat as far as I can. Even my soul aches. I just want to retreat into my shell and lick my wounds for a while. I close my eyes and allow the whirring of the jet's engines to soothe me, and before long, the pilot's voice comes over the intercom. "Welcome back to the United States," he says.

I swear that's the sweetest thing anybody's ever said to me.

CHAPTER 15

Dreams

Shoot for the moon. Even if you miss it, you will land among the stars.
—Les Brown

November, 2004

There are places on earth where the energy level is supposed to be higher than normal. I don't know exactly what that means, but Maui is supposed to be one of those places, and Machu Picchu and Stonehenge. Maybe Cabo is like that too, since I've had supernatural experiences there twice now, but I've searched the Internet and can't seem to find anything. What I do find though, is that early civilizations in the area were thought to have been female-dominated societies. And I think it's kind of interesting that I've been getting the idea that there is something feminine about Land's End all along. I was calling her a goddess and writing poems about her before I ever knew about the legends.

Tonight I'm bent over my notebook and working on a poem about all of this, but it's really hard because I feel like I'm trying to relate emotions or feelings that have no description. Since I can't seem to get hold of what I want to say, I decide to print out what I've written thus far. Usually when I see words on paper, it makes more sense to me than looking at the computer screen.

I put the poem on the counter next to the soap dish as I'm brushing my teeth at the bathroom sink, hoping inspiration will filter down on me from the spirits of the great writers of the past. Or the bathroom fixtures. All of a sudden, Sammy's song, "Eagles Fly" comes into my mind. Not the song itself, but how it makes me feel when I hear it.

I look into the eyes of the woman in the mirror. *Yes! This is perfect!* Grabbing a pen, I scrawl "takes me away, lifts me up" on the edge of the paper, to help me remember what I want to say. Before I finish writing, the phone rings. It rings and rings and rings. Dee and the boys are downstairs watching TV. I have toothpaste in my mouth! Why doesn't somebody answer the phone? No one does. It keeps ringing. I wonder why the answering machine doesn't intervene. Its job is to answer the phone after the fourth ring, but tonight it is ringing well past that. Annoyed, I trudge across the bedroom floor to the nightstand where the phone continues its insistence.

"Hello?" My mouth is sticky from toothpaste.

No one says a word. Except Sammy Hagar. He's singing into my phone: "Take me away, come on fly me away. Lift me up so high . . . ." [2]

I stare at my paper, where I've just written those same words. My eyes water. *How can this be?*

I almost drop my toothbrush as I search my brain for a rational explanation, because I know there has to be one. The call is probably from a friend attending a live concert somewhere. Yes, that must be it. It's just a coincidence. And yet, I'm so shocked, my insides feel like moths are bumping around in there, leaving their powder on everything they touch.

A wee voice inside of me whispers, *I don't think it's a coincidence.*

Twenty minutes later the phone rings again. I pick it up and hear Sammy singing "Dreams" —the song that started everything for me. As the muffled music comes out of my phone, I feel as if a cord has been extended to me through the mist of reality. It's the same song that presented itself to my friend Liz a while back, telling her to tell me to contact Sammy.

Just when I've almost convinced myself that all of this is nothing but a bunch of odd coincidences and flukes, and just when the memory of my mystical experience was beginning to dissolve around the edges into forgotten-ness sufficiently for me to look back on it and say, "My imagination was only playing tricks on me," and when I'd finally convinced myself I was being ridiculous thinking there was any sort of connection between myself and a rock star, that he's only a person like the rest of us and that there is nothing extraordinary about him other than the fact that he's a talented musician, now *this* has to happen. I didn't ask for any of this; it came to me of its own accord.

Why is this happening to me?

If there really *is* a connection between Sammy and me, it's not an earthly one; it's something that transcends my definition of reality. Maybe if I could look back far enough in time—I'm talking centuries—I'd be able to see where and why this connection began. This thought makes me feel like there's a huge hole in my world and I don't know what it is I'm supposed to be seeing there, so I just stand in the middle of the room—staring, thinking.

I know about the concept of past lives, but I've never been sure what to think about it. My Catholic voice always told me that there was no such thing as reincarnation—after you died, you went to heaven, hell, or purgatory to wait for Judgment Day. After that, you either burned for eternity or dwelled upon the clouds with God. Gnashing my teeth and shoveling coal in hell didn't sound like my idea of a good time. On the other hand, cloud-squatting didn't sound too stimulating either. And what about forgiveness? I thought God forgave us our sins if we repented and were sincerely sorry for them. He wouldn't send us to hell after we were forgiven, would He? These were more questions no one could answer for me in a way that made sense.

But maybe there's some validity to this past lives thing after all.

Days later, my friend Steve tells me that he was the one who called that night from the Van Halen concert in Boise, Idaho. He says he tried calling several times but every time he called, the line was busy. He was about to give up when he decided to try once more. That was when I picked up the phone. "Did you know I was going to be at the show that night?" he asks me. I tell him no, I had no idea. "Whoa, there's some kind of freaky connection between you and Sammy," he says sounding completely dumbfounded.

Uh . . . yeah. I couldn't have made this happen if I tried. But I'm not going to tell Steve that I agree with him, because it's kind of embarrassing really, that I might even have that thought to begin with. And yet, it's rather odd that Steve would say it. Where would he get that notion? Is it really that obvious? People just don't go around saying stuff like that so flippantly. Besides, he doesn't seem the type who believes in spiritual realms. He's a financial planner; for him, everything's black and white, like with Dee.

I tell Steve that the song "Dreams" that was playing when he called from the concert the other night was the same song Sammy was singing when I had my mystical experience in Cabo. He knew about my mystical experience because the night it happened was the same night Dee and I met him and his wife. We've been friends ever since.

I hear him gasp, then he says, "Are you shittin' me?"

I guess it's futile to deny this energy any longer. All I know for sure is that none of this was a conscious part of my life before my out-of-body experience and now there's a supernatural force at work here that I can't grasp and can't control, even though something in me is deluded into thinking I *can* control it, or whether somebody loves me, or whether it rains in Pakistan. But I'm terrified to surrender. What would become of me if I did? Maybe I'd become a permanent resident of the loony bin.

And yet, when I did surrender and I stopped looking so hard for the answers, that's when the answers found me. Now do I get it all back? Does enlightenment just descend on a person, then take off again like a silent hummingbird? But I don't feel enlightened, I feel like there's a whole lot more to come. In the Bible, it says, "Ask and it will be given to you." Okay, God, I'm asking—*give me more!*

I think someone upstairs must have heard me, because when I check my e-mail, there's a letter from one of my professors at the college I attended. He writes that the editors of the college literary magazine want my permission to print one of my poems, and he says they'd be honored to have me read some of my poetry before a live audience.

They'd be honored to have *me?* I can hardly believe what I'm seeing. For the first time in my life, I feel like I have done something that matters (besides raising three great kids, but that wasn't all my doing; Dee did help a little). I have created art—and someone *wants* to hear it. Not only that, but my first piece is going to be published! If I were six years old, I think I'd be jumping up and down right now.

My confidence is now at an all-time high, so I send Sammy another letter. I figure since he seemed interested in what I told him before, he might be interested in hearing about this too, since it involves him. I explain how this entire experience is opening my eyes and because of it, my dream of being a writer is coming true, not to mention my even greater dream of integrating God into my life and getting closer to self-realization all the time. I tell him that I'm going to try to write a book about all the amazing things that are happening to me. I want, no, I *need* to share this tremendous feeling with others. I hope to inspire people to keep their hearts and minds open, because it's possible that their answers could be hiding in unexpected places too, like mine were. If it can happen to me, it can happen to anyone. Then I tell him that I don't know what to think or do about the way all of this is being delivered to me, though—all this paranormal stuff—and that part is scaring the shit out of me.

CHAPTER 16

Glimpses of Birds and Sammy

The kingdom of God is within you.
—Luke 17:21

December, 2004

The calendar on my desk says December 31. The barrenness of winter clutches my world in its icy grasp. Mentally I'm somewhere between the hustle and stress of Christmas and the readiness for a new year. I escape to my bedroom and close the door for a few moments of solitude. The odor of the bacon I cooked for breakfast hangs in the air and I wonder why it takes so long to dissipate. Now the greasy smell almost makes me feel sick. I can still hear the TV blaring from downstairs as I sit on the floor and get into my meditation posture.

Taking three deep breaths, I close my eyes. The wind bashes itself against the outside of the house and rattles the windows as I bring my awareness to my breathing. After a few moments, my head tilts back and my mouth falls open. Maybe I'm doing something wrong; I don't think this is normal. My tae kwon do master used to say that we must sit perfectly still without moving and fight through the pain of sitting still because maintaining the proper posture is important for the flow of *ki*. I force myself to pull my head back into position and close my mouth.

Quit concentrating on your posture—that means you're thinking, I scold myself. You're not supposed to be thinking; you're supposed to be releasing your thoughts, not dwelling on them. Of course, this becomes a wonderful dichotomy. The more you concentrate on not concentrating, the more you defeat the purpose of meditation.

While meditating, I'm never quite sure what is real and what I'm imagining. Or perhaps in that state of mind, I experience reality more profoundly than in any other state of consciousness.

My head falls back farther, farther, and my mouth opens again, as if it's trying to take in something. Then I see my mother off to my left. She's speaking to me but no sound is coming out of her mouth. She's also pointing at an eagle hovering in mid-flight. When I look closer, I see that the bird is stuffed, covered with dust, and suspended by wires, preserved forever, like a diorama at the Natural History Museum. Then I notice that I'm part of the exhibit. Standing amongst the throat-cinching smell of sand that hasn't seen moisture in thousands of years and the vague scent of formaldehyde, I look up. One bare, red light bulb is hanging from a wire directly above my head, casting its shadow over me. The rest of the scene is in muted colors. Then it fades.

When I open my eyes, I feel as if I've been asleep for hours, but I tell myself not to lose the images before I can write them down.

Afterward, I grab a sponge and a can of cleanser to clean the bathtub. I hate this job. No matter how careful I am, I always manage to get bleach from the cleanser all over my shirt. Where's the magic fairy to come in and do this for me? As I'm scrubbing and cussing because my back hurts in this position (we have these ridiculous glass shower doors and I have to contort myself to be able to reach everything), the word "bluebird" pops into my head. It's not a voice; it's a rogue thought.

What does that have to do with cleaning the bathtub? I straighten up, drive the back of my wrist into my lower back, and wait for a moment. Nothing more comes, so I go back to scrubbing, not giving it another thought.

Over the next few days, more images of birds come, so many that I don't know what else to do but record them in my journal. I don't even know why I'm so compelled to write about them. It feels like I'm painting a wall, filling in a spot over here and another area over there but never connecting them. There's no one around to tell me how to paint that wall or why I need to paint it in the first place. I just know I do. And every now and then, the paint glides on so smoothly and effortlessly, I'm encouraged to keep going.

After I finished meditating the other day, I saw the image of a blackbird in flight and in the background I heard Paul McCartney singing "Blackbird." Then, that same night, before I drifted off to sleep, I saw a blackbird flying through the air and feathers, like a close-up of giant wings. Two days later, a friend and I were having lunch together, when out of the blue, she says that her sister had spoken with the spirit of their dead mother a few nights earlier, and that her mother's spirit showed her sister a blackbird and wings flapping. When she told me this, I was so shocked, I almost fell out of my chair, because it was the same night I had seen the same thing. And for some reason, I happened to have my notebook with me during our lunch that day, something I never do, and I showed her where I'd written all this down. I don't know who was more freaked out, her or me.

What are all these bird images—eagle, bluebird, blackbird? I'm not a bird person. Birds scare me. My friend Nancy had a pet sparrow once. She rescued it after it fell out of its nest. She was always rescuing weird animals. Anyway, whenever I'd go over to her house, the sparrow would greet me by dive-bombing into my hair and then leaving a nice little liquid surprise on my shoulder. I couldn't understand how Nancy could have a pet like that.

When I sit back and look at what I've just written about all the birds, it makes me feel so odd. All this paranormal stuff just keeps building but it never breaks open.

Then, I don't know why, but I get mad. I slam my pen down on the notebook with such force, it spins itself over to the edge and nearly rolls off the desk.

This is reality, I remind myself—this desk, my house, my husband and kids, our mortgage, and the fact that I need reading glasses now to see the computer screen. I've had enough of all the otherworldly nonsense. I can't even tell what's real anymore.

I was just a boring wife and mom on vacation with my husband, minding my own business, having a little fun, when out of nowhere all this supernatural stuff dropped into my lap because of some rock star—then heaven smiled on me. And that's all great, but I'm tired of having it consume my life. I don't want to become a fanatic. I have a life and a family who are important to me. What am I doing here anyway, believing in this force, this connection between a rock star, his music, and me? Why should I care about any of it? It's stupid. I'm going to turn my back on pandering to all these ridiculous mystical matters and go back to my life of washing mini-blinds and wiping boogers off the railing instead of searching for higher truth. I'm going to drop the lead ball right here on the floor at my feet, see if it puts a dent in the linoleum.

"It's part of you," comes a thought. "Relax. Let it happen."

Oooh, this feels like something shadowy is tempting me, but it's also so sensual that maybe it's worth the risk. The image of a vampire comes to mind. Oh, that's great—vampires/bats/ wings. Here I go again.

"I can't let it happen anymore. It's all too freaking weird!" I say to the air, as if something up there can actually hear me. Then I sigh so heavily that my body seems to deflate. "Okay, listen . . . if you're so big and powerful, then where's my technique for saving the world? If you really have the ability to contact me from another realm of consciousness, why do you waste my time with all this mysterious and piddling bullshit? Why don't you get to the stuff that really matters instead of breaking glass votives, whispering in my ear, bringing me to a rock star, and sending me all these images and messages that make no sense?"

But of course, there's no answer. Apparently whatever it is, it doesn't care if I'm mad. Maybe it's up there laughing its ass off. I probably should be too. I must look like a complete fool talking to the air. My pen and notebook don't offer any consolation either, the traitors.

And just when I think it can't get more intense, a few days later I pull an envelope out of our mailbox that's hand-addressed to me in black ink. The logo is "Cabo Wabo" and it's kind of square like an invitation. Saving the letter for when I get home, I walk down the street wondering, did Dee put my name on a mailing list for an exclusive tequila-tasting event? That doesn't feel right. Then how did this person get my name and address? Maybe they're holding some kind of art exhibit like the gallery here in town holds occasionally. Dee and I went to one of those once. It was an exhibit of rock and roll photography. There were photos of Jerry Garcia, The Rolling Stones, and The Beatles. I felt uppity, sipping wine and sampling little cubes of cheese while mingling with artists and commenting on the work on display, while those who weren't invited had to stand outside on the street and peer through the plate-glass windows.

And now I figure that's what this must be—an invitation to a similar event. But inside the envelope is a hand-written note and it's signed "Much love, Sammy" with a big swirling "S." My body seems to shut down for a few seconds, then it lurches back to life with a thud. In the note, Sammy encourages me to write my book and to say whatever I want in it. "You go girl," he says. Then he suggests some books for me to read, to help me understand what's happening to me: *Autobiography of a Yogi* by Paramahansa Yogananda and *Aliens Among Us* by Ruth Montgomery.

As I stare at the little card in my hands, I feel like I have a wonderful secret inside me, although I'm not quite sure what that secret is. It's much more important than receiving letters from a rock star though, as if that's not important enough. But why does Sammy care what's happening to me? What's in it for him? I can't imagine why he would take the time to write to me again. *Because there's a connection between you . . . .* Oh man, I wish this thought would go away. It's not doing me any good. Because even if there *is* a connection between us, what can I do about it? Nothing.

It feels like the life I have always considered normal is now upside down.

When I calm down, I check the Internet to see if our local library has either of the books. It takes an eternity for the pages to load on the screen, but eventually it pops up. They have one. The other I order online. Then, like a hypnotized person, I drive to the library.

The rocks at Land's End, Cabo San Lucas, Mexico

Cabo Wabo Cantina, Cabo San Lucas, Mexico

Fans sleeping on the streets of Cabo for concert tickets

October, 2005

October, 2006

October, 2008   *May, 2009*

A kiss from Sammy, May, 2006

View from on stage, Las Vegas, July, 2006

With David Lauser, October, 2006

With Aaron Hagar, May, 2008

With Victor Johnson, October, 2007

*With Michael Anthony of Van Halen
and Chickenfoot, April, 2010*

South Lake Tahoe, Nevada, May, 2008

*Singing Onstage, South Lake
Tahoe, May, 2008*

Cabo, 2005

Photo by Dee Walker

Michael Anthony and Sammy, Tahoe, June, 2006

Photos by Dee Walker

Eddie Van Halen, Van Halen Reunion Tour, Denver, CO 2004

Eddie and Sammy, Van Halen Reunion Tour, Denver, CO 2004

CHAPTER 17

Kindergarten Games for the Soul

Do not seek to follow in the footsteps of the wise. Seek what they sought.
—Matsuo Basho

February, 2005

The black and white photos in the book are from the early to mid-1900s. They show serious-looking, dark-skinned people wrapped in robes and sitting with their legs folded in the full lotus position. There's also a map of India, pictures of buildings, and photos of large groups of people. Flipping through the pages and looking inside, I see that it's clearly philosophical. I can't wait to dive in.

After dinner, I take the book upstairs to the bedroom and stretch out on the bed. I'm going to need it quiet in order to concentrate.

It's hard to get into at first. The author is extremely articulate, proper, and well educated. I'm not used to the way he writes, so it takes me a while to feel comfortable with it. But *Autobiography of a Yogi* makes what's happening to me seem like kindergarten games. Yogananda describes supernatural meditations and experiences infinitely more interesting than any of mine. He writes about human beings who make solid objects materialize out of thin air, yogis who never eat or sleep (hm—that sounds like me), and those who are capable of literally being in two places at once (moms do this too).

At first, I find some of the stories a little hard to believe. Anyone can write fiction, disguising it as fact to make it more exciting than reality, but this book is a cherished account of a highly acclaimed man's life. It's a reference still used today for those not only interested in studying yoga, but also for those who want to expand their minds.

I shift my weight and push my back up against the dark wooden headboard. The older I get, the harder it is for me to get comfortable but I finally manage.

Although a lot of the circumstances Yogananda describes seem impossible, I see shadows of my experiences woven into his words, and I know they must be true. Maybe if none of this had happened to me, I'd be less inclined to believe what he says. On the other hand, a man of his spiritual stature didn't have to make up stories. His beautiful life gave testimony to the truth of his words.

I consider my own experiences in relation to those of this holy man who lived and died before I ever heard of him, as if by absorbing his typewritten words on the page deeply enough, some understanding would come to me and sweep me into a camaraderie with him. It never does. Instead, I'm left standing on the precipice of a mountain, gazing at the drop far below, and wondering if I ever gained the courage to jump, would I have wings to fly?

The second book Sammy recommended is *Aliens Among Us* by Ruth Montgomery. Here's that name again, the woman who inspired the song "Love Walks In," where I heard Sammy describing what happened to me during my mystical experience. And now he has personally delivered this concept right to my front door.

The book arrives in the mail even before I've finished the yogi one. But this one looks even more enticing, so I put the other one aside for the time being. Fixing myself a glass of iced tea, I plop myself down on the living room couch to read.

I don't know about this. *The cover has a picture of a space ship on it, for crying out loud!*

I open the book, and before I even read any of it, I feel a strong pull, like uncovering the main source from which *everything* springs forth. Strange.

I sink deeper into the cushions for reassurance.

The author writes about her Guides—souls or spirits who speak through her typing fingers. I've felt this way occasionally on this journey too. When I'm writing sometimes, it's as if the words aren't coming from me. Could that maybe explain what's been happening to me?

Montgomery talks about how her Guides pushed her to write the book. She says she resisted writing about aliens because she was already a highly respected author and worried that people would think she was crazy. She had no personal experience with this sort of thing. But inexplicable events began to happen and she knew they were messages from her Guides convincing her to write the book. She mentions several episodes: a photo taken of her that included ethereal figures not physically present when the picture was taken, an airplane that arrived to take her home even though all other planes were grounded due to bad weather, and her ability to rejuvenate her plants by talking to them although she didn't believe it was possible.

Tears come into my eyes. Not because of the words I'm reading, but because something beyond the words feels familiar. Inexplicable events seem to be pushing me to write a book too. Maybe I wouldn't have ordinarily considered this to be the same thing Montgomery is talking about, but there have been so many inexplicable events since Cabo, and I've never had weird stuff like this happen to me before. Not to this extent. I mean, don't we all have those little moments that make us stop and question if we really heard or saw something out of the corner of our eye or if we just imagined it? I sure have, but the episodes I've been experiencing lately are nothing like that. And they're not like déjà vu either, because those moments feel like a speck of time, a snapshot or flash with feelings attached, lasting a split second or less. This feels more like I'm opening a photo album of someone I've never met before and looking at their pictures. The only problem is that I'm in the photos and I don't recall ever having seen anyone capture them on film. But they're also much more than photos. It's like they're all chapters in an epic novel that's loaded with color, background, richness, depth—and reality. I can feel the breath of the others in the pictures on my skin. I can taste what they were tasting. I can feel their emotions, feel their clothing on my body. That's not the same as thinking I heard or saw something.

Montgomery also mentions Paramahansa Yogananda, saying that Hindu yogis altered atoms, allowing themselves to disappear and reappear—the same method aliens use to come to earth. I know this is a book about aliens, but she's talking about yogis and aliens in the same sentence! And is it just a coincidence that she's also writing about Yogananda—the author of the other book Sammy recommended? Perhaps.

The further I read, the more similarities I find between this book and my life. But I don't ask myself if I believe what the author is saying. This is entirely different, it's as if some kind of otherworldly intelligence has reached across time and space, drilled a hole right into my soul, and is peering into me without my permission. *Why am I reacting like this?* It's just a story! Why do I care what happened to this woman?

My mouth suddenly feels dry, so I reach for my glass of tea, and as I do, I realize my hand is shaking.

When I go back to reading, I feel more tears falling from my eyes—from sheer astonishment—as an almost pleasurable sensation of fear moves through me, rising and expanding with each paragraph. Its roots are sprouting right out of the words, growing out of the pages, and wrapping themselves around me like in some low-budget horror movie. With each sentence, it gets more intense, like a thunderstorm brewing, and along with it comes the thought, *Does all this have something to do with me?*

Yes. You know it. You feel it.

No way.

I can't take it. I push my face away from the book with the palm of my hand and force myself to look out the window for a moment. That doesn't help. I have to close the book. *Aliens? Come on . . .* Just because Sammy says it happened to him doesn't mean that's what's happening to me.

Folding my arms around myself, I gaze around the room looking for something familiar to keep me grounded. Ah yes, there's my overstuffed, brown, floral print chair sagging in the middle, my lamps, my end tables with the water stains on them, my kids' school papers in a pile on the fake-wood desk. I must be in the right house.

The concept of aliens has absolutely nothing to do with me.

I go upstairs and find my notebook and attempt to write what I'm feeling:

> The author first shocked me when she said, "a significantly . . ." (Oh God, I can't even write it. I am so freaked out I want to cry . . . .) Holy shit, what if it's true? Oh God, Sammy, what the fuck happened to you? What the fuck did you do to me?? I'm really scared!

When my mind comes back around (sort of), I find myself thinking, *Oh man, this is no joke. This woman is serious and I believe her. Why do I believe her? That's what scares me . . . .* I'm afraid to pick up the book again. It's presenting a theory beyond the scope of what I consider possible—ideas my rational mind deems preposterous. At the same time, I recognize a truth within its words. And yet, there seems no way to bring both sides of my mind together; it's like trying to blend oil and water.

I've never seen or experienced aliens. If they're real, what else is out there in the universe that we don't know about? And what's the capacity of our minds to comprehend and create this stuff?

All these outrageous notions are making me feel sick to my stomach. The back of my neck tenses up like a rock. I start looking for any excuse to do something, *anything* to keep from thinking about this, so I scan the first few pages into my computer and e-mail them to Nancy and Leann: *"You're not going to believe this . . . ."* I need validation. I need something to grasp. Never in my life have I reacted so strongly to a book. Ordinarily I wouldn't even have considered reading something like this— it's too "out there" for me. And yet, Sammy has shared something very deep and personal with me by recommending it. Was he saying he believed that what happened to him all those years ago with aliens was also responsible for what happened to me in Cabo?

Yes.

That his experience influenced mine or planted something magnificent inside of me, advancing my understanding of my self and showing me the purpose of my life?

Yes.

Was he saying that he believed there is a spiritual connection between him and me?

Yes.

That can't be right. Aren't aliens considered sinister beings who want to take over our world? If my Cabo experience had something to do with aliens, why has everything that's happened since then been nothing but positive and wonderful? I can't allow myself to subscribe to the notion of the existence of aliens. But what if they *are* real? Nah, I can't go there. If I choose to deny this, it won't affect me, right? Or do perfectly normal people really believe this stuff?

I need to talk to Sammy so bad, it's tearing me apart. I certainly can't tell Dee about any of this. He'd think I'd lost my mind. I can hear him now. He'd sing that stupid song from the '60s about being taken away to the funny farm. Since he won't even consider philosophical and otherworldly theories, I've learned through the years not to mention stuff like this to him. I'm already wondering if I'm going crazy; I don't need him confirming it simply because he doesn't understand the concepts. I feel so fragile right now. But it's also getting to be a rather heavy load to carry all by myself and I long to share it with him—if for no other reason than to keep me grounded. And yet, I know he'd laugh at me, so I force myself to bury my feelings. Keeping them on the surface is just too much to take. It's like holding a smoking gun in your hand and wondering what you've done, how you were even capable of it, and how to dispose of the evidence before it all becomes too real.

Two weeks later, Sonia Choquette prances onstage before a packed auditorium wearing a lime green skirt, five-inch stilettos, and a big smile. She's a world-famous psychic and although I have an intrinsic distrust of people who call themselves that, because the word "psychic" usually elicits images of dark foreboding in me, with everything that's been happening to me, I'm beginning to rethink my earlier doubts.

But the things she talks about make sense. She tells us it's more important to live a spirit*ed* life than a spirit*ual* one. I love her attitude. She's exhilarating and uplifting.

I hadn't planned on buying any of her books, but afterward, as I walk past the table where they're selling them, I change my mind.

The next day as I sit down to read *Ask Your Guides*, I'm still in my pajamas. I shouldn't be doing this, I know. There are so many other things I need to get done first. *Just a few minutes . . . .*

Sonia writes about being psychic and she doesn't apologize for it. She says that a lot of people worry that following their intuition puts them out of touch with reality, but the opposite is actually true. You can't nurture your sixth sense unless you're fully in tune with the world around you. That makes sense. Why then, am I so anxious? Is it wrong for me to investigate this part of me? Am I encouraging something evil here? And yet, everything Sonia says is positive and full of light. But how can she act so confident and normal if she has psychic experiences? Having conversations with spirits would scare the shit out of me! But maybe that's precisely what's happening to me. And if I weren't so freaked out about all this, I think I'd be laughing right now.

Since there's no one else I can turn to for advice, I might as well consult Sonia's book. She makes everything seem so natural, as if there's nothing to be afraid of. Besides, God isn't striking me down for it. Not yet anyway.

Sonia's book leads to more books. Nancy even has a suggestion. She says I need to read *The Alchemist* because it sounds exactly like what's happening to me, and *The Celestine Prophecy*, but I read that one years ago. I guess I'll have to revisit it.

When I open up *The Alchemist*, inside the front cover, it says, "To realize one's destiny is a person's only obligation." I already like this book.

It's an easy read. I can't put it down. Page after page sounds as if it were a fictionalized account of what has been happening to me. It's as if the author, Paulo Coelho, saw what was going to happen to me years ago and wrote it into a different form. Even the similarities between Coelho and me are uncanny. He too had an encounter with a stranger he met in a foreign country, which caused him to write about his experience and his "discovery that the extraordinary occurs in the lives of ordinary people."

When I finish it, I turn the book over in my hands, as if I can't believe there are no words left to read. The strangest thought occurs to me, that *The Neverending Story* has been passed on to me to write the next chapter. I don't feel capable, but I sit down at my desk anyway. "It can't be sheer chance that all these books and Sonia's lecture have all surfaced at the same time," I write. Then comes another thought: "You're having difficulty accepting all the wonderful things that are happening to you. You're worried about your sanity, but these mystical things are means to convince you to trust your spirit and the spirit of this force that has come to you, because as you now see, these things happen to other people too. What you are experiencing isn't wrong. Quite the contrary. *The path you are walking is the way to your soul.*"

I pick my eyes up from the page and stare at the light blue wall in front of me—beyond the wall. How does one know if one is slipping into one's mind in a manner from which there is no escape? Is there an edge one crosses over before plummeting into insanity? And does one know where this lip is in order to turn one's self around before it's too late? The Bible talks about dark angels and Satan misleading us into thinking we're on God's side, when all along he's deceived us so he can sweep us over to the side of evil. But none of this feels evil. Not even Sammy's aliens. The only negative consequence I can see is that I used to know exactly what my routine was every day, every month, every year. And most of the time, things went smoothly. I had them under control. Things got done. On time. I had it all down to a science. Or so I thought. But before, it was predictable. Now I'm spending so much time writing that the bills are late and the bank accounts unbalanced. I'm forgetting my friends' birthdays, meals aren't being cooked, the bathroom sink is growing an attractive pink coating, and the living room carpet is developing a new design of dark stains. I'm staying up too late at night, getting up too early, eating on the run, and neglecting my workouts. I'm tired all the time. No, exhausted. And I've never been happier.

Dee comes into the bedroom where I'm sitting at the computer, madly typing away. I came upstairs after cleaning up the dinner dishes and now it's almost midnight.

"Is your butt glued to that chair?" He walks past me and slaps me with his shirt.

I suddenly feel tired. Life was so much easier before all of this.

CHAPTER 18

Maybe We Can't Get There Through the Doors of Knowledge and Logic

I love those who yearn for the impossible.
—Goethe

March, 2005

It snowed again last night. Now it's 6:30 in the morning and the purple-pink sky is alive with huge, fluffy flakes that are still falling like millions of ballet dancers. They cling to the bare branches of the cottonwood tree and the green needles of the Austrian pine in our backyard. It looks like the scene from a Christmas card. As I look out, my kitchen window acts like a mirror, reflecting my image backward and superimposing it on the outdoor scene. My face, the kitchen countertops loaded with empty cups and dirty silverware splayed out like wounded soldiers, my teakettle on the stove, and my white kitchen cabinets all fade into the morning sky and ice-laden trees like some other dimension. What if my interpretation of all these paranormal experiences is backward like that too? I've heard of people given to so much lofty thinking that it literally made them crazy. I can't allow that to happen to me, but I've been wallowing in my own pool of thoughts for so long now, I'm not sure what to do anymore.

Tucking my robe closer to my body, I pour myself a cup of coffee and mutter how thankful I am for the invention of programmable coffee-makers. Then I go back to contemplating my sanity. Maybe all the wonderful things that have happened to me since Cabo really aren't any big deal. Perhaps they mean nothing. And if they mean nothing, then that means I'm wasting my time chasing concepts that brought tremendous love and light into my life, something I had asked God for as long as I can remember and had finally been granted. Why would I want to let go of something that has given me so much joy?

Scuffling into the family room with my cup, I turn on the gas fireplace. My dog Sam stretches, yawns, and comes over to put her chin on my leg as I scrunch into a ball on the couch. I pet her soft little head and wonder what I would do if I found out that all my supernatural experiences were merely incidental. And yet, there have been *so many* and I know I didn't imagine them, so they must mean something. Why do I always think I have to disprove all this stuff before I can consider it believable? Is it because I think I'm neglecting my intelligence if I don't look to reason first? But maybe my skepticism comes from my questioning the Catholic faith, because although I was taught that Catholicism was "the truth," a lot of what I kept hearing didn't feel right to me and yet, I was terrified to challenge "the truth." I also have to be careful because I've been burned more than once by trusting in beliefs or people I shouldn't have.

One time I attended a lecture where an ordinary-looking woman said she interacted with angels. She said they were in the room with us and glanced at the ceiling as if she were seeing something, looking quite benevolent herself. She asked us if we could see them. I couldn't. Then she said that each angel had a different vibration. Now I'm an extremely sensitive person.

I often feel vibes when no one else does, but I did not sense a thing that night and I really tried. I wanted to believe her. Toward the end of her talk, she said her angels had a message for someone in the audience, so a middle-aged woman came forward, but she kept shaking her head "No" to every statement the angel lady told her. Even sitting in my seat in the back of the auditorium, I could see how mortified that angel lady was and I felt kind of sorry for her. But I also felt sorry for myself, for being there in the first place, although I didn't have the guts to get up and leave.

I'm not saying there aren't people who can and do talk to angels, because I do believe in angels. I'm just saying I don't trust every spiritual guru who claims to have the answers. Or maybe I should say that not everyone's interpretations resonate with me. We all have different roads.

"Just what do you think about that, little girl?" I ask Sam, scratching her ears.

She wags her tail and looks up at me as if everything I'm saying is gospel, then walks over to the door and waits for me to let her out. When I close the door again, I sit back down on the couch.

When I think about all the spiritual gurus out there, it's almost comical how gullible a lot of us are—we're lost and starved for spiritual direction, so we're sometimes willing to go along with some pretty outlandish propositions. I have to remind myself not to be so open-minded that my brains fall out because if I don't watch it, I can be one of those trusting souls too, like with this book I've been reading—*The Divine Matrix* by Gregg Braden. And yet, Braden's theories make sense to me, mostly because he uses science to back up his claims, but also because the things he talks about seem to explain, in more concrete ways, exactly what's been happening to me. And this is what I so desperately need—to prove to myself that these things are real and not imagined; maybe then I can rest with the knowledge that I'm not crazy after all.

Braden says that we're all connected to one another and to the universe by an invisible web made of energy. It's here and there, then and now, us and them, all wrapped up into one. That's what I saw during my out-of-body experience too—how every*thing* and every*one* is connected. And he talks about this "double-slit experiment," a test that was performed back in the early 1900s (and repeated many times since with the same results) that proved how our thoughts alter our physical world. I guess a particle, (otherwise known to us non-scientists as tangible substance) was passed through holes in a barrier and in the first test, where the particle passed through only one hole, it came out on the other side unchanged, just as expected. But when two openings were used, it passed through *both* of them, something that required the particle to change its form into a wave (otherwise known to us non-scientists as energy). Supposedly, these experiments suggest that a solid can and did change into an energy wave and that it actually made a decision of how to solve the "problem" of having to choose between two paths. According to Braden, the only thing that could have influenced the behavior of the particle (telling it that there were two openings instead of one) was the minds of the observers.

I heard somewhere that we can alter our dreams while we're dreaming them. I tried it once. For weeks, I kept dreaming that a horrible man was chasing me with a huge dagger in his hand. Before I fell asleep one night, I told myself that if I were to have that dream, this time I would stop running and confront the man. That night, the dream came again. It was dark. I was running in and out of dilapidated buildings, and a man was chasing me. He was dressed in dirty rags and dripping with green slime. All of a sudden I remembered that I had the power to change my dream, so I stopped running and spun around to face the man. Although I was terrified and shaking, I told him, "You're not real!"

"I'm not?" He looked like he was going to cry.

"No, now go away!"

He did. And he never came back.

So if we can change our dreams during sleep, why wouldn't it work while we're awake too? Maybe it all boils down to our perception of reality, or particles, or solid substance, or matter—whatever you want to call it. And maybe it all has something to do with what's been happening to me, like an overlap of dreams and reality in conjunction with the power of my mind.

The coffee must be affecting me because my brain is entertaining concepts way too heavy for this early in the morning. But I like it. I'm starting to see a correlation between what all these authors are saying and the things I've been experiencing. I need to figure out exactly what the correlation is, though, because these things just don't happen to ordinary people like me, do they? Rock stars, concerts, music, out-of-body experiences, God, Cabo, me, connections, psychic abilities, synchronicity, serendipity, aliens, visions, spirits—*lions and tigers and bears, oh my!* And I'm almost there; I can feel it.

I go over to the door to see if Sam is ready to come in. She isn't, so I sit back down on the couch to wait. Must be nice to be a dog—having somebody who adores you catering to your every whim. But then, I think she'd do the same for me if she could.

All my thoughts about particles and waves make me remember something else Braden said, that quantum physics proves not that particles exist, but that *possibilities* exist. That's what particles really are—possibilities. Yogananda concluded the same thing almost a hundred years ago. He said that electrons had characteristics of both particles and waves, and the smallest known piece of solid substance, the atom, contained both positive and negative forces, as the sacred texts of India had been saying for thousands of years and calling "duality." Or as I interpret it—all opposites in the universe.

So if our bodies are made of particles, that's what *we* are too—possibilities. The sky's the limit! That's another thing I saw when I left my body that time, not in images, but in feelings—that we're not just stuck in our positions in life with no way out; no matter how hopeless things may seem, there always remains the possibility for us to improve them, if we choose.

Yogananda also said that science proves that there is no material universe and everything we think is real is just illusion. To me, this means that we each create our own definition of reality. I've always wondered why certain things appeal to some people but not others. That goes for just about anything—music, cars, food, clothing, art—so it makes sense that if we create our own reality, perhaps we really *aren't* perceiving things the same as the next person. Because everything that's ever happened to us throughout our entire lives has an impact on how we perceive the world. Maybe that guy who cut you off in traffic last night didn't do it to be a jerk, he did it because he just found out he has cancer and he was so shook up, he wasn't paying attention to his driving.

It all seems too simplistic on one hand and too philosophical on the other. And then I remember something I saw on TV—pictures of 8-year-old girls in South Africa, forced to sell their bodies to keep themselves and their younger siblings from starving to death because their parents both died from syphilis. To say it broke my heart is an understatement. I cried. I took it personally. How is *their* world mere illusion? And how can they change it? Since I'm just a mom and not a philosopher or yogi master, the only thing I can think of is that since I believe anything we desire is possible for us to achieve, that goes for *everyone,* including them. And since I also believe we're all connected, maybe if I make a positive change in myself, it will send a ripple out into the world that will somehow affect those girls in a positive way too. All of this sounds airy fairy, I know, but I truly believe it. No, I *know* it, because I've already seen how the change in me has affected Dee and the rest of my family and friends—even total strangers. As the saying goes, "If you want to change the world, start with yourself."

Sam paws at the back door, so I let her in. "On your rug," I tell her. "Your feet are wet." She lowers her head as if she's being chastised and saunters obediently to her small, braided rug in front of the fireplace. Then she lies down and starts licking the little white tips of her black paws.

I've already had too much coffee, I'm sure, but I still want more, so I go into the kitchen to pour myself another cup. As I pass by the window, I steal a look outside again. A polite frosting of snow and ice covers the neighbor's house and cars, and the sky is getting lighter by the minute. There's a mystical beauty in moments like this, when everything's silent and cold and purple—and it fills me with such emotion that goosebumps pop out on my arms and not just because it's cold outside.

That's another thing I keep hearing in all the books I've been reading and the lectures I've been to lately, about emotion, and how it's not enough to merely desire change; in order for it to come about, our dream needs to be fueled by intense emotion, because emotion is what connects us to the Divine. It makes me think of the many times I've felt intense emotion throughout this entire ordeal, like my out-of-body experience during Sammy's concert, for one, and the time I was awakened from my sleep and went out onto the balcony of our hotel room to connect with the spirit of Land's End. And the many times I've experienced all human emotions at once. Is it possible these things were signs that I'm on the right path with what I'm doing? Because what I've been pursuing—my need to understand all the supernatural events and to write about them—has been with the greatest amount of passion I have ever felt. So how do I channel that emotion and *make* stuff happen? Then it occurs to me that perhaps that's what I've been doing all along with the writing of my book. This thought makes me warm all over. Or maybe it's just the coffee.

In any case, I think the purpose of the soul is to *become* God—perfect love. Love is an emotion. Knowledge isn't, so maybe we can't even get there through the doors of knowledge and logic. And maybe God too is made of emotion. I wonder if anybody's ever thought of that before. I kind of like how that sounds.

Sam raises her head and lets out a small whimper. She seems to sense something and is asking permission to get off her rug and come to me.

"No, you stay there, Sammie; your feet are still wet," I tell her.

She gets a sad look on her face, but stays put. I whisper, "That's a good girl," then allow myself to further indulge my thoughts. I have to. I'm finally starting to gain some ground here in my need for understanding and man, is it exciting!

If particles and waves can change properties, and our bodies are made of particles, could this explain how human beings and perhaps non-human beings could change from physical form to spirit form? Not only at the moment of death but also at will or *accidentally at a rock concert?* That's pretty much what Yogananda said, and Montgomery said her in book about aliens. If that's true, then what we think we see with our eyes isn't necessarily real. There's a loaded topic, one I've held near and dear to my heart ever since I can remember. And for some reason, it triggers a picture in my mind of Sammy performing. I can see him clearly—T-shirt, long hair, sweat, sunglasses, microphone—and attached to this picture is the thought, *What if all this mystical stuff is simply due to me falling down the well of being seduced by a rock star and all the rest of it is just my mind playing tricks on me and making me think this is some kind of transcendental shift when it's really not?* God, I hope not. *Why did I have to think of that?* Even though I'm coming to the conclusion that having tangible proof may not be the most important thing, I feel I owe it to myself to investigate this, because this could be a deal-breaker.

And yet, I don't think I would have been changed permanently as a result of what happened to me if that were the case. Besides, it wasn't like I went to the show that night looking for a way to connect with a favorite singer; I didn't find out who Sammy Hagar was until *after* I had the mystical experience. Not only that, but the "something familiar" I sensed about him from the very beginning was not, and still isn't, physical. It's something beyond that—a spirit I sense which is altogether separate from the physical that feels so familiar it's almost painful, like a phantom limb—something that was once a part of me and had been cut off.

And through all of this, I feel like I'm being led by the fire of an energy I can't explain. It pulls me along like an addiction. Not to the celebrity, but to a cause that still remains obscure. I'm becoming obsessed with the notion that something so important has happened to me that I need to take it somewhere. First, maybe I'd better take it somewhere where someone with experience in this sort of thing can give me an unbiased opinion.

With questions in hand, I go to see Bob, a licensed psychologist.

CHAPTER 19

Psychologists, Mystics, and Fanatics

Life does not control you. What you believe about it, does.
—Alan Cohen

March, 2005

I'm a little nervous as Bob directs me into his posh office with its massive, wooden desk, a glass of water sitting on a green felt coaster, and thick bookshelves loaded with books whose titles are both technical and philosophical. *Autobiography of a Yogi* by Paramahansa Yogananda catches my eye.

Unsure if I should say it or not, it comes out of my mouth anyway, "Hey, I've read that!" I sit down—delicately—in a leather chair across from him. "Wow, this is weird . . . ."

As I start telling him about my mystical experience, I'm not sure how Bob's going to take what I have to say. But the more I talk, I see that if he's finding anything unusual about any of it, he isn't letting it show. He's smiling and nodding as if he's hanging on my every word.

"I like Sammy Hagar. I like his music," he says when I've finished my story. His closely cropped gray hair seems to enhance the blueness of his eyes as he leans back in his chair with a look on his face that conveys both understanding and amusement.

I wouldn't have thought Bob would be interested in rock and roll. He seems more the earthy, intellectual, grounded type. He's also studied folk healing arts, tae kwon do, tai chi chuan, and jujitsu. I'm impressed.

"So, in your professional opinion, was my experience real?" I drop the bomb right up front and wait to assess the damage.

"It was a legitimate and genuine experience. I don't have any doubt about that," he says. "As you expand your awareness to the universe, other connections start happening that might not have been there until you expanded it. And you expanded it through, in your case, this sense of love and connection."

I instantly feel lighter, as if the fear I'd held inside me, the fear that he would say "Hmmm . . . Pat, maybe I'd better start seeing you on a regular basis. I'm a little worried about you . . . ." has dissipated. I want to jump up and hug him, thank him for confirming that I'm not crazy. But of course, I don't. I behave myself, as usual.

He continues. "Psychologically, it sounds like something opened up perceptually for you, and energetically. It was one of those perfect moments in life, where you had a perceptual shift or an energetic expansion. What you describe is similar to other mystical experiences that other people describe, for sure. Professionally, it sounds genuine."

All of a sudden I notice that the room is bright and cheery, with a smattering of Asian décor here and there—a single symbol on a framed green canvas and a tiny statue of Buddha sitting on the shelf. It's as if my eyes are now open, or the blinders taken off.

I look into Bob's eyes. I'm braver now. "So, is it possible for human beings to exchange energy?"

"Oh yeah, sure we do! You see it in the various forms of pranic healing or reiki, where the healer never touches the patient, but the energy apparently shifts and the recipient may be improved or cured. I've definitely observed it in healing. And I've been able to do it with other people where their illnesses improved. In many of the Shaman experiences, meditative traditions, yogic traditions, and various religious experiences, people report energy changes and transformations."

This makes me want to learn all about this, or at least witness it happening with my own eyes. As long as I can remember, I've ached to know what's out there in the depths of the mind and how it connects us to other dimensions of consciousness and worlds we can't comprehend yet sense the existence of. I should have been a psychologist.

There's a scene in the movie *Contact* with Jodie Foster that touches on this. It deals with the possible existence of life in other solar systems, and is based on the novel by Carl Sagan, who was a highly acclaimed professor of Astronomy and Space Sciences at Cornell University and chief advisor to NASA. In the film, Foster's character volunteers to be the sole passenger in a spacecraft built to specifications dictated to her from another world. As the rocket launches, she meets a being in another dimension with whom she has a conversation. Upon returning to earth, she's astonished at the implications of what happened to her, but no one believes her. The controllers in the tower and scientific experts consider the flight a malfunction. The ship hadn't gone anywhere; it just dropped to the ground. Furthermore, only a few minutes had passed, so obviously she hadn't traveled anywhere. However, the video recorder onboard the ship shows 18 hours of static that can't be accounted for.

The possibilities expressed in the film make sense; they're based on mathematics, science, philosophy, and psychology and I believe that somewhere in those theories lies a bridge between the mind and the physical world and a very important link between time and space. It may also provide a doorway between our minds and the minds of other beings, which is why

I can't rule out the existence of aliens, spirits, or angels. It has to do with dimensions of consciousness.

A buzzer goes off on Bob's desk; he has another appointment. I thank him for his time and he walks me to the door, insisting that I keep him posted on my book.

On my way home, I stop at the library to check out some of the books and videos Bob recommended. I also download several professional articles dealing with the fan/celebrity dynamic.

The articles and books say that the public's obsession with celebrities stems from the theory that human instinct dictates that we're drawn to and follow the leader of the pack. And, being the herd animals we are, we tend to imitate those qualities we admire in the leader. At the same time, the media turns famous people into ideals the ordinary person can't possibly achieve. (I recently saw pictures of celebrities without makeup and I was amused to see that they looked just like the people I might run into at the grocery store.) Some people get so carried away trying to "be" that other person, or become so wrapped up in their mania, that they lose their own identities and during the process become frustrated, depressed, and sometimes deranged. Of course, there are varying degrees of all of this. Not only that, but I think that when actors or musicians are performing, there's a certain magic in the moment—in the bright lights, the exaggerated set design, and in the fact that the stage is literally elevated, sending a subliminal message that they're "above" the rest of us. Perhaps this is why I was so surprised when I met Sammy and he seemed shorter than I expected.

And maybe all of that is just a reflection of me anyway. My dad always tells me that the traits we admire (and dislike) in others are traits we also have inside of us. "Tell me who you hang by and I'll tell you who you are," he says, imitating his parents' thick, German accents. Maybe if we put as much focus on ourselves as we do on other people, we might see that.

And now, being perfectly honest with myself I have to ask, *How does all of this relate to my situation?* For one thing, what Sammy does in his personal life is none of my business and I could care less. I don't need to know when he goes to the bathroom or where he ate dinner last night. I love what he does onstage, *how* he does it, and how it makes me feel. Period. I don't read magazines about celebrities (although I do flip through them while waiting in line at the grocery store sometimes) and I don't watch TV shows about the latest celebrity gossip. That kind of stuff doesn't interest me. Never has.

The more I think about it, the more I realize that what's been happening to me isn't simply the result of my being swept away by a celebrity. I haven't lost myself through this means, I've *found* myself. It also explains why it bothers me so much to call myself a fan—because that word feels like the embodiment of relinquishing my power to control my own life. I've already done that enough over the past fifty years, beginning with my religion and then with my first husband. All it did was make me feel inferior. I don't want to feel like that again.

On to phase two—the books Bob recommended on mystical experience. At first, when I look through them, they seem too technical for me, but book after book validates mysticism and mystical experience, describing them almost exactly as I did. One says: "identity with, or conscious awareness of, ultimate reality, the divine, spiritual truth, or God through direct experience, intuition, or insight . . . characterized by a fading or loss of self, or a perceived interconnection with all existence, often accompanied by feelings of peace, joy or bliss."[3] Another describes it as the realization of "a greater intelligence at work far more powerful than any merely human intelligence . . . something beyond our own physical organism, personality, and life circumstances,"[4] and yet another defines mystical experience as "the experience of everything and nothing, of knowing all yet being empty, of hearing within silence all sound . . . . those very rare moments of total understanding that can arise in connection with works of art are clearly in the same category—that clarity of vision and sense of contact with some archetypal personality."[5]

Yes! Music is art. I think I'm onto something here. I can't read fast enough.

The next book says that many who have had out-of-body experiences have developed psychic abilities afterward, and in the same sentence it says "mystical and psychic experiences are often associated with UFO encounters."[6] *UFO encounters?* This is from a professional compilation; it's not some crackpot website. Could this confirm that Sammy's aliens really did play a part in what happened to me? When I talked to Bob, the psychologist, I also told him about what Sammy had said about aliens, and Bob told me that it didn't matter if it were "true" or not. What mattered was that Sammy acted "as if" it were true and had built his life and philosophy around his belief, which of course, certainly seemed to be the case. The way Bob explained it, it all sounded perfectly normal and not the least bit unusual, so maybe it isn't, I don't know.

When I sit back and look at all the books piled up on the desk in front of me—thick ones, thin ones, old ones, new ones—it all feels so overwhelming. I'm sure Dee would tell me not to believe everything I read, but these researchers have analyzed mysticism from a scientific perspective after studying lots of cases. There must be something to it after all. If nothing else, it proves that I'm not the only person who has had an experience like this.

I exhale hard. The past few years of worrying about my sanity have been like praying I didn't have some life-threatening disease, doing everything possible to ensure good health, waiting for the test results, and finally getting good news. And yet, I could go around and around, forever dissecting these theories, but the more I learn, the more I recognize that having tangible proof for everything may not be the most important part of my journey because in the first place, science can't measure spirit. What we believe is just as if not *more* powerful than any amount of scientific justification. Therefore, I choose to accept the theories in these books as proof of the supernatural things that have been happening to me. I believe them. It's *my* reality. That's all that matters.

Over the past few years, my definition of reality seems to change on a daily basis anyway, swinging from one extreme to the other, then back again. I'm trying to balance both sides—the spiritual and the physical. I can't leave either world and ignore the other for long, and there seems no bridge between them. It's tearing me apart.

Interspersed with all the supernatural revelations, my dog Sam's cancer has returned and is now exacerbated by diabetes. I have to give her shots of insulin twice a day. She's not going to last long; she looks like a walking dog skeleton. How can I deal with this? I can't. I just give her the shots and hope for a miracle. She's my only girl (besides my mom) in this family of boys. Sam fell in love with me the first time she saw me—a little mutt puppy sitting all alone in a cage at the dog pound—the name "Samantha" scrawled on her paperwork. When I picked her up, she put her chin on my shoulder and fell asleep against my chest as if to say, "Ah, everything's going to be all right now."

Worse, my mother's mental capabilities are declining fast. The doctor says it's Alzheimer's disease. I talk to my parents on the phone at least three times a week and lately it has gotten to the point where I can no longer carry on a conversation with her. It's almost more than I can bear. I don't know what to do to help her and Dad doesn't seem to want my help.

I'm living two different lives and my heart aches in both of them. On one side is the pursuit of that elusive something that has grabbed hold of me and captivated me in joy, while at the same time, I sense that despair such as I'll never be able to prepare for is rapidly closing in—losing the ones I love. I've been trying so hard to disprove all the mystical and paranormal stuff so I could dismiss it as folly and get back to concentrating on the serious issues in front of me, but apparently that's not going to happen. I guess the meanings of the supernatural episodes are much more complex and important than I thought.

Now which is reality? Both.

CHAPTER 20

Enter the Dragon

Passion, it lies in all of us, sleeping... waiting... and though unwanted ... unbidden... it will stir... open its jaws and howl. It speaks to us.. . guides us... passion rules us all, and we obey. What other choice do we have? Passion is the source of our finest moments. The joy of love ... the clarity of hatred... and the ecstasy of grief. It hurts sometimes more than we can bear. If we could live without passion, maybe we'd know some kind of peace... but we would be hollow....
—Joss Whedon

May, 2005

When one is plugging along on her merry way, happily following her life's calling, there always seems to be somebody who has to throw a wrench in the works (besides my own thoughts of course). In this case, it's Dee.

After breakfast he's sitting at the kitchen table, reading the paper. "You need to get a job outside the home," he says. "You can't make any money sitting up there in the bedroom writing."

If he's said this to me once, he's said it a million times. I try to keep my cool as I pick up the dirty plates and move them into the sink.

Apparently, it isn't as obvious to him as it is to me that writing can be a noble profession. *If* of course, one can sell books. However, following my heart's desire means more to me than money. I've heard that when you feel so much enthusiasm about something that you're willing to do nothing but that one thing, would even be willing to do it without expecting pay, that's what you're meant to do with your life. And for me, it's writing. Funny how it never occurred to me that writing was my life's purpose. It took a complete stranger to point this out and make me believe my dream was possible. And that's just it—it's *possible* and it's coming true, but not fast enough for Dee. He continues his assault. "I don't see where any of this is taking you. Do you have a guarantee that all your hard work will pay off?"

"No."

"*Then why do it?* It makes no sense. Why waste your time?"

"It's not a waste of time, Dee. This is my dream. I've always wanted to be a writer."

"Having a few poems published doesn't make you a writer."

"What do you call it then?"

"It's a hobby; you're not making a living out of it."

"Well, I'm *trying* to. Besides, if my words can bring joy to just one person and give them the inspiration to pursue their dreams, then what I will have accomplished means more than all the money in the world." I hate feeling like I have to defend myself.

"But money makes the world go 'round. Without money, *you can't survive.*"

Here we go again—the money issue. I want to tell Dee that I think money is a major source of a lot of the world's evil, because it's about the furthest thing from "spirit" there is. Money lures us into always wanting more *things*—a bigger house, a newer car, a different lover, because the more things we get, the more things we want. We're never satisfied for long. If we concentrated more on looking inside of ourselves, maybe we would realize that we already have everything we need because of *who we are*, and be satisfied with that.

I want to tell Dee that I'm seeing evidence of this in my life more and more everyday—and *doesn't he see it in me?* But I also know that I won't be able to get him to understand. I may as well speak Vietnamese to him.

"You just don't want me to be happy," I say instead, trying hard not to let him upset me. Then I start scraping the residue of dried egg off the plates.

"I do want you to be happy. I love seeing you so positive; that's great. But we never see you anymore. You're always upstairs in front of the computer writing. There comes a point where you just have to quit messing with your book and be done." His voice is growing louder with each word.

He's right about that. But my spending so much time writing is due to two things. Number one: I'm a perfectionist to a fault. I think that came from always trying to please God so he would take me to heaven when I died. The other reason is because I desperately want to make a difference in the world and maybe it's selfish, but I'd really like to be around to witness it, no matter how big or small it may be.

"I know, but I'm not there yet," I tell him. "Writing a book isn't like going to your nine to five job. You don't leave it at the office. I have to run with it when I feel inspired and sometimes that doesn't happen for months and sometimes it's in the middle of the night . . . and stop shouting at me!"

"I'm not shouting. You just think I'm shouting; I'm just talking."

"Raising your voice is shouting."

One of the wet plates accidentally slips from my hands and makes a loud crash in the sink.

He shakes his head. "I think you're just doing all this to piss me off. You just don't want to spend any time with me anymore."

"You should know me better than that. I don't have it in me to do things to purposefully piss anybody off. It takes too much energy and I don't waste my energy like that."

I agree with some of what he's saying. I don't know how to balance my writing with the rest of my life. My heart is on fire; what can I say? I've never felt so much enthusiasm for anything.

"I don't know who you are anymore." Dee lowers his voice as if he's giving up on me.

"You know what? I finally *do*. And that's what all of this is about."

A big smile covers my face. This realization brings me so much joy that even though Dee is angry, I can't help myself. I go to him and give him a hug. "You don't have to understand it—are you coming with me? I'm flying!"

I kiss him on the lips but he doesn't react. Maybe he thinks I'm asking him to accept things he can't. He never asks me what I'm writing about and he's expressed no desire to read my book thus far. When I offer, he says, "I'll read it when it's done."

He doesn't like to read anyway. In all the years we've been together, I've never seen him read anything but the newspaper. And my book contains a few, well . . . *sensitive* subjects. I don't want any of it to come as a surprise, so I guess the best thing to do is break the news to him in bits and pieces.

"Sammy talks about aliens and some of the stuff he says sounds an awful lot like what happened to me. I wonder if his experiences had something to do with mine." I don't waste time with the piddling stuff—I go right to what I assume Dee will have the most difficult time accepting, because after that, the rest will be cake. Then I cringe, waiting for his response.

"Do you think you've been abducted by aliens?"

I get the feeling he's going to assess his judgment of my mental health based on my answer.

"No."

"Are you sure?" He tips his head sideways and looks at me.

"Yes, I'm sure, Dee. I've never experienced aliens."

"Okay, 'cause I gotta know whether to drop you off over there or not." He nods his head to the right, toward the mental health hospital a few blocks from our house.

Seeing that he's being rather humorous, I take it one step further. "Just because I've never seen aliens doesn't mean they don't exist."

He fans out the newspaper and shoots me a look as if to say, "Don't push it!"

To appease Dee, I apply for a job at a local grocery store. An attractive young woman interviews me and tells me to come back the following day. When I get there, she shows me into another room and sits me in front of a computer.

"Follow the directions on the screen," she instructs. Then she walks out.

Is this some kind of pre-employment test?

The computer is in a small, windowless room—the employee break room. People keep coming in and out, talking to one another or watching the chattering TV mounted on the wall above a set of gray lockers. The room smells as if a pile of dust and old sandwiches have been stashed in the corner behind the door. I picture myself as an employee punching the clock and shoving my clothes into one of those lockers like in high school and it doesn't produce a good feeling in me. Nevertheless, I do my best to answer the questions. For hours. The computer does its damnedest to overwhelm me with what seems to be worthless information: how long the shelf life is for macaroni salad, how high to stack cases of canned pork and beans. My mind floods its capacity for new information and I grow dizzier by the minute. *After this section, maybe someone will come in and offer me a break.* But there is always one more section and no one comes to check on me. My neck aches. The text on the screen begins to blur. My back hurts and my butt has had enough of sitting in this plastic chair. Finally, the computer locks up when I'm supposed to take a test on how to spot a bogus check. Thank God! Is this how they treat everyone?

I get up from the chair and my knees don't want to straighten out at first, but eventually I find my way to the customer service desk, looking for the manager who sat me in front of that machine.

"Who?" The woman behind the desk eyes me suspiciously. "Oh, she went home hours ago!"

The next shift manager had no idea I was back there.

The following day, the manager tells me to come in "whenever" so I show up in the early afternoon. A heavy-set man about fifteen years younger than me takes me in the back of the warehouse and hands me a uniform sealed in a plastic bag.

"Go into the restroom and put it on," he says.

It's not that any of this is beneath me, but it feels like a cruel joke. My entire being screams *No! Quick! Run the other way!* When I step out of the stall and see myself in the restroom mirror, there's a heterosexual rodent staring back at me.

All my dreams instantly sink into a pool of thick, greasy sludge. The experiences over the past few years have shown me something more magnificent than I ever dreamed possible. And now I feel like I'm prostituting my heart, allowing my dream, which has brought me so much joy, to slip from my grasp after having spent my whole life searching for it and finally finding it. The upswing, however, is that my conformist façade will please my husband and society's role for me; but I've spent all my life doing that.

I want to throw that uniform in their industrial-grade trashcan and sneak out the back door before anyone sees me. But that wouldn't be right now, would it? Apparently they've hired me because now I have a uniform.

I stay for the first day's on-the-job training only to find that my requested twenty hours per week have turned into fifty.

"Yeah, I know you said you could only work twenty hours, but we really need people for this shift," the woman in charge of the schedule snips, looking down her glasses at me.

I was taught to respect those in authority and although I want to say something that isn't so nice back to her, I hold my tongue. Bite my tongue actually. Then I wipe my hands down the side of my stylish, brown plastic apron and return to work, wondering how my knees, which have been the curse of my life (three surgeries and a huge metal screw) are going to tolerate me being on my feet for fifty hours per week or rather, how long it will be before they rise up in protest.

I left home this morning thinking I was just going in for another interview and I'd be home within an hour, but now it's well past dinnertime. My kids have been home for hours and I'm sure they have no idea where I am. For all I know, the house could have burned down.

I finally ask the supervisor for permission to leave for the day. He says they need me here for training, and his lips form a solid line across his face when he says it. Then he plants his hands on his hips and gives me the strangest look.

"I know, but my kids have been home for hours and I didn't know I was going to be gone this long," I plead.

He sighs and looks away as if he is anything but impressed with his new employee. Then he says, "Yeah, all right, but come back early tomorrow so we can get started. You have a lot to learn."

I can't get out of there fast enough. I don't look anyone in the eye as I punch out on the time clock and hurry to my car. I don't want them to see me. It feels like I've done something wrong for which I will soon be caught and severely punished.

When I climb into my car, I slump down in the driver's seat, relishing the familiar feel of its cushions on my back—heaven. I sit there for a few minutes, trying not to cry and wondering why I want to cry in the first place. Driving home, it feels like all the spirit has been wrung out of me, as if I'm being pounded like a nail into a brick wall.

"This opportunity will be good for you," my ego mind states emphatically. "You can work yourself up within the company to create a career for yourself. Lots of people have done it; so can you."

But my inner voice tells me differently. "This is *not* what you are meant to do with your life. You haven't been led so mysteriously down this path for no reason; there's a higher purpose involved. You can't continue to follow that calling working fifty hours per week. Plus there'll be no time left over to take care of your family and your parents. They *need* you."

My blood seems to freeze in my veins. I slap my hand down hard on the steering wheel. "Am I just being a spoiled brat?" I ask the interior of my minivan. "I know I'm luckier than most, staying home all these years to raise my kids, but we also do without a lot of things. And yet, most people don't have this option and I'm truly grateful for what I have."

"Oh come on, give it a chance," the other side of me presses. "Maybe you can work until fall and then save the money to go back to college and get your journalism degree."

"That sounds reasonable. I could finish school in less than two years if I went full time."

I recently put myself through a few years of college—not an easy task when you have a family to raise. But I stayed up late, got up early, and earned excellent grades so I could get merit-based scholarships. It took me six years to get my two-year Associate of Arts degree, but I did it. I had planned to pursue a bachelor's degree in journalism but then all these amazing things started happening since Cabo and they insisted on dominating my time. This put going back to college on hold.

But my heart knows that going back to college at this point isn't likely. The reality of it is if I stay in this job, I'm flushing my dream down the toilet. The thought of having meaningful conversations with crates of limp lettuce on a daily basis does not correspond with my idea of a rewarding life.

When I get home, I fall onto the couch and cry. I can't eat, so I go upstairs to bed. I can't sleep.

This goes on for days. I just plain feel awful inside and out and I don't see any way to improve it, except for the one thing I don't know how to do: quit. But how can I quit after only a few days? That's going to make me look like a fool. *I shop there; people know me.* What would they think of me? Maybe they'd say, "See that woman? She lied and told us she wanted a job. She just wasted our time. Who does she think she is, some prima donna pretending to be like the rest of us?"

I don't need God to punish me; I'm more than capable of doing a stellar job on my own. But I can't keep doing this to myself. I've made myself such a wreck that even Dee says, "Quit then."

With great anguish, I phone the manager and quit, apologizing profusely for wasting their time. When I hang up, I am overcome with a relief such as I've never known before, but it's also short-lived. The old beliefs of being a failure once again assume their positions. *You can't do anything right. You're not good at anything,* they sneer. Then guilt steps in right beside failure, because guilt is my middle name. The nuns in Catholic school taught it to me well: *You should have at least given it a chance; you're not getting any younger. Now what are you gonna do? You've let your husband down; he's going to be furious.*

But I don't have to listen to failure and guilt for long. Perhaps the horrible feelings I keep getting are really the voice of my Higher Self trying to get my attention for more reasons than simply falling off the path to my dream. It's screaming at me because it knows something "I" couldn't have known. The next day, Dee's brother-in-law calls and tells him that his sister had a heart attack and they don't know yet what they're going to do, probably surgery. She's already had several that we know of and luckily she keeps bouncing back, but how many heart attacks can one woman endure before it kills her?

As if this isn't bad enough, my little dog Sam finally succumbs to her diabetes.

I know she's gone, but I keep thinking I see her lying under the kitchen table. I even catch myself pulling out a chair so I can reach down and pet her. Although I knew she wasn't going to get better, to brace myself, I tried to imagine ahead of time what my life would be like without her following me around everywhere I went, or how it would feel to miss her brown eyes gazing up at me. I thought I could prepare myself for not being able to hear her "talk" anymore in her soft, grumbling little voice or chirp whenever I came home from being gone somewhere. I've never heard a dog chirp like that before.

No matter how hard I tried to imagine what it was going to be like, it wasn't even close to what I'm feeling now. The little brown, braided rug in front of the fireplace is empty and cold.

And things are about to get a whole lot worse.

CHAPTER 21

Plates Across the Sky

If you fall down seven times, get up eight!
—Japanese proverb

July, 2005

The answering machine is blinking. I exhale hard as I drop one of the bags of groceries down on the kitchen table. I'm tired. It's the Fourth of July. I have to get all the food together for a barbeque with the kids before we go to watch the fireworks over the lake tonight and I still have all these groceries to put away. It's already late and they'll be here any minute. I don't have time to sift through all the telemarketer calls, but I push play anyway.

It's my mother's voice. "Oh, Honey, this is Mom, call me please."

Beep.

"Dad is lying on the floor next to the bathroom and he won't get up."

What?

Beep.

"Pat, please call me; I don't know what to do, I'm so scared."

Beep.

Sounds of my mother crying.

Oh my God.

Beep.

My hands are shaking. My chest feels like there's a house sitting on it. Mom hasn't dialed the phone in months. She can't remember how. How did she do it this time?

I call and ask her what happened. She can't tell me.

"Mom, let me talk to Dad."

"No, he can't talk to you." She sounds confused.

My whole body is trembling. My mind is racing. My father has never been seriously ill a day in his life. Is he unconscious? Dead? Oh my God, oh my God, oh my God, please help me. I'm more than an hour's drive away, what do I do? Wait . . . try to think. Mom probably can't call 911 and it won't do any good if I call; they need someone on the phone who's at the scene.

I tell my mother to sit tight. I know their neighbors, so I call them and ask if they will please go over and check on my parents.

Of course.

With phone in hand, they go across the street. I can hear the sound of their footsteps crunching the ground as they walk and I can only make out little bits of their conversation as they talk in lowered tones. I'm afraid to breathe; afraid I might miss the sound of my father's voice that I'm desperate to hear.

The wife finally comes back on the line. "He seems okay; he's sitting up, talking and making sense." Thank God.

Chills wash over me. "Can you stay until I get there?"

"Sure," she says.

Instead of spending a fun evening with Dee and the kids, I find myself speeding through the night and showers of colorful lights as I rush to my father's side. I can't get there fast enough. I usually enjoy this drive because I can crank up my stereo and surround myself in music, but now it's taking an eternity. And I feel so horribly alone.

Passing through the center of town, I have to wait at a stoplight while globs of people stroll across the street in front of me—families with excited children hauling their blankets, coolers, and lawn chairs back to their cars. How dare they laugh and walk so slow when something is wrong with my father! Hurry up! Hurry up, dammit!

My stomach feels like a vat of sour milk. This can't be real. *Don't jump to conclusions; everything's going to be okay.* But I don't really believe it. Something sinister and black is lurking. I can feel it.

When I get there, my father is standing up and talking normally.

"I'm fine, Pat." He forces a little grin. "See?"

He looks okay, a bit thin, but otherwise fine.

I thank the neighbors and they leave, but within a few minutes, Dad collapses again. It's as if his knees have just given out on him and yet he's still conscious. He's lying in the doorway from the garage into the family room. I can't shut the door and I can't get him up either. He's not a big man, but he's too heavy for me. And he must have hit his head when he fell because now his forehead is bleeding. I have boys. I'm used to seeing blood, but now it's making me sick.

"I'm calling 911," a voice coming out of me says. It's that authoritative voice that takes over when my brain knows it absolutely, positively can *not* fall apart under any circumstances because the situation at hand is dire.

"No, I'll be fine. Just give me a minute." With me holding his arm, Dad tries to stand and falls back onto me.

I call the ambulance.

After an excruciatingly long night of doctors, tests, and trying to make sure Mom gets some rest, at 5 A.M. the doctor informs me that Dad has bronchitis, chronic obstructive pulmonary disease (COPD), and emphysema from smoking a pipe all his life. They put him on oxygen, give him antibiotics, and release him. As I drive us home from the hospital, I'm seeing something I never thought I'd see. Only hours ago they were my parents—self-sufficient and wise. Now they're suddenly and unexpectedly my children.

It's odd how life can take such twists sometimes. Just when you think you've got things figured out, the bottom drops out and you have to switch gears in the middle. And I'm not one of those roll-with-the-punches-type people. Even small things have a big impact on me. But I'm the oldest child. I can't panic now or this will suffocate me. There's no time or emotional space in my heart to allow feelings, because if I acknowledge them, then all of this will be real and it isn't. It's just a bump in the road. So I go through the motions. I do what any daughter would do—move into my parent's house.

I take all the clothes out of Mom's closets and drawers and wash them—they're loaded with stains and they smell like yellow perspiration and greasy skin. Then I put masking-tape labels on all her dresser drawers: "Sox," "Underwear," "Bras," "Pajamas," "Long pants," so she can find them when she needs them. I call the oxygen company to arrange regular deliveries and teach Dad how to operate the machine. I go to the drugstore to pick up prescriptions. I cook pancakes for breakfast and whatever I can find for dinner. I fix ham sandwiches for lunch. I drive Dad to the pulmonologist and Mom to the dentist. And I burn—like a small campfire whose warmth doesn't seem adequate to sustain us all.

After several weeks, Dad is regaining his strength and his eyes look clearer, so I move back home with Dee and the boys. My only other sibling, my brother Tim, and I take turns going every day to check on Mom and Dad. Their neighbors send over casseroles in plastic containers and freshly-baked cookies on fancy plates.

At first Dad is cooperative, but it's not his nature to accept charity or help. One night after he's finished his supper and I'm at the sink, cleaning up the dishes in their kitchen, he confronts me. "You and Tim are getting too much into our personal business."

I've never heard him talk like this before. Dad doesn't usually let anything upset him—he plugs away at whatever task he's been assigned to. So now, his behavior concerns me. I feel a pinprick of pain in my heart and I'm torn between being afraid of offending him and insisting on helping make sure things get done. I can't let something bad happen to them.

"I don't mean to, Dad, I'm just trying to help. I'm worried about you guys," I say over my shoulder, intentionally avoiding eye contact.

"I know you are." His voice sounds like he's back to his old self again. "But we're fine."

I'm sure he views our help as infringements of his dignity and freedom as an adult. How can I possibly know what they're going through? How would I feel if somebody told me I couldn't drive anymore? Or that I smelled bad because I'd forgotten to take a shower?

Out of respect, I promise to back off a bit.

As I'm driving home it's dark out, darker than I've ever seen it. It's as if the mountains off to the west, which I've always considered some sort of terrestrial guardians, have deflated, and the sense of security they've provided for most of my life has disintegrated with them. Now I'm left out here to wander the prairie and it's midnight.

But I know Dad will get better. He always gets better. It's Mom I have to worry about. Her confusion is getting worse by the day. It's becoming a health risk for both of them. She forgets and leaves stove burners turned on, doesn't take a bath for weeks, forgets where she's put things. Her friend across the street confides that sometimes Mom goes over to her house and cries, saying things that make no sense.

It's becoming harder for her to find the right words, and the worst part is that she knows it. My best friend in the world is slipping away right before my eyes. Maybe if I back off like Dad wants me to, I won't see it on a regular basis and it will all just fix itself. Yeah, my dad can handle anything; he'll make everything all right again. But damn, it sure is dark tonight.

On a warm fall evening, I'm sitting outside with Mom on the front porch of their house. The trees in their yard are still green and leafed out; they've grown to the point where they make terrific things for visiting grandsons to climb. The street is quiet and the air has only a slight hint of autumn.

"We love to sit out here and have a cold can of beer in the summer," she explains. She are I are sitting on the freestanding swing I bought her for her birthday last year and she's pushing it with her foot, swinging us back and forth.

"Yeah, it certainly is beautiful out here."

A passing airplane leaves its vapor trail overhead as we speak.

"We like to watch the plates go across the sky." Mom points at the plane like a little kid and then her face changes. I can see the confusion and anger in her eyes. She realizes she's said the wrong word and she's trying desperately to think of the right one, but it doesn't come, so she attempts to cover up her mistake before I notice. "We call them plates because they look so flat."

My hearty German mother, who loves to hunt and fish with the best of them, who, at 83, shot a record antelope in Wyoming, suddenly seems so fragile. I put my arms around her thin, freckled shoulders and squeeze her gently. "I love you, Mom."

She looks puzzled as to why I'm saying this in response to our conversation about airplanes.

My eyes fill with tears; but I don't let her see them.

While driving Dad to his doctor's appointment, I glance over at him in the passenger seat of my minivan. For the first time, I don't recognize my own father. He is suddenly a little old man—his glasses too large for his face, oxygen tubes up his nose, the tank tucked into the seat behind him. My dear father, forever the anchor in my life, now appears vulnerable and gray. In some strange way, it feels like I'm being disrespectful to him—me being his caretaker. An unfamiliar feeling begins to grow inside of me, as if it knows what I refuse to admit to myself—the unspeakable, the unthinkable—my father is dying.

"There's a song I'd like to play for you. It's a Van Halen song, but it describes exactly how I feel about you, Dad. Do you mind if I play it?"

I don't know why all of a sudden this idea has occurred to me, but it's perfect.

"Okay." He's looking straight ahead, out the windshield at the world passing by.

"From now on, this is your song." I turn on my stereo and play "Can't Stop Loving You." As Sammy's voice sails out of the speakers, my father listens intently, politely, his tired blue eyes trying to focus inward, on the meaning of the words. When the song ends I ask him, "Did you like that?"

He runs his hand over his little mustache. Funny how I hadn't noticed before now that it's become more gray than brown. "Yeah, but why do they have to scream all the time?" he replies.

When I get home, I write the lyrics down and mail them to my dad so he can understand the words. I tell him how much I love him. A few days later, he phones me to tell me that he received the letter. "That's a really beautiful song," he says.

I can tell by the sound of his voice that he's choking back tears and it makes me cry too because we're both well aware of what it is we're not saying.

CHAPTER 22

Eagles

Well-behaved women seldom make history.
—Laurel Thatcher Ulrich

October, 2005

The sky is full of birds. As I drive down our street, they appear to be just floating there, like they're waiting for me to acknowledge them. Pulling up to the stop sign, I glance up to get a better look.

They must be pigeons. No, crows—no, blue herons; they're bigger than pigeons or crows. I watch them sail effortlessly, sliding above me in gentle circles. They come so low, there is no mistaking them—bald eagles. Seven of them. One of them flies right over my car. Seven eagles, what a positive sign!

When I finish running errands and get back home, I do an online search to find out what the eagle symbolizes. Eagles aren't just your ordinary bird. In a lot of cultures, especially Native American cultures, they represent the highest of rank. Their eyes are such that the higher they soar in the sky, the clearer their vision becomes. That's how they can see a fish swimming below the surface of the water from hundreds of feet up. Some people even consider eagles to be liaisons between humans and God—carrying our prayers to the heavens.

Since eagles keep making appearances in my life, perhaps they're trying to tell me something, but whatever it is, I'm still not getting it.

A friend and I discussed this once—how do you know when something is a sign? We came to the conclusion that if you think it's a sign, it probably is. I guess it goes along with learning to listen to your Higher Self, which I'm getting better at every day.

About a week later, Dee and I find ourselves at another concert at Cabo Wabo in Mexico. We're up at the front of the stage for the show—the front! There's nothing between the raised, open floor and my stomach. I dig my fingers into the carpet on the stage. It feels matted and brittle; I'm sure I don't want to know what's imbedded in it. The room is crammed with people as usual. Tonight, some form of infectious, mass adrenaline seems to permeate the air. It begins to smolder.

Assistants bring out two metal buckets filled with ice and sports drinks, beer, Cabo Wabo tequila, and bottled water and set them on the stage. The show begins. Sammy and the Wabos—Mona, Vic, and Dave—start out lit up and gain speed with each note. Energy pours from them like an erupting volcano—thick, hot, machismo liquid. It seems to flow over the edge of the stage, taking me with it, as if some sort of locomotive is rolling over me, smashing my guts into the gaps between the railroad ties, then releasing me into the world gasping for air.

This fascinates me, maybe because the musicians are up there on the stage, revealing their hearts, their souls, their act, and it touches something inside me that I desperately need to make contact with. And when I see them doing it, it reminds me all over again that that part of me exists—that part of me where unlimited possibilities and dreams are, just waiting to be unleashed—and tonight the music is filling that need, like giving sight to a blind person.

The more I watch Sammy sing, the more I sense something beneath his performance. Maybe it's because I'm already feeling so emotional, but when he bends down and puts his face in front of mine, I notice gray hairs in his beard and little bumps on his neck from shaving, and I realize that rock gods don't have gray hair or bumps from shaving—*real* people do. It makes me think that he probably feels insecure sometimes, and that his kids probably get hurt by other kids just like mine do and as parents, we want to protect them with all our might, but the awful truth is that we can't always do that. And I bet he has moments when he just doesn't want to get out of bed in the morning. What is it that separates a famous person like him from the average person? Is it because he gives himself permission to follow his dreams while the rest of us are scared to try? Is it because he's allowing himself to tap into that part of himself where he's creat*or* and creat*ed* at the same time—that realm of the Divine? What about those of us who also need to do that but don't know how? Maybe a lot of us aren't finding our answers because we don't even know the questions. All we know is that something is missing and we have a hunger that won't go away.

Or maybe Sammy just got lucky.

As I watch the sweat pour off his face and the stage lights bounce off his mic stand, something about it reassures me that doing what we love most is an avenue available to all of us, and that's what our lives are all about. Maybe when things don't happen the way we think they should or as fast as we want them to, we give up and that's one reason nothing changes.

But something about this night also makes me know that one day I'm going to be doing what Sammy's doing—living my dream. If he can do it, *so can I.* I'm already halfway there, maybe more.

He looks down at me and smiles as if he knows what I'm thinking. I'm so happy right now.

A woman standing next to me bumps into me. She came in here wearing red devil horns, but now she's handing them to Sammy. Then she shows him the tail. He turns around and bends over for her to put it down the back of his pants, kind of like he's teasing her, "touch me/no don't." Before long, he takes it out and shoves it down the front so it looks like a long, red, pointy penis. And he starts stroking it up and down, up and down, dancing around with the devil tail in one hand and the microphone in the other and grinding like a stripper. He's seems to be doing a pretty good job of it too. Rather interesting expertise for a man his age.

Michael Anthony then comes onstage and the crowd cheers louder. He teaches his bass who's boss by pounding on it and offering the unique vocal accompaniment that can only come from Mikey. He feeds off Sammy's sexual innuendoes and shoots them right back with his body and guitar. They are even more uninhibited than usual and the show is cranking itself up into an out-of-control frenzy. I can't imagine what it would feel like to be up onstage like that, doing whatever you want and having people cheer for everything you do.

With the two of them at the helm, the band launches into a Van Halen tune. It's a song called "Poundcake." I know what's coming. Since I've been to a few of Sammy's shows now, I've seen him do the same thing every time he performs this one. Yet, somehow, he always manages to do or say something that shocks me. I think he likes it that way. He gets off on crossing the line and seeing how much he can get away with.

Part way through the song, there's a moment where the only sound is that of a few notes with a chord at the end. Sammy uses this as an opportunity to demonstrate what the song is really about. He tilts his head back and licks his fingers one by one, then goes into exaggerated theatrics to suck one finger. The audience screams. Wanting to drive his point home, he grabs his goatee and rubs it all over his face with his open hand.

"I thought about shaving this off," he says afterward. "But the ladies really like how it feels." He doesn't mean on their faces.

Okay, he got me with that one. I'm blushing.

Then Sammy goes into "Finish What Ya Started," another Van Halen song. But he doesn't just sing it, he crawls right into it. He plays with the melody rolling out of him, sliding the notes up and down, in and out, embellishing the sound, slathering us with it, winding around soft and low, taking each of us along for the ride.

"*I want some, I need some, mmmm, got to have some . . .*" he taunts.

Seeing the effect he's having on the audience, he smiles, sweat pouring off his face and dripping onto the stage floor and into the faces of those of us in the front row. It doesn't get much more personal than when someone else's sweat stings your eyes.

He seems to absorb the emotion of the crowd, and he's toying with us, turning us over and over in his hands, tossing us up in the air and catching us again—basking in the feeling of sustaining the emotions of an entire roomful of people. I can see where this could get addictive. For him, I mean. But I'm being pulled into a moment created by the human voice in a way I've never experienced before. It makes me want to laugh, cry, scream—something—but I don't. It's not that I can't react or, yeah, maybe that *is* it. But it's not because of the words he's singing, or the melody, or the way he's acting; it's because Sammy's voice is taking me on a trip in and out of reality in a way I don't know how to deal with. I love it/hate it, only because it wants to incite a loss of self-control in me that I fight against.

With his mouth at the mic, and both hands gripping it, Sammy closes his eyes and whispers the final word of the song, like letting go of the string of a balloon and watching it float away, "*Pusssssssy . . .*"

The audience is spellbound. Some of them scream, some shout, some clap wildly. Fists go up in the air. I just stand there. My internal fight to control myself versus the intoxicating lure to *lose* control is just too much, so I sink in between like a coward. Why can't I just allow myself to experience the full impact of the moment? Why do I always have to be so damned proper? Because adults aren't supposed to let themselves be swept away? But isn't that what life is really all about? Experiencing each and every moment to its fullest?

I'm about to find out.

The band is taking a short break as their leader decides what to play next. Sammy gulps down a bottle of water, lifts up his sunglasses, and puts his arm around Vic. The two of them stand looking at the setlist, which is taped like a long, white runway onto the vertical stage speakers. In the meantime, his bass strapped around his shoulder, Mikey smiles his beautiful smile at the audience, runs his fingers through his sweaty hair like a rake, then grabs a full bottle of tequila from the bucket onstage. He bends over backward and slams it down his throat for a good ten seconds or more, then he looks right at me and comes over. Without a word, he kneels down in front of me and starts pouring tequila straight from the bottle into my mouth. This is not a quick shot; he keeps on pouring like it's just water. I have to swallow fast to keep it from spilling all over me. It's ice-cold, then it turns warm and velvety-smooth as it slides down my throat.

I feel like I'm melting, as if my body's turning into a pool of warm syrup.

The front of my shirt and my whole face are wet and sticky from tequila, and before I can wipe my face or stop to wonder what this is all about, Mikey grabs me around the neck and pulls me toward him. Then he starts kissing me. His mouth is slippery and warm and the kiss is more than a little peck, lasting longer than it probably should. I can feel his soft tongue on my lips, and for a split second, I wonder if I should see how much I can get away with. Should I open my mouth and suck him in? Because then things could get really intense, and I sort of want them to—my brain and my clothes are drenched in tequila— what do I care? He might even go further than that if I let him, because he's still going at it. Oh, it would be so easy right now, to just let go and blame it on the alcohol.

But somehow I catch myself before I go over the edge. I can't do that to my husband. I can't do that to Mikey's wife— even though *Mikey* started it. But damn, he's sure making me feel good.

It's me that ends the kiss. I can hear my friends now, "*What are you, nuts?* You had a chance like that and you didn't take it?" I know. Sometimes I get so mad at myself for being so frigging responsible. It could have been even more fun, but . . . .

My heart is thumping hard.

There's no time to think or even feel guilty about it. I hear Sammy's voice talking into the microphone, "Be careful, Mikey; she's jail bait, she's only 12 years old!" like it's something he sees every day. Maybe it is.

The booze is really starting to hit me now. My head is swimming in a tequila-infused, sensual blur, like floating in the warm ocean and letting all my inhibitions dissolve with the current. Is he talking about me? I hear myself say it out loud, "Me? You mean *me?*"

He does. He's looking right at me, holding the microphone at an angle and grinning. Mikey's not the only one with a beautiful smile.

This is not happening.

The concept of time seems to grind to a halt. I'm not even aware of all the people around me. What happened to the sensible old lady who always tried to act respectable? Here I am guzzling straight tequila and making out with a rock star! The sensible old lady must have gotten left behind in the shadows under the stage floor, in the dark with the sticky cups, because the other rock star onstage just announced as a joke that I'm 12 and suddenly I am. Only 12-year-olds don't know what they're doing and I know what I'm doing... *or do I?* I feel so amazingly, gloriously, fabulously *fine.*

Then the thought occurs to me, "Oh man, Mikey's wife's gonna kill me. I hope she didn't see that. Oh God, I hope *Dee* didn't see that." I look around to see if either of them noticed, but I don't see Dee or Mikey's wife. At the same time, I don't care who saw it. I know everyone did.

There is no high like this in my life in Colorado. Or anywhere else but right here, in this moment. I feel like a star myself. Up until now, even tonight, I fought against letting myself go, fought against allowing myself to get swept up in the moment, and then the Universe *forced* me to lighten up—with a little help from Mikey, and I still somehow managed to hold myself back. That was probably a good thing in this case—wasn't it? Breathe, Pat. Sometimes I guess I just need a little push though. I need to loosen up more often. My life is so much more fun when I do. And I need to remember this concept next week and next month and next year and not let it get lost in the memory of making out with a rock star. *Even though that part was so nice.*

Maybe it's all part of what I'm supposed to learn from this spiritual journey, I don't know, like the Zen theory of Beginner's

Mind—be fully present in the now. It's funny though; I'm learning all these spiritual lessons through an avenue that seems about as un-spiritual as you can get—sex, drugs, and rock and roll. And if my brain weren't so high on tequila right now, and things weren't moving so fast, I'd really like to think about that some more because it's such an amusing idea—discovering myself and God in the most unlikely places. My entire mystical journey has been about that. It reminds me of the yin/yang symbol, because inside the circle, the yin always contains a bit of the yang and vice versa. It's never all one side or the other, never all black or all white and within each side, there's always a little seed of the other.

A man behind me taps me on the shoulder. "Was that as good for you as it was for him?"

I can't even answer him; I'm still trying to process what just happened, so I just smile instead.

When the show is over, the crowd inside the building shuffles outside to get some air. They spill out into the courtyard, the sidewalk, and down the street, drinking and visiting with one another and the road crew.

I've assembled a bunch of happy, sweaty people under the neon Cabo Wabo sign and I'm getting ready to take a picture, but as I hold my camera up to my face, someone comes up behind me and puts an arm around my shoulder. "Let's take a picture," he says.

He wants me to get in the photo with the other people, I assume, but when I look to see where the voice is coming from, I realize it's Sammy's drummer, David Lauser. Before I can react, he grabs my camera out of my hands, turns me around and holds the camera in front of us at arm's length. He puts his face next to mine. Snap! Then he jumps into a waiting car and disappears into the night.

I'm thinking, *Wow! Everybody's giving me attention tonight; I wonder why.*

Security guards back the next getaway car down the driveway. Mexican men with biceps the size of my head surround an SUV that stands waiting with its doors open. When Sammy and his wife come out, bodyguards usher them quickly toward the waiting SUV. As he passes by, Sammy sees me. He squeezes my hand and gives me a big smile.

"Keep on writing, Pat," he says. Then he's gone.

I suddenly feel like I can accomplish anything, that all I have to do is ask and the Universe will provide me with whatever I need. How can four simple words from a stranger make me feel like that? And David and Mikey . . . .

Back in our hotel room, I feel I owe it to Dee to confess. "Did you see Mikey kiss me during the show tonight?"

"No," he says. He's busy looking at his pictures of the concert and doesn't even look up from his camera. Since he doesn't seem even the slightest bit irritated, I drop the subject. If it's bothering him, I'm sure I'll find out sooner or later.

A little smile spreads across my face as I climb into bed, and when I close my eyes, I see the heads, beaks, and wings of eagles rushing toward me, enveloping me, *becoming* me. They fly toward me, straight on, and go into me. Then they carry me into my sleep singing, "Keep on writing, Pat," as if it's the answer to all my dreams.

There is no difference between miles and hours, but on the trip home, when I step off the plane, returning from feeling like a celebrity in paradise and 95-degree weather to a 40-degree October chill and cloudy skies, the stark contradictions of reality make me feel that maybe my latest adventure was nothing more than a dream. A dream of being an eagle that soared into the heavens, gaining a new perspective and delivering the prayers of the people to God. Ah yes, that must have been it.

CHAPTER 23

I Can't Stop Loving You

The greatest discovery of my life is that a human being
can alter his life by altering his attitude.
—William James

December, 2005

Hobbling drunk with sorrow to the podium, I'm acutely aware of how the incense the priest has just released into the room lingers, its saintly aroma a representation of unseen worlds. My father's body is ensconced in a gray, metal-colored box and draped in the American flag, with bouquets of sad flowers cascading over the sides—sealed up now, for good. The saliva in my mouth feels thick and hot, and it's all I can do not to throw up.

I glance at the rows of downcast faces before me, all arranged in church pews. Red poinsettias and evergreen branches decorate the room because tomorrow is Christmas Eve. My mother is sitting in a wheelchair, comprehending one minute and looking confused the next. They're all waiting for me to say something to make them feel better. But I am overcome with how frustrating and inadequate my human love is, and how frustrating and inadequate my words are to describe that and all the other feelings inside of me—millions of them, all vying for my attention simultaneously—and raping each other, stabbing each other, bleeding, pouring, and rising in revolt.

With Dee, Tim, and my sons at my side holding me up, I manage to deliver the final farewell to my father, or rather, a voice coming out of the woman in the blue dress with my shoes and hands delivers the final farewell. Then I dedicate "Can't Stop Loving You" to Dad one last time.

"I won't play the song because my dad didn't like rock music." The words trickle out of me sounding like they're coming from down a very long hall. Instead, I read the lyrics to the congregation.

Where are God's angels? I expect that they are here right now, flowing in great arcs above our heads, in the highest lofts of air, dropping mists of love and comfort on all those who grieve. I strain with all my might, but I don't see them. And I don't feel God either. I feel completely abandoned by Him, even in His church, with the candles, the holy water, the priest in robes, and the singing of "Amazing Grace" and "Ave Maria" at my request. He took my daddy from me—at Christmastime no less—family time, happy time. Now the holidays are a farce. I feel like I'm floating on a plank of two-by-fours that are nailed together, the sole survivor of the Titanic, rising and falling in the middle of an endless black and stormy sea while I watch those boards disintegrate beneath me with each barbaric wave.

You can't prepare yourself for this. I thought I would feel empty, or that I could psych myself into believing, even if just for a little while, that my father was on vacation and would be back in a few weeks. Those are just words. Words without any depth. There's a nervousness in my stomach and I want to run away. If I run fast enough, maybe I can get away from the monster. I see where the face of evil comes in to haunt the tormented souls left behind to pick up the pieces. I see where the fear comes from. It feels like I've swallowed chunks of decayed cement and it's breaking apart further into dust or sand in my guts—throat, stomach, intestines—trying to digest that which can't be. It tastes like dry, caked-on dirt that was tread upon by dinosaurs—smells like the inside of an ancient Egyptian tomb—stale and stark, with scents I cannot identify.

My parents were staying at Tim's house for the weekend and Tim went to check on them one morning because they'd been sleeping later than usual. Dad was ashen and cold in the bed, his oxygen tube askew on his nose. Mom was asleep beside him, unaware that the man who was her whole life had slipped away into the night without her.

Paramedics worked on my father for nearly forty minutes but it was too late. My daddy checked out without saying good-bye, without telling me how I was supposed to go on living without him.

My body can't figure out how to react; it breaks into a sweat and shivers at the same time. I feel like I've been flipped inside out and my muscles and vital organs are exposed to the open air, while my skin, hair, and senses are now on the inside and suffocating. My brain is somewhere else.

I slip into that autopilot mode again—the one where I become mature and take my mother into our home, feed her, bathe her, dress her, and brush her teeth. It's the same mode where I was able, along with Tim, to choose a suit for our father's burial and secure their house, Christmas presents thoughtfully wrapped in Santa Claus paper with "to" and "from" cards containing little notes like, "To our wonderful son with all our love," positioned under the tree, a bright red hand-towel hanging on the ring in the powder room proclaiming "MERRY! MERRY! MERRY!" Fuck merry. Fuck you, red towel.

And through a blur of sleeplessness and unimaginable shock, I somehow composed the eulogy for the man who had been the rock of stability all my life, the man who still had my baby teeth in an airtight film canister stored in his filing cabinet in the upstairs bedroom.

How weird this all feels. Reality on one hand, dreams on the other—black versus white, darkness versus light. A feeling like attachment, belonging, joy, dancing, warmth, honor, friendship, privilege versus despair, alone, abandoned, fear, cold, hard, gritty, swallowing sand and blood, nervous. And here I am right in the middle, desperate for any small light to cling to. Hanging on every word like dogma. At the same time waiting for my head to be chopped off and never resting again. Never trusting. And yet God has delivered an alternative that can never taste the same but maybe it can take my hand and teach me a new way. If I let it. If I can find it again—the light that poured into me during a rock concert in Cabo eons ago. I don't know where it is right now though. And where am I? Between the sheets— ice and glass, feathers and fur. Forlorn. First born.

And then Dee tells me that he had a spiritual encounter with my dad, something about geese flying overhead and them being a representation of my dad's spirit. Although I'm too numb to give it much thought, this is kind of shocking, coming from him. Maybe something's changing in him. If I still had my mind right now, I'd ask him more about it. But I don't.

In my bed at night, I pray and ask for help from God, the Universe, my father, the angels. Mom isn't going to last long. It's only been a few days since Dad's funeral and now that she's come to live with us, she suddenly can't walk. She refuses to eat. Even when I make a special trip to the Chinese restaurant and bring back her favorite—sweet and sour shrimp, she won't eat it. She gets mad and tells me she's full and why do I keep insisting that she should eat when she's full? I'm getting more terrified by the day; what will become of her? How can I help her? I can't lift her by myself and our house isn't set up for someone who can't walk. It will take months to reconstruct the downstairs to accommodate her. She's confused most of the time and doesn't realize that Dad is dead. She asks me if she can take an extra cookie for him, tells me she hasn't seen him in a while and by the way, where is he? When I explain, her eyes widen and her mouth drops open as if I'm some heartless beast who has been purposefully withholding information. Then she becomes furious and tells me that I'm lying, as if I would lie to her about something like that. I don't know what's worse, seeing her shock and insurmountable pain several times a day, each time she learns the truth anew, or seeing her physically shutting down.

In the morning, when I go into her room to check on her, she won't open her eyes.

Oh my God, this is my mother, my darling, my sweet and dear mother. Just yesterday, she was sitting on the floor and showing me how far she could stretch and touch her toes and now she's lying limp in her bed.

Dee and I take her to the emergency room.

That sick feeling, the one that tastes like cement in my gut, which hasn't really left me since losing Dad, flares up again.

After three days of tests, the hospital can't find anything wrong with her. I need to find a place for her or take her home. If she could walk, it would be different, but . . . I have less than twenty-four hours to find a place for the most cherished woman in my life. And it's New Year's Eve.

There's not much to choose from on a holiday and on such short notice but I finally find a nursing home. They drug her because she keeps falling and nothing else works to keep her

from hurting herself. I hate them for it. Hate myself for sign-
ing the paper giving them permission to do it. Then I watch
my mother's mind undulate between drugs, fear, confusion,
and—once in a while—understanding. Even writing these
words makes me sick. I'm the worst daughter ever, the scum of
the earth. What's the matter with me? I can't even take care of
the woman who gave me *everything*. How can I do this to her?
She must hate me. I feel like Judas betraying Jesus in the Garden
of Gethsemane. What else could he have done? Could he have
stopped it? I don't know how to stop this.

Jesus' words keep going though my mind: "The spirit is
willing but the flesh is weak," and it infuriates me to see how
true this is. Why do I have to be so goddamned human? My
mind feels like it's on backwards . . . oh God . . . my daddy, my
mommy—is there any solid ground left to stand on? I want to
cry but I can't. I'm so out of it, I can't even describe my emotions. I sit down to meditate and see an eagle coming straight
toward me, its legs and talons extended, to pick me up.

Less than two months later, at 3 A.M., there comes a call
from the nursing home. "You'd better come soon," the nurse
tells me.

I tried to decorate her room to make her feel at home.
There was her favorite picture of Jesus over her bed, a vase of
fresh flowers I'd brought her a couple of days ago cheerily sitting on her nightstand, a photo of her and Dad smartly dressed
up at my friend Nancy's wedding on the table near the TV so
she could see it every day, and the stuffed toy cat I bought her
to help ease the pain of not being with her beloved Persian cat
on a daily basis.

The clock on the wall glows 6:38 in big, red numbers. I'm
holding her hand, which is scrawny and covered with age spots.
I don't think it looked like this yesterday. I'm telling her how
very much I love her, but I don't know if she can hear me. Not

sure if she heard me last night before I left either, when I read her the 23rd Psalm, her favorite Bible passage. I tried to do it to bring her some comfort, but I kept crying in between the words. And then I had to stop because the words in the nursing home's version weren't the same words I was used to hearing in the 23rd Psalm, and I didn't want to upset her by getting the words wrong.

And now, just like that, she doesn't take another breath as if it's no different than her *taking* a breath, her beautiful eyes fixed on something I cannot see.

The sun is rising in the sky. Its beams are shining in the window and onto my mother's face. Her straight, white hair seems to glow in golden light. I look to see if I can see her spirit rising out of her body, or some sign of change. There is nothing.

That's not my mother lying there. It's not. Who or what is that, pretending to be her, dressed in her nightgown, that which used to be my mother? The one whose lips kissed my "owies" when I was small, who taught me how to bake apple pies and Thanksgiving turkeys, the only one who never grew tired of looking at every single photo Dee and I took on our vacations, the one whose warm smile filled her whole face and made you know that everything was all right, the one who was sincerely grateful for the bright, orange "zee-ray" fishing lures she was given for her birthday (because they caught the most fish), the one whose soft touch always soothed my soul and made me feel cherished.

The room is suddenly filled with women in nurse's scrubs. I don't know where they came from. No one seems in any kind of hurry though. I think someone must have taken a heavy blanket and thrown it over my head. I can hear them talking, feel my body moving, but the light is suddenly dimmed and my eyes won't focus and it's hard to breathe under all this weight.

The next morning at 6:38 I'm wide-awake. There's no commotion like there was yesterday. Yesterday my mother was still alive just seconds ago. Today something makes me get out of bed and walk downstairs. Opening the front door, I step out into the icy chill. The trees are bare, the grass is frozen and crunches like plastic straws as I step on it in my slippers; the air hangs as heavy and bitter cold as death. The sun is a thin slice of pink just above the silhouette of the neighbor's houses to the east, and lights twinkle from distant buildings, gearing up for business as usual.

I turn my eyes to the sky. The stars seem farther away than before, except one, which is very bright—the planet Venus, for Virgo—my mother's star. I'm here at the exact time she passed away yesterday, perhaps it's to try and grasp some part of her, as if by entreating the stars, I might see her lovely face there or a sign from God that she's all right now. But there's only a dull hum. My brain and body are beyond exhaustion—I don't have to go to the nursing home like I did yesterday, my heart filled with confusion and fear, waiting for her to die. Would it be hours? Days? Weeks? There's no longer a part of my mother there. Maybe she's with the sky.

The frosty air blows my hair and does its best to attach itself to me, but it doesn't penetrate my skin. I'm already numb.

Tears fall from my eyes.

"God," I cry. "*Where are you?* I don't feel you with me. How come you don't reveal yourself? You took *both* of my parents, God, why?"

But God is silent.

"I thought during times of great strife, I could turn to you and my church for support and comfort. But that's not happening. There's no solace for me in you or the church. You didn't show me what to do when I looked to my church for guidance other times either, like when our priest was convicted of molesting those boys. When I asked the parish officials about it, they made it sound like I was the one being disrespectful." I laugh. "I guess everything I believed in my entire life turned out to be nothing but a lie."

I'm well past being angry with God now; I'm through with him/her/it. Strike three—you're out. I've never felt so alone in all my life.

"You're just a fucking joke, God, a lie they told us to keep us in line in Catholic school. There's no such thing as God. If there were, you would have heard my prayers and saved my daddy. You could have given me a few more years with one of them before you took the other. You could have sent your angels to my side. You could have given me some words of encouragement and strength in a vision or a dream. But no; I don't feel your presence anywhere."

Tears flow with such intensity, they hurt coming out, as if my soul is bleeding acid. My breath makes puffs that hang in the air.

"You've always deserted me when I needed you most."

Remember the story "Footprints?" Where God said that when you saw only one set of footprints in the sand, it wasn't because God had abandoned you, it was when God carried you?

"Just a touchy-feely story," I sob. "I'm done with God and done with the church."

The front door opens and Dee steps out.

"I thought I heard you come out here. What are you doing out here, Honey? It's cold."

He walks up to me and puts his arms around me.

I just look at him. I don't even know who I am this minute; how can I possibly describe what it is I'm doing out here?

"Come inside," he says.

I take another look at the sky. The sun is rising higher now and it's getting light, but Venus is still shining brightly. I allow Dee to guide me back into the house.

The day after Mom's funeral, I'm getting myself a glass of water at the kitchen sink and happen to look out the window. My pine tree is loaded with birds. There must be at least forty of the same species on my tree. I've never seen this before. I wonder if it's happening at Lois's house too, so I call my next-door neighbor. "Do you have a bunch of birds all over your trees?"

"No," she says. "What do they look like?"

"Come on over."

While she's on her way, I look online to see what kind of birds they are—flickers, a type of woodpecker.

She arrives about a minute later, and as we proceed to the window to see the birds, I fill her in on what kind they are. By the time we look out though, the flickers are gone. *Thousands* of robins have replaced them.

It barely registers in my brain that this is something unusual.

"I thought you said they were flickers?" Lois isn't quite sure whether to believe me.

"Uh, they *were*."

We stand looking out my dining room window at them. Our trees and roof, along with those of nearby neighbors, are black with robins. They even land on the gutters right above the window while we're looking out. I've never seen the underside of a robin before. It's almost as if they're trying to be near me.

"How strange." She leans in to see better.

Very uncharacteristic of robins to congregate that way; you usually only see one or two robins at a time, but not *this* many, and not in February. What happened to all the flickers? I didn't imagine them, did I? No, because I even looked online to see what they were. My mind feels like the piles of dirty snow along the fence in the backyard—frozen and compressed. Something in me wants to acknowledge how extraordinary this is, but that part of me feels like it's under a silk veil and it will take more effort to lift it than I've got right now. The other part of me just wants to shut down.

I go into the other room and open the back door to get a better look. The robins don't move. I step out onto the porch. Surely, this will scare them. Again, they make no attempt to fly away; they just sit there watching me. Thousands of them.

"Maybe it's a sign from your parents," Lois says.

I look up at her. She's a good five inches taller than I am and she looks a bit rumpled, as if she'd been taking a nap when I called. "You think?"

She says, "When my dad died, their neighbor saw three large, bright, white birds, bigger than a hawk, that came to my parents' house. This was in January. They landed in the pine trees at the end of my parents' driveway. The neighbor had never seen that type of bird before, so she looked them up in her bird book, but couldn't identify them. They were bright, like glowing. The birds stayed around until the hearse came and took my father's body out of the house; they weren't scared away by all the commotion. And after they took Dad away, the birds were just gone. No one saw them fly away and they were never seen again."

It makes me think about the many times I've seen birds over the past few years, since my out-of-body experience in Cabo that time. It's as if they're a representation of something watching over me and guiding me.

"That's weird." Tears well up in my eyes. "Do you think birds could have something to do with angels?"

"They both have wings; I don't know, maybe." She shrugs. "Or spirits."

Or God.

My parents both loved to carve birds out of wood. I was continually amazed at their talent because creating tangible art with my hands is not something I can do. They won a lot of ribbons for their outstanding work and were well known and respected in the world of woodcarving. They also loved to camp, hunt, and fish. Mom always said that she'd rather spend vacations camping in the woods than go to some fancy hotel in a tropical place. They had a little room in the basement of their house, affectionately known as "the sporting goods room," where they stored all their gear.

Now my brother and I have the horrible task of going through all of their belongings, and as we're sitting on the cement floor and cleaning out the sporting goods room, underneath several elk carcass bags and fishing reels, I find a small "survival kit" Dad had made.

I remember him taking Tim and me to wilderness survival classes when we were teenagers. Having been an eagle scout, Dad liked to be prepared for any emergency, and he thought this would be good training for us. The instructor taught us how to put together a kit with necessities in case we ever became lost in the woods. It contained matches dipped in wax to waterproof them, flint and steel to start a fire, a signal mirror, a "space blanket" that looked like a wad of aluminum foil, a candy bar, a piece of wire with jagged edges to use as a saw, a plastic whistle, and a few other items.

I stare at the small blue nylon bag that my father had painstakingly assembled. Then I pull out its contents one by one. It contains all the items I expect it to except for one. Wedged thoughtfully between the mirror and the space blanket so it won't get bent is a picture of my mother.

CHAPTER 24

The Language of the Drum

People frequently believe the creative life is grounded in fantasy. The more difficult truth is that creativity is grounded in reality, in the particular, the focused, the well observed or specifically imagined.
—Julia Cameron

April, 2006

As I step inside my house, the TV's blaring commercials touting mascara that plumps your lashes in two easy steps and how the local hamburger chain has converted to using non-trans fat oil to cook their fries. Then I watch my neighbor jump into his car, slam the door, and drive off like he always does, leaving little oil spots behind on his driveway. Why am I noticing oil spots all of a sudden? And why does everything look the same as it did when I had parents?

I fall onto the couch. *What's wrong with everybody?* The world has ended and they don't even know it. I don't understand how they can *not* know. I put my hand on my heart and feel it beating—even my stupid heart mocks me. I wish I could just tear it out and stomp on it.

I think spring, with its lies of hope and rebirth, should never come again and the tulips in my front garden should keep their bright faces hidden beneath the ground forever. But they don't; the damn things come up anyway. And why does the sun keep coming up every morning like somebody's idea of a cruel joke?

Every day I try another tactic to deal with the demon that has taken up residence in my heart. I can see him clearly. His lumpy, toad-like body towers over me, bigger than a mountain range. His yellow eyes pierce my soul and his dagger teeth drip with the blood of generations of fury. His breath smells like a thousand decaying corpses.

"I'll drown you in booze," I tell the seething, crawling agony. "You won't be able to find me if my mind is numb." And for days or weeks or months—I'm not sure anymore, they all blend together—I try to mask my pain with booze, but its anesthetic properties fall far short of their intended results. Actually, it only seems to enhance my feelings of helplessness and makes me feel even more worthless.

"I'll run away from you," I sputter. I try to outrun it, but my legs can't carry me fast enough or far enough to escape it. Besides, I wonder what my neighbors think watching me scuffle down the street in my snow boots, my waffle-stompers from the '70s, and my big, fluffy, down coat that makes me look like the Michelin tire man.

"I'll kick the shit out of you!" I go into the basement and kick and punch my heavy bag that's still hanging from the rafters from my tae kwon do years. I beat it until my body aches and my throat is sore from screaming. And although the bag is more than happy to absorb my blows, it never offers any solutions.

No matter what I do, the emptiness and despair are always right there in my face every time I wake up.

Dee says he's worried about me and that I've been down way too long. I'm sure he means well, and it's got to be frustrating for him because he doesn't know how to help me—men always want to fix things—but he has no idea what I'm going through. His parents are still living. I know I need to allow the light to come back into my life though; I can't spread light if I'm in darkness. I also see that you can't fully appreciate the value of light until you've known darkness intimately. *Intimately.* And I don't think we're meant to wallow in darkness because all that does is create barriers between ourselves and others, as seems to be the case between Dee and me lately. He keeps telling me, "You need to get over this." Why do people say stuff like that? Probably because most of us spend our whole lives pretending that death doesn't happen and when it comes, we don't know how to deal with it. But telling me to get over my grief makes me feel like I'm supposed to deny that I ever had parents, like they weren't important. It's not really his fault, though; most non-grievers don't know what to say or do. At my mom's funeral, a well-meaning friend put his arm around me and in a very kind and loving manner, said, "Don't take it so hard, Pat, this is just a test. God has something even worse coming up for you and all this will make you stronger so you'll be able to deal with that." *Oh my God,* I thought, I've just lost my dad and now my mom—*how can it get worse?* Is God going to take my kids and my husband too?

Maybe this is all a big test for me in another way, though. When I had my mystical experience, God introduced herself to me and introduced *me* to me in incredible light, and as I struggled to grasp it, she then showed me the opposite of light—a darkness so terrible that my mind wasn't capable of accepting it, so it caved in and shut down. I thought I understood how opposites defined one another, but now I see that the concept of light versus darkness is by far the most powerful. (I've also come to accept that my definition of God is composed of opposites—male and female—God is the ultimate duality that is *one,* so I refer to God as "he" and "she" interchangeably now, although I don't believe there is a pronoun that adequately describes God.) And like all the other lessons I'm learning on this journey, I realize that before I can feel whole again I need to embrace my pain and *celebrate* it, because it's part of who I am. In tae kwon do, I learned that my most formidable opponent wasn't that other person facing me, ready to kick me in the face or punch me in the gut, but myself. Now I'm seeing that truth all over again.

I sign up for grief counseling. There I discover that you don't get over grief, you learn to live with it. To know this, is such a relief that I'm not even sure there are words to describe it. I can function with the knowledge that my parents are gone instead of telling myself that I have to "get over" them ever having been my parents.

I also undergo Eye Movement Desensitization and Reprocessing (EMDR) sessions. It's been used extensively for victims of post-traumatic stress syndrome.

As I'm sitting in the overstuffed chair at the hospice center, the counselor gives me a round buzzer to hold in each hand. She holds a small box about the size of a slice of bread that controls the frequency of the vibrations. It's connected by wires to the buzzers, which pulsate gently, one then the other, in a hypnotic manner to guide me into the proper state of mind.

I close my eyes and before long, I see myself in a room without doors or windows. It's the color of midnight blue. I'm standing in the center, turning around in circles trying to figure out what to do. I decide that since I can't get out, I'll invite someone in. No sooner do I have this thought, than the room is filled with shining, silvery-white, human-like beings. They don't appear to be male *or* female, which I find ironic since my recent conclusions about my concept of God, and I can't see any of their faces.

"Where am I?" I ask them.

"Heaven."

"This doesn't look like heaven to me." I think I'm being duped.

Then I see my mother's death scene and it quickly turns into my dad's death scene.

"Oh no, I can't go there right now," I tell the beings made of light.

One of them grabs my hand and pulls me up into the air and back to that blue room, saying, "Come with me."

"Only if you're good and not bad." I feel like a five-year-old accepting candy from that dreaded, faceless menace—the stranger.

They assure me they are good. Back in the dark blue room, I suddenly have thick, white paint on my fingertips and I start making fingerprints on the walls. Each mark I make turns into a star and together they become a constellation, which then comes alive and starts to spin in all directions. I make constellations all over the place. Then I see that I'm painfully alone—cold, helpless. Who am I? Did I ever really exist? Has anything I've ever believed in really existed? Has my entire life been a dream? A dream where I'd been under the impression that I was awake? Where does "being" end and "not-being" begin? Or do they?

"If this is heaven, then where are my parents? I want to see them. I need to see them," I begin to cry.

Suddenly, a cold puff of air rushes past my face. I gasp and open my eyes, pulling myself out of the "dream." Did the counselor move somehow and cause the puff of air? No; I would have heard her. She's sitting perfectly still in her chair across from me with a puzzled look on her face.

"What's wrong?" She can't figure out why I've suddenly opened my eyes.

Was this a message from my parents' spirits? And what do the beings of light have to do with this? Were they angels?

The grief counselor then convinces me to attend a three-day retreat for people who have recently lost a loved one. It's a weekend of arts, crafts, writing, and music. Right up my alley, except for the crafts part. When it comes to cutting, pasting, and putting things together, my brain stages full-out mutiny. It's the same with math—it ain't gonna happen. I would rather shovel horse poop nonstop for a month than do one craft project. It makes me feel like I'm in preschool. I'm always impressed with the work others do; I just have no desire to do it myself.

The retreat is held on property so hidden by a forest, you wouldn't know it existed unless you proceeded through the gate and down the dirt road. It twists and turns revealing scenery you'd expect to see in the mountains rather than in town like this.

As I walk into the building, I feel like I'm wearing a neon sign on my chest that reads "Mourner" like something's wrong with me. Well, there is of course, but I don't like feeling so conspicuous.

To the right of the entryway is a large room with walls of windows on two sides. The windows overlook a patio that opens up to a vast, manicured, green lawn and a pond, beyond which are nothing but dense stands of mature, green trees. I could live here. I could spend forever just sitting in this room, looking out those windows and watching how the trees react to fall and winter, then spring again. And maybe if I watched closely enough, they'd let me in on some of their secrets. I think nature holds lots of secrets; we just need to learn how to hear them. One of these days I'm going to figure it out.

There are about twenty of us in the group today and we're all wearing that same sheepish expression, like, "If you talk first, that would make me really happy, just please understand if I don't answer you."

We do crafts (or rather, I *limp* through this part), meditate, write poetry, give each other massages, and make sand sculptures. It's all very Martha-Stewart-nice—an attempt to reach inside myself and make contact with the part of me that's wounded and needing to heal.

And then comes the music . . . .

In the center of the room is a circle of large, wooden drums, each with a chair behind it. The drums are conical shaped with ropes zigzagging up their sides. We each choose a drum and sit behind it.

A man in his late 40s, with choppy brown hair and a warm demeanor, walks into the room barefoot and dressed in a native costume I can't place. I want to be barefoot too. I didn't know it was allowed. I kick off my shoes and socks. This is already cool.

The man is wearing a small, round hat decorated with mirrored sequins and bright colors. His eyes are filled with kindness. He introduces himself as Gregory and says his Sufi name is Gayan. I don't know what Sufi means, but I like it. I expect him to be rather passive, maybe because of the way he's dressed, but as soon as he starts talking, I see a man with fire in his soul. His voice is confident, knowledgeable, and vibrant. For some reason, he makes me feel safe.

Gayan shows us how to hold the drum with the head facing us. As I open my legs to position the drum between them, a very distinct, sexual spark zaps me quite unexpectedly. I feel my face getting red, as if the people around me might have somehow noticed, and quickly turn my head so no one will see that I'm blushing. Is something wrong with me? Or are drums known to elicit this type of response? But it feels good, as if my body's saying, "Here is my soul, opened completely unto you, enter me and take me back to you—back to God, back to paradise." I don't know why something in me would even consider that a mere drum could take me to paradise. And what is it with me and sex and music the past few years? If no one else was around, I think I'd be laughing at myself right now, because it's kind of funny and I kind of like this sexy feeling. It's animal-primitive. Jeez, I'm really a mess.

While we wait for everyone to get situated, some people can't resist thumping the drum, while others sit quietly, looking bewildered and intimidated. I, of course, can't resist. *Thunnnnggggggg . . . thup, thup.* Smoothing my hands over the drumhead's tight surface, I feel energy moving from the skin of the drum into the skin on my palms and fingers, as if it, too, is being awakened. And I don't know why, but I'm astonished at how wonderful it is—all these new sensations stirring in my body. I wonder if this is happening to anybody else. I glance around but everyone else looks so serious.

Gayan teaches us a simple beat. It looks easy when he does it. "Don't worry; there are no mistakes, only solos," he says smiling, revealing deep dimples in both cheeks.

I find I am instantly an expert at solos.

"If you're embarrassed to move out of your comfort zone, you will never get ahead," he says without missing a beat.

How true. In music as in life.

We play the rhythm Gayan has demonstrated: *boom, boom, boom, boom.* Steady. Then he adds a few more beats in between *taka, taka, tin . . . taka, taka, tin* while the rest of us maintain the rhythm. The sound absorbs me. *It's only a simple drumbeat.* How can that be? As I'm drumming, I'm no longer conscious of what's happening around me. I'm in some sort of trance, transported deeply into the sound—like the scent of jasmine, tranquility, and communion with spirit. With earth. With All That Is and All That Ever Will Be.

And then the entire room—all of us complete strangers—
melt together into one. Pulse. Intense. Emotion. Every single
one of us is on beat. For these moments. We are. One. Living.
Spiritual. Body.

First it was my sexual energy coming to life, then my skin,
and now it's my spirit. Even my breath moves in and out of me
in time with the drums. Music is entering my soul again, taking
me to that place inside myself where God is—that place I went
during Sammy's concert a few years back. And like before, it's
all very sensual and sexual. Oh, it feels like it's been ages since
I've thought about any of this. I didn't realize how very much I
missed that part of me, what a huge part of me it still is, and how
magnificent it makes me feel. What emancipation it is to realize I can still feel this way after everything I've been through! I
thought all of this died along with my parents.

Gayan starts the next beat and everyone joins in. Then people take turns playing their solos, most of them looking embarrassed, but when it's my turn, I'm like a lit match to gasoline.
Where only a moment ago I'd been concentrating so hard on
making sure I did everything right—holding my hands in right
position or hitting the drum in the right place—suddenly I
don't care. I have no idea what I'm doing, I just let loose. This
isn't like me. I'm usually content to blend into the background.
But now I hear the throaty voices of the drums roaring inside
the room like an avalanche, rattling the walls and all those windows and it fills up my soul. The throbbing of the main beat
and my little noise in the middle of it feels like a spiritual trip
into God's ecstasy, a connection with worlds one can only reach
through the doors of death, drugs, or deep meditation. Or
maybe orgasm. All sorts of images go through my mind: water-
falls, tree roots, huge boulders, an endless blue sky and puffy
clouds, women dancing with their hands in the air and spinning
brightly-colored scarves—and I'm soaring—high above them

and moving in and out of them like steam, as if I have been there before, as if I am part of all those images. I don't care how bad I sound. I'm loving every moment of it—even the stinging sensation in my palms and fingers. And I don't even mind the attention, actually. But maybe no one's noticing because they're too worried about what they're going to do when it's their turn.

I could do this all day, and the day after that, and the day after that. I wonder if this is how professional musicians feel when they're performing, like another force is taking them over.

I think Gayan must have read my mind, because he starts talking about how the beat of the drum is like the beat of our hearts and that our very lives are made of rhythm—our pulse and our breathing. He says that sound involves all of our senses because we don't just perceive it with our ears; we hear it with every part of our bodies. And he says that the mystic Sufis teach that rhythm affects the circulation of our blood, causing us to feel relaxed or energized. I feel how right this is with each vibration in my hands. It's an introduction to the world of sound on another level and I feel a part of my voice coming back because of it—like a conversation with the god of all beliefs, the truth of existence.

It makes me want to know more about the mysticism of sound, because I'm getting the idea that Sufism is a connection to the Divine through music, like what happened to me at Sammy's concert. Maybe this explains a lot of the things that have been happening to me. Even my mind is dancing.

Gayan also has a large, round drum that sits on the floor. Next to it are long-handled sticks, each with a padded ball on the end. It reminds me of the drums where several Native Americans sat around it, dressed in the tanned hides of animals and necklaces made of bone, each person holding a long stick and beating the drum while chanting.

The face of the drum looks like a full moon. I can't resist. When I lift the stick, it feels like I'm choosing power, power over my destiny. And as I strike it, the drum sings out with a deep tone. Its voice is like being lifted to the center of the earth—dark, warm, and comforting—then slowly floating back out again. It isn't like falling; it's like soaring within something earthy, resonant, vital, pure, succinct. The sound shakes my skin and travels through my body like ocean waves, all the way down my legs, out the bottoms of my feet, and into the earth beneath me. Each time my stick strikes the drum, it shakes me all over again—washes me up, slides me down. And as I play, I think I see spirits rising from the sound and swirling over the trees, the pond, and the lawn of green grass outside—misty figures that could be those of my parents and my relatives who have passed on, and some I don't recognize. Maybe they're the spirits of the loved ones of the other people here today. And then I see something else—a naked man dancing with eagle feathers in his hand, moving within the haze like a memory from many lifetimes ago. Has the drumming summoned them? Is that possible? I'm so emotional right now, I'm thinking anything is possible.

When the session ends, it doesn't feel like an end to me. It feels more like a beginning because the vibration is still moving within me even as I get up out of my chair: *It's something in the music . . . a cosmic connection with the Divine, through the music.*

As I drive back through the groves of trees on my way home, it occurs to me that the drum session provided a lot of lessons for me, lessons that could not have been conveyed through words, and when I quit worrying about getting the technique right, that's when it happened. Like life. When I quit trying so hard to be perfect, that's when magic happens. Every time. You'd think I'd have figured this out by now, but apparently I haven't.

And I know that's what the tequila did for me during Sammy's concert when I had that mystical moment too. It forced me to stop thinking about having to act a certain way and to just let go—experience, let it enter me.

That's why I was brought here today. I'd been so wrapped up in grief and anger, and judging God and even myself, perhaps I was blocking anything positive from coming to me. I forgot about my passion and my connection to the Divine Spirit. I forgot all about my mystical journey. And because of that, I forgot how to live.

It's time for me to remember again.

CHAPTER 25

Out of the Trenches

*Music raises the soul of man even higher than the
so-called external forms of religion.*
— Sufi Hazrat Inayat Khan

May 6, 2006

Sammy makes eye contact with me. He's in the middle of his concert, the room is packed, his band is still playing behind him—*what's he doing?* Then he grabs his drink, takes a sip, and hands it to me—blue liquid in a plastic margarita glass.

"This one's for Pat," he says into the microphone. "She sent me an awesome poem. I *love* it." His words echo all over the room.

What? Did Sammy Hagar just say MY name? Over the speakers for thousands of people to hear? Even stopping his entire show here in Tahoe to do it? I'm stunned, I'm flattered, I'm a little embarrassed. For one thing, I haven't been one of his followers for thirty years. Why should I have something they deserve more than me? This makes me want to shrink so small no one will see me. Not only that, but *I've just been called out from the stage* and if my brain weren't so fuzzy from everything

I've been through for the past several months, I think I'd be freaking out—big rock stars don't say my name into the microphone. Big rock stars don't even know who I am!

Hell, *I* don't even know who I am anymore. I've been feeling sorry for myself for so long now and telling myself that it really *is* okay to go on living, because after all, I am still living and I deserve to be happy again, but I still feel so all alone. And yet, when it all comes down to it, all I really have is myself, so maybe I should be a little kinder to myself then, and a little more tolerant. I guess I *do* deserve this drink after all. And I deserve to enjoy it.

I take a sip—it's thick and cold and sweet. The cup makes my hands sticky. I feel like I'm being pulled up and out of the trenches, mud still dripping from my legs, and it's kind of bittersweet, like, "Leave me alone; I don't want to be a burden—oh please, take me out of this."

My heart is beating fast, and I feel a little choked up. I haven't told anyone except Sammy about my book and now my secret about my writing is out. Does that mean I have no choice but to produce a book? That I can't back out now because the words have been spoken publicly? And why do I feel like I need to put out a book in the first place? It seems impossible, but it's almost as if he's prodding me to do it. Anyway, he didn't say I was writing a book, so maybe that buys me some time. Yeah, maybe it went right over their heads and no one noticed.

I take a few more sips and it isn't long before I feel the alcohol beginning to take effect, relaxing me and making me warm all over. Maybe I don't have to mourn the loss of my identity as a daughter. Maybe I'm so much more than a daughter, a wife, or a mom. And while all those things are important, maybe I have value for reasons based on the woman I am underneath all of that. What a great thought. I wonder why it never occurred to me before. I feel my façade start to slip a bit—the mask I think

I'm wearing, pretending that nothing's changed in me. But I've never been very good at putting on a front. What you see is what you get.

I allow myself to fall into the music, forgetting about everything else. It's easier now. And I notice for the first time tonight that the whole atmosphere is bright and cheery—the stage, the colors, the crowd, the songs.

When the show ends, Sammy turns to leave the stage. But as he's walking, I swear he's looking straight at me. It's hard to tell since he's wearing sunglasses. I can't imagine what he might be thinking. Then he comes over and extends his hand to me. I figure we're going to bump fists because I've seen him do that to people before, so I offer him my hand, fingers pulled back in a relaxed fist. Instead, he takes my hand and squeezes it. His fingers are wet from just having poured a bottle of water all over himself and the front of his shirt is drenched. I'm thinking how cool this is, that he's acknowledging me. He does this all the time to his fans. But then he pulls me to him.

"I'm so sorry about your parents, sweetheart," he coos. He knows about my parents because I told him about it in the letter I sent him with the poem.

All kinds of thoughts are swirling inside me—I can't believe he remembered that about my parents . . . he's giving me attention *again* . . . I'm sad . . . I'm excited . . . I'm confused . . . I'm sweating like crazy. . . This is *Sammy Hagar* saying this to me, as if he really cares.

"Thank you, Sammy," I say, lowering my head.

He's still holding my hand tight as he leans over the stage amps and pulls me closer, putting his face in mine. Suddenly there are bursts of light, as cameras flash from all directions. I can feel Sammy's breath on my face, and before I know what's happening, he's kissing me on the mouth. Hard. His lips are thick and soft and his mustache pricks my upper lip.

It's not a passionate kiss though; it's quick, the way one might kiss a friend.

Before it fully registers in my brain that *Sammy Hagar is kissing me*, it's over.

I realize Sammy did this as a token of condolence. Still, where does one file being kissed by a rock star in the cabinet of life experiences? For that matter, where does one file *any* of this? I guess in an entirely different cabinet.

He turns, waves to the audience, and walks offstage.

I can see his son, Aaron, squatting down just offstage with his camera up to his face and looking astonished. The people around me are looking quite astonished as well. Some are even smiling and hugging me. I feel like one of those balloons that gets swatted back and forth by the crowd before a concert. I hardly feel real. Then I notice that my fingers are touching my upper lip because there's a small burn there from Sammy's mustache. I didn't even realize I was doing it. What kind of weird— and I hesitate to use this word because it's not quite accurate, but—"relationship" is this? The big star calls all the shots and tosses gold coins to the woman on the ground once in a while. And it makes her feel valued.

I must keep my head on straight though. I'm just a fan. *Don't think you mean anything more to him than that; don't go thinking you're his friend or anything,* I remind myself. *The concert tickets and CDs you buy pay for his Ferrari.*

But I also realize that this is one of those moments that makes life so wonderful, when someone goes out of his way to let you know he cares, and when you're doing the things you love most with people you enjoy being with. I don't think I fully appreciated this concept until recently. I mean, I knew it, but not to the extent that I do now—life is too short to be miserable, and Sammy has just reinforced this in me. He's reminding me of that magic that came to me through him in his sweaty bar in Mexico a few years ago.

It makes me wonder if all the pain I've suffered recently could have caused me to fall off my path to self-realization or if it was something I needed to endure for the advancement of my spirit. Because all that overwhelming joy, that magic force, feels like it's left me. Or perhaps it isn't gone, it's just buried beneath my wounds and since I've been wallowing in negativity and grief, I haven't been able to hear its voice. Maybe it never really came to me either. I've heard it said that enlightenment isn't something out there we need to achieve, but something inside of us we're giving birth to. We will find what we want to find, but what we're searching for will escape us every time, and not because it isn't attainable, but because we don't understand that we already have it. So maybe I've always had it and my "event" in Mexico simply revealed a part of me that had been hidden all my life, maybe for many lifetimes—my Higher Self.

Perhaps I just need to open myself back up to receive it again, like I accidentally did with the drums recently, but how do I do that?

And why am I crying all of a sudden?

A woman behind me taps me on the shoulder and shrieks, "Oh my *God!* You just got kissed by Sammy Hagar! I'm so jealous of you!" She's jumping up and down. "Let me touch you! Tell me about your poem; I want to hear all about your poem you gave Sammy."

"I . . . I . . ." my voice sputters.

I cover my mouth with my hand as tears keep running down my face. That woman probably thinks I'm crying because of a kiss.

CHAPTER 26

On Top of the World

*Humanity has advanced, when it has advanced, not because
it has been sober, responsible, and cautious, but because it
has been playful, rebellious, and immature.*
—Tom Robbins

May 10, 2006

Dee's sitting in front of his laptop, listening to some Internet
program that's blaring from his computer's tiny speakers.
It's about 11 P.M.

"I hope that doesn't wake up the kids. They have school in
the morning," I tell him.

"Sammy's on some radio show," he says. Dee is like a kid
himself; he gets so into certain things. I know, I'm not the one
who should talk, but it feels like I have four boys sometimes.

"That's nice. I'm going to bed. I'm beat," I say, padding past
him in my slippers.

The male voice coming from the speakers chirps in that for-
mal "on-air" singsong manner, "Call 1-800-344-ROCK with
your questions for Sammy Hagar and Michael Anthony," he
says. It's giving me a headache because he's saying it too much

if you ask me, so I do my best to ignore it, an acquired trait necessary for survival when you're the mom of three boys. Four.

"You should call in," Dee says. Beneath his seemingly gruff exterior, Dee is the one who unwittingly keeps making it possible for a lot of my amazing experiences to take place. Of course, if I were to tell him this, he'd roll his eyes and give me that look I always tell him reminds me of his sister who, by the way, has fully recovered from her heart attack, thank God. But Dee's the one who arranged our trips to Cabo and Tahoe; he introduced me to Sammy. And every now and then, he comes out of his shell and tells me something like this. It's so not-Dee that it makes me wonder where all this comes from—he keeps delivering me right into the lion's mouth as if it weren't his choice. I'm beginning to think maybe it isn't.

"Why would I want to do that?" I finally ask.

He doesn't answer, as if it's perfectly obvious.

I sit down in a chair next to him, but I don't plan on staying here long. "If I'd known ahead of time, maybe I could have come up with something interesting to ask," I say more to myself than to Dee. Then I look over at the suitcases filled with dirty clothes, souvenirs, newspapers, and toiletries that are lying like gaping mouths on the family room floor because we've just gotten home from Tahoe, and I think about all the laundry I need to do. Combined with the kids' stuff, I'll bet there are at least fifteen loads. This thought makes me even more tired, so I squeeze my eyes shut for a moment. This is what I need—sleep. But my mind decides to take on Dee's challenge anyway. Lately it refuses to shut itself off; it goes and goes and goes until I force it to take a break by going to bed or meditating: otherwise I wouldn't get any relief. Besides, now I have new stuff to think about—Sammy telling everyone about my writing and kissing me like that the other day.

"I guess I could ask Sammy why he isn't coming to Colorado this year and I could ask Mikey if the 'V' on the back of their new tour T-shirts is a jab at Van Halen."

"Say Baja Rock Pat," Dee says. He's doing it again—*encouraging* me. He probably doesn't even realize it. Or maybe he does since this is the name Sammy has come to know me by because of the first poem I sent him.

"Nah."

"Why not?"

"I'd never get through anyway. I'm sure they're swamped with calls."

Dee punches in the numbers on his cell phone. "It's ringing," he says, handing it to me.

A male voice says, "Rockline."

They actually answered the phone. What are the odds of that?

I tell him that I have a question I'd like to ask Sammy and Mikey. I sound very confident, as if talking to rock stars is something I do on a daily basis. Dee is watching me with a big grin on his face.

The voice on the phone asks me what my question is, but he also sounds rather condescending. Why do people in the entertainment business always seem to treat the fans like they're not much above the intelligence of an amoeba? This is another reason I don't like being a fan. It feels disrespectful to me. Or maybe I'm misinterpreting his tone because I didn't expect to be doing this tonight and I'm grouchy because I'm tired.

I tell him what I want to ask. He informs me that I can't ask about the tour because it's international radio and nobody wants to hear fans calling in asking that over and over about their hometown. "But you can ask the other question," he says. "Hold on."

I don't look at Dee. I'm suddenly in my own little world—thinking too much and getting nervous. I now have more energy than I know what to do with, so I walk around the kitchen and into the family room and back again. After a while, a woman's voice comes on the line and asks me what my question is. I tell her.

"Okay, you'll be on right after the commercial. Get away from the speakers or turn them down. If you don't, there'll be too much feedback and Sammy won't be able to hear you." Her words suck every ounce of confidence from me. *Sammy won't be able to hear me?* I'm actually going to get to talk to this big star personally. Well, it really isn't going to be me talking to him personally; it's more me talking to him publicly. *Oh God, please don't let me make a fool out of myself.*

With phone in hand, I tramp upstairs to get away from the speakers. My heart is racing as I plant myself on the edge of my bed in my nightgown. I have to sound intelligent. I don't want to come across as a giddy teenager. What about this—"Hi guys! It's so nice to talk to you." No, that's stupid. Maybe I should comment on the weather. No. The concerts in Tahoe. Yeah. Tell them how great they sounded. But wait, if I say that, I'm going to sound like I'm kissing ass. Oh quit being so overly critical of yourself.

I sink into the puffy bedspread, but it doesn't offer any comfort; I'm getting more nervous by the minute. I hope it doesn't show in my voice. They've giving me waaay too much time to think about this. Now what was I gonna say again?

Suddenly the line is connected to the host of the show. "We have Pat here from Colorado."

"How's it goin'?" I ask, wanting to kick myself because they told me not to ask that. My voice falls away for a second. How can people who are in the public eye all the time be so careful of what they say?

Then I pipe in. "This is Baja Rock Pat."

Sammy makes a sound of recognition.

"I just wanted to tell Sammy, Mikey, and Dave what awesome concerts they did in Tahoe. I am still high from those shows." My voice sounds hoarse from being around all that smoke in the casinos for the past few days and from not getting enough sleep.

Sammy says, "Well, we're high too, Pat, but it's not from the shows, but thank you." He pauses. "I know *exactly* who you are."

I picture him sitting with his feet propped up on a table and a drink in his hand. He's not freaking out like I am. He says that he loves my poems but they are all about him and it's hard for him to be objective. (This isn't true, of course, but I didn't think he'd be interested in anything I wrote about other subjects, so I never sent him stuff like that.) Then he tells the audience that this isn't a set-up call because I guess it's looking decidedly suspicious.

It never occurred to me that he would promote my writing over the air, not to mention the fact that I'd be talking to him on the radio in the first place. I'm suddenly up against someone with the power to make or break people's careers, and he's praising *me*—again. (Sammy helped launch the band Def Leppard, and many others.) I'm trying to stay cool, but the words are getting all jumbled in my head. What do I say now? That I didn't mean for him to say those things? Then I hear words coming out of my mouth in a knee-jerk response. They're a feeble, "It's all true though." Now that was a dumb thing to say! Here I am on international radio and all I can say is "It's all true though!" I meant to say, "I write about what I feel, that's what writers write about—their feelings." Why didn't I? I'm not given time to explain and I have no experience dealing in a public forum where my words will be forever immortalized. And now I'm projected into the spotlight again and feeling mighty inadequate. I'm sure Sammy didn't intend for me to feel that way. He meant it all as a compliment. Besides, he's used to being interviewed, I'm not. What would someone ever ask me any-how? "Mrs. Walker, will you please tell the audience how many loads of laundry you do a week? The fans are *dying* to know."

The host of the show quickly scoops up the ball and takes it out of my court before I can say any more. He's working frantically to convince the audience that this isn't a set-up call. He then tells me to ask my question. Sammy explains that the graphic is unique and not a jab at Van Halen.

The host doesn't permit me another chance to respond. He simply adds, "And Pat, quit flattering Sammy." Then my phone goes dead. There's that "barely above the intelligence of an amoeba" treatment again. I feel kind of embarrassed because of what he said, but there's nothing I can do about it now. I guess it could have been worse.

When I go downstairs, Dee is still sitting at the kitchen table listening to the show. There's a time lapse in the program, so I hear the conversation played back a few seconds later. Sammy said, "This girl here will have a book out someday." I didn't hear the last part because they cut me off before he said it.

A small, electric surge goes through me and I feel my face turn red. Oh my God, he said *a book!* And the way he said it makes me feel like he knows something I don't, even though I know that sounds ridiculous. *A book?* My heart is pounding. Dee doesn't say anything, but I think he might be a little bit proud of me because he's trying to hide a smile. I wish I could explain to him about the spiritual connection between Sammy and me without sounding like some screwball fan with an over-active imagination, because I really do see the immense power of my mind to create and implement these things, and I recog-nize the will of the human spirit to believe it and keep going in spite of ridicule—my own, mostly—which is the worst and hardest to ignore. I want to tell him about all the other super-natural stuff, and how it sure looks to me like it's pulling him in too, or give him some indication of how important all of this is to me. And sometimes I try, but he just doesn't get it. There's always been that wall between us. But he has a soft side to him too, and just when I think his black-and-white way of looking at things is going to drive me crazy, he brings something like this upon me and it allows me to see through that wall. And what I see there makes me know that if we stick together, we can accomplish anything—him and me against the world. Then things are so amazingly, incredibly wonderful for a while that I'm willing to put up with the wall until the next time I get to see through it again. I guess everything in life has its price and if you love somebody, you're willing to make concessions.

And then I can't imagine why a celebrity, a man I don't even know, has so much faith in me. It seems so easy for him. But maybe he's just that way and it has nothing to do with his having faith in me. Or it could be that all it really is, is a mutual appreciation between artists. Sammy can certainly relate to the need for self-expression. And yet, if that's all it is, I don't think he would keep going out of his way for me like this, would he?

The song "Love Walks In" enters my mind, the part about how aliens were responsible for all the amazing things that were happening....

My phone starts ringing.

"I just heard you on the radio!" Friends are calling to congratulate me.

I am thrust into center stage once again, drawn into a world an ordinary housewife like me never dared dream about—bright lights and color, non-stop action, pulsating sound and excitement. Most of all, I am given license to release the artist screaming inside of me. All my life, when I experienced something that moved me, I allowed myself to become swallowed up in it—in wonder and awe—but I never allowed myself to fully acknowledge the feelings it caused in me, because those kinds of feelings might force me to look inside myself to determine their significance in my life, and I was scared of what I might find there. What if it was something bigger than me that I wouldn't be able to handle? What if I really was the person everyone else *thought* I was?

And now, I'm finally allowing myself to acknowledge my feelings, to put them into thoughts and words and on paper. It's all suddenly acceptable. *I* am suddenly acceptable; me—the timid Catholic girl who worked so hard to be everything others expected of her. Me—the naïve young wife whose husband convinced her that she was so uncool and undesirable that nobody would ever want her. Me—the middle-aged wife and mom who long ago accepted that she was doomed to a life of mediocrity. Me—the newly-orphaned daughter who is finally beginning to emerge from the haze.

I feel like that little yellow canary my grandma used to have—Robert Goulet, she called him, after her favorite singer. And I feel like someone has just opened the door to my cage and set me free. My wings have been cramped from lifetimes of lethargy but now I'm flying! Does this mean that I'm back on my path to self-realization?

All I know is, I'm soaring on top of a world I could never have seen from the ground.

CHAPTER 27

One Foot on the Path, Body and Mind to Follow

Instead of searching for meaning and purpose at the literal level, you will find it at the mythic level, where the stories are epic and sacred. When this happens, you will die to who you've convinced yourself you are and become a mystery unto yourself . . . and realize that you're made of the same stuff of stars, that you are God appearing in the form of yourself.
—Alberto Villoldo

September, 2006

I guess the supernatural force is back, because strange things are starting to happen again.

While I'm meditating, as my mind settles into a relaxed state, I begin to feel a presence within me. It grows stronger, accompanied by an emotion I don't recognize. My eyes open partially. I feel very sleepy—stoned maybe. My unfocused gaze falls to my folded legs beneath me. And although they are clearly attached to my body, these are not my legs. It's not like they're numb from sitting on them—these legs are definitely not mine. They're the hairy legs of a man and they're tanned deep, golden brown, as if he'd been lying in the sun for hours. Then I see a woman's silky white skin. I can smell the scent of her—perfumed soap, as if she has just stepped out of the shower. She's smiling a quiet smile and whispering. The man who belongs to the legs that are attached to me is about to make love to her. He reaches over and strokes her breast, delighted all over again at how soft it is. Then he slides his tongue around her nipple and feels it getting hard in response to his touch as he sucks it into his mouth. I can feel his thoughts and the tension of his body's adamant desire.

I see all this as if I'm peeking out from something slightly obscuring my view. My partially closed eyes perhaps? I'm there in their bed, but I'm not the "me" who is here meditating. Then I snap back to reality. My skin feels different for a moment—thicker. It's as if my mind has returned to the present before that other body has had a chance to melt off me. It doesn't feel creepy though; it feels natural, like walking from one room to another.

I've heard of the concept of simultaneous time, where past, present, and future are happening all at once, but that just seemed like an esoteric theory. Maybe that *is* what's happening. Or perhaps all these sensations are glimpses of past lives. Is there really such a thing as past lives? With each passing day, it's becoming more important that I find out, because this happened to me once before, and not too long ago.

My friend Jill and I went to a Zen lecture at the local college. As we sat in our chairs waiting for the talk to begin, suddenly my perspective flashed back and forth between the man seated behind the small table at the front of the classroom and me. It was like flicking a light switch on and off quickly several times, or how the mood seems to fluctuate when they change camera angles on the TV screen; you hardly notice it. One moment I was in my head looking at him and the next I could literally see from his point of view as he sat watching all the people waiting for the lecture to start.

Then it happened again. And again. All within a millisecond. I could see out of his eyes, hear his thoughts, feel his emotions. He had no thoughts. He wasn't nervous, he wasn't excited; he was just waiting. I couldn't figure out who this guy was. He couldn't be the Zen master; he certainly didn't *look* enlightened. He looked like your average next-door-neighbor-type person, the kind you'd encounter taking out the garbage after breakfast on a Saturday morning. And yet, I could see Jill and me sitting in our metal chairs and the rows of people in front of us, next to us, behind us, and those still coming in the door. I could see groups standing around talking to one another—all from his perspective.

I blinked my eyes, unsure of what had just happened, and I shook my head, thinking something must have come loose in there. Then I started telling Jill about it, and as I was telling her, a woman introduced the man in the front as Zen Master Gerry Shishin Wick Roshi.

I got goose bumps all over me.

After the lecture, I thought I'd tell Shishin Wick what just happened to me, because being a Zen master, maybe this stuff wasn't unusual for him. But I chickened out. I was afraid he'd think I was crazy.

That moment has haunted me ever since. It was so strange, I wondered what it meant. I came to the conclusion that it was a by-product of his superior spirituality and had nothing to do with me. And now I'm beginning to wonder if my incident with the Zen master that day was similar to my meditation taking me inside that man's body, mind, and spirit recently. Maybe I should try to get in touch with the master and tell him about this. Maybe he can help me figure out what's happening to me in the other instances as well. I know I kept the newspaper clipping announcing his appearance at the university. Maybe I can find it.

I dig into the bottomless pit that is our walk-in closet. A most dreary place with its narrow tunnel, it swallows up anything stupid enough to get shoved way in the back. I find the article easily. Now I have his name, which I'd long forgotten, and information on his Zen Center.

I send him an e-mail telling him about what happened to me at his lecture that day and asking if I can talk to him. The next day there comes a reply. He graciously agrees to meet me. I'm not sure whether to be nervous or elated.

Driving to what appears to be an ordinary middle-class neighborhood, I stop in front of a bi-level house with a small sign in the front yard unobtrusively stating "Zen Center." As my car pulls up, Shishin Wick emerges from a house across the street. He apparently lives in one house and uses the other for the practice of Zen.

Shishin is middle-aged, thinner than I remembered him, and dressed in tan pants and a short-sleeved, button-down shirt. He has dark, balding hair, a beard and mustache, and a quick smile that flits across his face and vanishes before I have time to smile back. I can't figure out what this means. Is he toying with me or are his thoughts so quick to come and go that the smile leaves his face before he realizes it? His demeanor seems to shift between childlike playfulness and intense seriousness, not as if he knows a secret, but as if he were a mighty mountain. He speaks in a soft voice, shakes my hand, and invites me inside.

The Zen Center is decorated with the scant décor of Eastern tradition, all very tastefully and sparsely placed. Upstairs, the meditation room has a statue of Buddha against the far wall and pillows placed in a circle on the floor. Its air of tranquility makes me want to join the school right then. There's spiritual wisdom here, but that's kind of exhilarating and disturbing at the same time. Do I really want to know what lies in the dark recesses of my mind? Because once I've witnessed my true nature, I'd be forced to act upon it, wouldn't I? It would be impossible to go back to the old behaviors because I could no longer use ignorance as an excuse. Do I really have the guts for this?

Shishin offers for the two of us to sit in the living room. As I make my way to the futon, I notice the difference between my manner of speaking and his. My voice is loud and when I laugh, it's gregarious and boldly indecent. Sinful almost. He speaks quietly and his laughter is more like a prayer—reverent and unassuming. And yet, he doesn't seem to be judging me, but my loudness seems like profanity in his presence, as if to advertise my lack of class. But there's nowhere to hide now; it's just him and me.

I came to the meeting prepared to bestow this master with the highest respect, deeply honored that he granted me his time and wisdom. And I'm well aware of protocol from my tae kwon do years—master is god, student ain't shit, so bow, shut up, and listen. (Our *sa bum nim* used to tell us, "We have two ears and one mouth, which means we need to listen twice as much as we talk.") But Shishin does not demand my respect, nor does he seem to want it. He seems indifferent to my display of admiration and it confuses me, because this isn't the kind of person I'm used to dealing with. His eyes are full, but not revealing; they hold no preconceived notions, as I do. They are more seeking to uncover what is beneath my physical appearance. But I'm not so sure I want him to know more about me than I do.

He also doesn't seem to have a need to impose any part of his truth upon me. This I like and it makes me trust him.

Shishin tells me about how he settled into Zen as his practice after searching many other avenues. One reason, he says, is that Zen doesn't have any dogma. "There's nothing you have to believe; it's all based on your own personal experience, your own personal effort. You have to realize it yourself, there's nobody there telling you what you should believe in or what's the truth.

But there are very clear instructions, parts of meditation or how to meditate and various cautions and traps you can fall into," he warns, his black eyes flashing.

I immediately assume that I will most certainly fall into these traps and maybe not find my way out again. It seems that whenever I learn something new, I make all the usual mistakes beginners make, plus two. I'd better be careful.

I explain about my mystical experience at Sammy's concert, and at his lecture that time, and about all the other things that have been happening to me. He tells me that these things indicate that I've gotten a taste of enlightenment. "One foot on the path, body and mind to follow," he says with that little smile breaking out over his face again and quickly dissolving.

Really? Enlightenment? That's a big word. I have deliberately avoided using that word in relation to my experience. There's a lot of responsibility attached to that word and people might expect me to be able to teach them too. But we all have to find our own way. Just because this happened to me through Sammy's music doesn't mean it will happen to someone else in the same way. Most likely, it won't. I think each person's awakening is tailored to his or her specific needs and way of understanding. But if Shishin says this is a taste of enlightenment, then I believe him. He should know.

I suddenly feel honored. Humbled. Blessed.

He explains that my experience in Cabo was due to both Sammy and me letting down our personal boundaries at the same time. He says this is common for musicians when they're performing, but in order for a connection to take place, both people have to be in that state. He makes it sound like I entered another dimension when this happened. "If you can transcend space and time, then you can transcend barriers between self and others and all kinds of things are opened to you."

Yes! Yes! Yes! *This is it!* Finally! After all these years. He *gets* it. He knows what I'm talking about! Here at last, is the road to my soul. And it's not weird, psycho crap—it's a revered philosophy passed down over thousands of years. I had a feeling that Zen would show me the answers I was searching for, I just needed someone to teach me. Now I've found him at last! I want to jump up and hug him. I want to thank him a million times over. But he'd probably think I was being disrespectful (to myself) if I did that, so I don't. I sit quietly all the while my spirit wants to dance. I can't wait to start learning more.

Driving home afterward, I turn onto the freeway and start heading north—four lanes each way, but not much traffic. I'm thinking about everything Shishin and I just discussed, when suddenly I notice that the interior of my car is very warm, as if the sun is shining hotter than normal on my arms. And I don't know how I know, but I feel a presence in the car with me, and it's kind of like a coating, like butter all over my skin. Even my insides feel warm. I wonder if Shishin's spirit has come to visit me because Paramahansa Yogananda talks about that in his book—how a teacher's spirit sometimes visits his or her students. Apparently our spirits converged once before, so why wouldn't they now?

As I'm noticing all these sensations, a Van Halen song starts playing. This isn't a CD I'm listening to, it's the radio. It's a song called "Déjà Vu."

"Come *this* way, my child," the energy surrounding me seems to say, and I literally feel my right elbow being pulled toward the empty passenger seat.

"What? Toward Van Halen? Toward Sammy?" I wonder aloud.

"This is where your answers are—*Déjà vu*," it's like a sigh.

"That's stupid. No," I'm confident. "Zen is the way for me. I've finally found a direct route to the meaning of my life. I've wanted this for as long as I can remember, and now I have a way to get there. Besides, I won't have to beat myself up for believing in Zen like I do for believing in a rock star and all that supernatural bullshit."

"It isn't quite right." The feeling is insistent, but it's also loving.

"You're wrong." I reach over and turn up the radio to drown out the feeling. It obviously has no clue what it's talking about. "If you're real, and what you're telling me is the truth, prove it. Show me CH0142 right now." I figure I'm being clever with this one; there is no way in a million years this will ever happen.

Just then, a large truck passes me in the right lane. I happen to notice part of its license plate number, but not the whole thing. It's going by too fast—something, something 0142. It's a California plate with the words "Salinas Safety" painted on its side. Before it even registers in my brain how unlikely this is, the song "Déjà Vu" gets even louder, so loud that it hurts my ears, even though that's not how the song was recorded and I haven't touched the radio a second time. So then, *who did?*

I nearly swerve off the road.

Following Shishin's advice, I attend *zazen* [formal meditation sessions] at a *zendo* [building for the practice of Zen] presided over by one of his students.

Upon entering the building, which is a converted, one-car garage, again I become acutely aware of the volume of my voice compared to that of the instructor. I'm like a wild horse kicking the walls in a holy place. I'm also laughing a lot because that's what I do when I'm nervous, but again, my laughter seems strangely vulgar. I force myself to speak more quietly and not laugh so much, to be respectful of the practice of Zen, as I learned to do as a child in church.

Other students arrive, and after greeting one another, each chooses a small pillow to sit on. They give me a chair because there's no way my knees are going to tolerate being folded up for three 30-minute sessions.

We sit facing the wall with our backs to the middle of the room. Having to sit perfectly still for this long should be interesting. I'm not so sure I can.

The instructor tells me to keep my eyes partially open, so fixing a downward gaze at the gray carpet, I try to find a position I can maintain without moving. A woman to the right of him taps a little wooden mallet against a brass bowl. Three times it rings out, then silence. A dog barks in a neighbor's yard. More silence.

As the room becomes infused with the calming scent of incense, I attempt to let go of my mind. This isn't so bad, I tell myself during the first few minutes. But before long, my lower back begins to object and my mind starts playing tricks on me. I've never sat in meditation for this long. I wonder how much time has gone by. Ten minutes? Twenty? I'd say about ten. Only *ten?* Nah, it has to be longer than that. I try to bring my awareness back to my breathing, but with each passing minute, it gets harder to do. Then my eyes join in the game—going in and out of focus. The white wall I'm facing turns blue and tilts at an angle. Patches of dark spots pulsate in front of my field of vision.

What are you trying to tell me? I ask my mind. It only seems to laugh, as if the devil is mocking me. It's a delusion, I remind myself. But how am I supposed to tell the difference between delusion and reality? Okay, back to breathing.

My muscles start to quiver and my right leg is numb. Beads of sweat break out on my forehead. I want to stand up and say, "Never mind, I can't do this," but what would everyone think? And just when I'm sure I can't take it another second, the bell rings, signaling it is now time for the five-minute walking meditation. Thank God!

This goes on for two more 30-minute segments. When the session ends and I get to my feet, my body feels like it's been ripped to shreds, but I also feel surprisingly cleansed. I've actually survived this. What a trip! I like it. Yeah, I can do this. This discipline will show me my soul, I'm absolutely certain.

I attend *zazen* several more times. I read the books the instructor recommends and try to absorb some of the wisdom. And I do learn something, but it isn't what I expected to learn.

Something is still missing.

Shishin told me that my mystical experience in Cabo and subsequent psychic experiences were validations of my budding soul's development, but he warned me not to focus too much on them. He said that they were illusions which could cause me to lose sight of my goal—self-realization. This could very well be true. And yet, I don't think I'm attaching to them, but merely acknowledging them because they're so unusual. I mean, I'm also trying to write a book about all this and how can I explain it if I don't break these things down into feelings, images, and senses? Maybe Shishin would tell me I'm just making an excuse for myself. And that could be, but even if it is, I think it's a good one.

For now, I want to immerse myself fully in this moment, experience *all* of my life, attach myself to all my emotions, feelings, and experiences without reservation. I want to let them show to the world without apologies—oh yes! It's all coming back! I want to share this love and joy openly and freely, not keep them quietly to myself and demonstrate strict discipline. I don't want to speak softly or live beneath diffused lighting and muted colors. I'm tired of beige. I want to scream at the top of my lungs, laugh out loud, experience vibrant red, yellow, orange, purple. I want to dance and make noise, let it all out of me no matter how long it takes. I don't want to feel holy and reserved. I want to grab hold of the tail of the tiger, feel his tight muscles moving beneath his skin, white fangs flashing as he thrashes and twists trying to devour me. I want to hold onto him with every ounce of my being for as long as I can before I release him to the universe, or he consumes me, then watch the effect float away like the text of a *Star Wars* film.

CHAPTER 28

Beings of Light

All that you behold, tho' it appears Without, it is Within, In your
Imagination, of which this World of Mortality is but a Shadow.
—William Blake

October, 2006

Our kids don't want to be seen with their parents anymore.
They're getting older and are much happier having the
freedom to take care of themselves and the house while Mom
and Dad spend a week together, so Dee and I come to Cabo
as often as we can now instead of camping at Steamboat Lake
like we used to. It makes the kids feel grown up. It makes *me*
nervous, but we haven't yet come home to find one of the boys
in jail, so I guess it's all good.

It's kind of a strange feeling though, like I have one foot in
two identities—a mom at home and a lover in Cabo and I have
to stop and switch gears when I go back and forth. It always
throws me off for a bit, that and the fact that we're actually able
to afford to keep coming here. Nothing's changed financially,
but a lot has changed in other ways since my mystical experience, so maybe there's a reason we're supposed to keep coming.

It's nearly midnight as Dee and I sit down in the sand to take in the view of the moon, the ocean, and the rocks of Land's End. The moon is bright with a luminous, misty ring around it. It's absolutely breathtaking. After a while, three people walk toward us, or I should say, "what appear to be people" walk toward us. Actually, from my quick glance, they appear more like undefined, elongated ovals walking along in the surf and my brain strings together the facts it's been presented and tells me these are people. What else would they be? I don't pay much attention to them because it isn't unusual to see people walking along the beach at all hours of the day and night here. For some reason though, all sound seems muffled as they approach, as if I suddenly have earplugs on, and I notice that the sky seems to be a very deep shade of purple.

About this time, Dee and I decide to call it a night and we stand up. In the few seconds it takes to get to our feet, I look, expecting those people to be much closer to us, but they're gone. They're not swimming in the ocean because I'd be able to see them. They aren't running up the beach because one can't run very fast in sand, and again, I'd be able to see them.

I ask Dee, "Did you just see those three people? Where did they go?"

He says he didn't notice.

They simply vanished.

An indescribable feeling runs through me, like trying to make my mind accept what it knows isn't possible. You'd think I'd be used to this feeling by now.

"That's weird." I'm hoping Dee will want to discuss it, but he doesn't say a word, which isn't surprising.

I turn and look in all directions but no one's there. Feeling cold all of a sudden, I grab Dee's arm and snuggle into it, then as we walk through the sand to our hotel, I keep glancing back just in case those people might still be there somewhere. Nope.

The next morning I'm up early. Dee is still asleep, so I fix myself a cup of coffee and step out onto the balcony to watch the ocean. Sweat rolls down the back of my neck and between my breasts, but for some reason, it almost seems cleansing. The idea then crosses my mind that maybe those three "people" on the beach last night weren't human. People don't just disappear and I know what I saw. Perhaps there was a reason I was supposed to see them. I wonder if it's possible to connect my thoughts to them through meditation, but I'm half-scared to try. What if it's something negative?

The gnawing inside me gets the better of me—I have to know more. I set my cup down on the plastic table next to me, and allow the sound of the ocean waves to lull me, "Shhhhh, fzzzzzz, shhhhhh, fzzzzzz . . . ." The waves are small and playful this morning. I close my eyes and before long my breathing falls into the same cadence as the ocean breaking the shore. I feel part of the earth in a profound way and a slight smile comes to my lips. I'm completely at peace.

Connect me to those people on the beach last night, I say through my thoughts. Focus on your breath. *But what if I'm asking for more than I can handle?* Stay positive. Calm. Surround yourself with white light and God's love . . . . Breathe. That's it.

A mental picture emerges. Everything is in varying shades of orange, dry and dusty with no vegetation. Rolling hills give way to a large, flat-topped, copper-colored mountain in the distance, which spans most of the horizon. The place even *smells* orange, like toast just before it's ready to burn. This is not earth. Another image floats into view. It's an empty, black, iron box about twelve inches square with slats spaced about an inch apart, perhaps some kind of cage to hold a bird.

The scene is gone as quickly as it came. I slowly drift back to consciousness and try to process the whole thing. When I think about it, the images felt kind of disturbing, but maybe only because they were so foreign; I didn't get any vibes, positive or negative. I've never seen anything like this though, never felt such *orangeness*. I've also never asked to be connected with anyone through meditation before. Maybe I did something wrong. Maybe there's a procedure you're supposed to follow to make sure you don't leave the earth, like how Shamanism teaches about finding a power animal to take with you for protection. Why didn't I think of that before?

Some people have no trouble accepting stuff like this, but I'm not one of them. That small, Catholic voice inside me still hisses that I'm delving into something I shouldn't, like Ouija boards—bad news. We don't initiate communication with spirits. But isn't this exactly what I've been doing all along? Communicating with spirits? I'm only half-admitting it though, because it's still freaking me out and I don't know what to do about it. Nobody has been sitting beside me when any of these things have happened and explained exactly what was going on. Like when you're a new parent and the baby won't stop crying. You can call your mom or your doctor or your friend and they can check it out and see if everything's going to plan, maybe offer suggestions, or tell you it's normal, sometimes babies are just colicky. But at least then you know it's not because of something you're doing wrong. These things happen to other people too.

All I can do now is write it down and see if it makes sense some other time. I step inside and find my notebook.

Five months later, I'm sitting in my living room, curled up in what used to be my overstuffed chair, which is now more of a pancake chair. I'm reading Sonia Choquette's account of being contacted by what she refers to as Light Beings. They sound a lot like the "beings" I saw on the beach in Cabo that night, except the individuals I saw had more of a dim glow, like a soft light behind a curtain.

Choquette writes about the time she participated in a retreat, and how she was leading the group in meditation when spirits unexpectedly contacted her. She describes the "beings" as tall, blue, and shaped like cylinders, and says that as they came toward her, she felt an enormous amount of love emanating from them. At that moment, she felt her head tip back as if to allow the thinking part of her mind to step aside in order to accept the message these spirits were attempting to deliver.

She goes on to explain that while she was experiencing all this, it felt as if there was a tremendous amount of energy and love surging through her—much more than her human body could sustain, but it was so great that it made her feel intoxicated and somehow transformed. And during the entire process, she sensed that she was at one with God.

Sonia says you know you've been contacted when love for self, others, and life becomes paramount—like what happened to me. Her experience sounds similar to mine in other ways as well, with her descriptions of the immense feelings of intoxication, energy, and love, and how her head tilted back during the encounter. This happened to me too; my head tilted back and my mouth fell open during meditation a few times. Whenever it happened, it worried me because I'd never heard of this happening to anyone before. And now Sonia's saying it. She's verifying a lot of things that have been happening to me. I'm relieved, but also a little spooked.

What are these light beings anyway? Angels? Spirits? God forbid—*aliens?*

People who have had near-death experiences say they sometimes see a white light, a religious figure, loved ones, or angels. If beings of light can exist in that capacity, in all probability, they'd be able to come to us under other circumstances too, wouldn't they?

I remember reading about how Yogananda said that Einstein's Theory of Relativity mathematically proved that light is the only real form of matter. Apparently this is how "perfected" yogis transcend time and space—they use light. So maybe these beings of light are messengers from God bringing me a clue to the reason everything is happening to me—like some kind of mystical guides. And maybe they're the same type of beings or angels that came to me during my EMDR sessions. Yes, this feels right.

My friend Gayan told me that in Sufism, they believe that our "inner parts" are made of sound and light. I guess by this, he means our souls. He said that the universe began with a vibration and everything that exists or has ever existed is made of vibration, which is first perceived as something audible before it becomes visible. He also said that thin rays of vibration produce sound and thick rays produce light, and that there are different forms of light—intelligence or consciousness, abstract light, and the light of the sun. All living things come from these, and they correlate to the Holy Trinity in Christianity—the Father, Son, and Holy Spirit. It makes me wonder if this could explain my beings of light in Cabo, because all sound seemed to stop as they came toward me. Same with my out-of-body moment that time. Everything went completely silent as I became engulfed in immense light. It's possible that the relationship between sound and light could have played a role in both these incidents. And it could also mean that what I'd perceived as light beings were created by something I'd projected from inside my soul, that "inner part" of me that's made of sound and light. This seems logical, that *I* somehow made it happen, or allowed it to because I think a lot of this, or maybe even *all* of this, has somehow originated from my own mind, my Higher Self. And like my concept of God, it's not something that's separate from me, but a very important part of me.

It seems like all the supernatural episodes are now starting to connect. As I sit here, a little person in my little chair, in my little house, in my little town of a great, big world, I can almost feel a thread of light extending from me, up through the roof and into the sky, then bouncing like rays of the sun in all directions.

I wonder if anyone else ever feels this way.

CHAPTER 29

Meeting God at 12,183 Feet

All true and deeply felt music,
whether sacred or profane,
journeys to heights
where art and religion can always meet.
—Albert Schweitzer

May, 2007

"I need to think. I'm going for a drive," I tell Dee.

So many things have happened to me over the past few years, it's gotten overwhelming. I barely see my family anymore. I also have a part-time job, so between that and working on this book, there's been no time for anything else and something tells me it's going to get worse. Dee says I never have time for him because I'm always writing. I assure him I'll make it up to him when I'm done with my book, but I secretly wonder—will I *ever* be done? I need a break—mentally and physically.

Climbing into my car, I drive out of the neighborhood. I have no real destination in mind. I'm just going to drive. When I get to the interstate, my car takes me south and then into the mountains. The road rolls through the canyon, twists back upon itself, and before I know it, I come upon the town of Estes Park, a quaint little mountain-village-turned-tourist-attraction. I pass the horses for hire, tied up to a long, log fence and patiently swishing their tails. I pass Lake Estes, the notorious Stanley Hotel, and head up into Rocky Mountain National Park. For about an hour now, I'm just following the road. It's cloudy today, as if the weather reflects my pensive mood. I'm just letting my thoughts be on hold. When they come into my head, I push them away by concentrating on the scenery rolling by outside my windshield. I have to, otherwise I think I'd burst.

I drive all the way to the top of Trail Ridge Road, which is often closed due to snow, even during the summer. Today the clouds are so low that my car almost has to break through them, like an important decision hanging over the world. When I get to the summit, I pull over and find a parking spot, then grabbing my blue jacket, I take a small trail that goes up the side of the mountain. You never know when it might start raining, or even snowing, in the mountains. You have to be prepared for anything, especially at this elevation, where there's no vegetation save for a few stands of eucalyptus grass here and there and some sparse, low-lying purple flowers.

My shoes make a crunching sound in the gravel as I hike up the path, which rises higher and higher into the clouds. As I walk, I think I hear a voice within the mist. Maybe it's the altitude, although I've lived in Colorado for over thirty years and am quite accustomed to the altitude. Or maybe it's my preconceived notion of God, brought about by the movie *The Ten Commandments*, where God visits Moses and God is depicted as a cloud. Either way, it seems to be a perfectly good representation of God.

By now I'm out of breath. It's a pretty long hike and the trail goes even farther than I can see. There are huge boulders strewn about the landscape as if they fell from somewhere higher up eons ago. I find one and sit down to rest. Glancing around, I notice a bighorn sheep watching me. He's just standing there silently, about twenty yards away.

"Hey there, dude," I say to him. "Are you real? Or is the altitude getting to me?"

The ram just stares, then flares his nostrils and snorts, his huge horns wrapped in corkscrews on either side of his head. I wonder if I should be concerned. What if he decides to charge me? I can't outrun him—his feet are built for this terrain, mine aren't. But he's not acting like he's going to charge me so I won't worry about it.

I guess the altitude does get to me because in my mind, the heavy fog and low-hanging clouds begin to swirl around the dirt pathway, the blue sky, and the bighorn sheep and then I hear *I AM THE LORD YOUR GOD*. It's a male voice and it's booming like thunder. Or maybe it is thunder, because it looks like it could rain any minute. I turn and look around me. Next thing you know, there'll be angels singing like in the movies. But there's no other sound and no one here but me. This thought makes me feel a bit uncomfortable. And yet, if God were to choose a place to speak to me, this would be as good a place as any. Okay, I'll play along.

"Hello, God. Maybe you're just a figment of my imagination, but I've wanted to ask you a few things for a long time."

The ram seems to relax a bit. His eyes don't look quite as alarmed as before. He twitches one ear then the other. The clouds continue to swirl.

I AM GOD.

The voice isn't coming from the ram or the clouds; it's coming from *everywhere*—the sky, the path, the rocks, the ram, the clouds, and my ribs. It isn't my voice, and yet I can feel my body vibrating with every word.

"I don't know how to deal with all these things that are happening to me, Lord. Are all the weird things caused by spirits?

Angels? Or are they messages from you or a part of my brain I don't know about? And what does Sammy Hagar have to do with all this?"

The answers are inside of you, comes the reply.

"Oh no, see, that's lame; I think I deserve a more concrete explanation than that. I mean, if you're God, you know everything, right? So level with me here: if the answers are inside of me, how come I haven't figured them out by now?"

If I were to tell you, that would defeat the purpose of your journey. You have to discover this for yourself. And you're doing just fine, dear. Keep up the good work.

"But this is huge; it's totally changed my life."

You have the power to change your life anytime you choose. You have always sensed this to be true, but you didn't know it. You do now. And this is your clue to the answer to your question. The voice seems to be my interpretation of someone else's words, as if they're being transferred into my head from somewhere else and the only way I can make sense of them is to translate them into my way of understanding.

"What do you mean?"

Throughout your life, you've repeatedly come across the same principles the enlightened ones have related for centuries. And though these concepts are really very simple, it hasn't been easy for you to incorporate them into your life.

"So true." I feel something within me shrink. "I don't know why."

What held you back was the belief that truth is obscure. And love. And happiness. And self-actualization. You've conditioned yourself to believe you're unworthy. You've conditioned yourself not to trust your heart, constructed a barrier and convinced yourself that it's an impenetrable wall preventing you from seeing beyond it. But it isn't a wall at all—it's an illusion.

My throat feels like the rock I'm sitting on—hard and dry. I turn to look at the ram and he has begun to wander a bit, his head down, foraging for food. He's apparently decided that I'm no longer a threat. But the cloud is still spinning and thick, as if it's alive and breathing.

"All my life, I've looked for you, God. I didn't see you in my religion, so I looked in other places," I confide to the faceless voice. "How could I tell what felt right and what didn't if I had nothing to compare it to? Native American philosophies refer to elements of the earth, sky, and spirit by names most of us use only for humans. To me this means that you are in everything—the plants, the animals, the land, the stars, and us. This feels right to me. What is the truth?"

Inside of you. The words are like a sigh floating on the light breeze that comes out of nowhere. It blows my hair.

Oh man, am I really talking to God here? Because it feels like it. I don't know why. Maybe it's because I haven't seen anyone else on this path up the mountain today and there are *always* people walking up here. Or maybe it's the presence of the bighorn sheep who doesn't seem scared of me. Or the way the clouds are swirling around me. It's possible this could also be the voice of my Higher Self, which connects me to God. Either way, I've never carried on a conversation like this with God before, at least not that I'm aware of. Why didn't I talk to him/her when I felt his/her presence so strongly as I hiked Maroon Bells years ago? Or when I had that encounter with Land's End in Cabo, when the rocks were glowing? Maybe because I figured I wasn't worthy or maybe it never occurred to me to try.

Now that I have his/her undivided attention, I may as well keep talking, because if this is a dream I've slipped into, I don't want to wake up yet without getting in the really important questions.

"I've read that early Christianity was similar to a lot of Eastern teachings, one of which is that we can aspire to be God. This makes a lot of sense to me, so I don't understand why it's considered a sin in Western thought for us to want to know you in such an intimate manner that we can be part of one another."

I am in you as you are in Me. The way to happiness is through Me. I don't rule over you by force. You've been given the intelligence and freedom to ask questions, along with a soul that yearns for understanding. You have an instinctive need to become part of All That Is Perfect where there is no separation between the human and the Immortal Sacred Being. This is a Universal need but it's more than that—it's soul sustenance. The voice is the same voice that breathes me and beats my heart. A tear forms in my eye.

"My understanding of my religion was that God was separate from me. Only certain individuals were qualified to read and interpret the words of God in the holy books and the only way for me to expand my soul was to abide by their interpretations. There was a distinct division between those who were considered holy and those who weren't. And it was clearly visible—there was no mistaking nuns or priests in a crowd.

"For me, this put you in an inaccessible realm. It wasn't possible for the average person to experience you personally because we weren't worthy of touching the hem of your sleeve, much less shooting the breeze with you over a margarita! And the only acceptable way for me to communicate with you was a one-way street—my prayers."

I keep going. I'm on a roll.

"It was a sin to question the rules, so I allowed them to manipulate my thoughts and actions because I believed I wasn't qualified to make my own decisions. Plus, how can any of us think clearly if from the beginning, we're *told* what to think? Anyway, if I allowed others to decide for me, when things didn't go the way I thought they should, I didn't have to take responsibility—it was someone else's fault! Ha! Pretty clever, huh? You wouldn't send me to hell for not knowing any better, would you?"

Many people speak the truth because they've memorized the correct answers given them by others, but they have no idea what they're saying. Since they haven't experienced it personally, they can't know it. It's like cheating on a test. The answers have to come from your experiences, not someone else's. Even if you arrive at the same ideas as the next person, you have to discover them for yourself or that truth becomes untruth.

"I meditated and prayed. I searched for you everywhere, but I couldn't find you. And then I had that spiritual experience in Cabo and it knocked the wind clear out of me. I knew you were there that night, God. I saw your beautiful face. I've heard of great gurus or holy people achieving enlightenment, but it always seemed like something reserved for those who *deserved* the honor because they worked their whole lives for it. Monks or nuns sacrificed and starved themselves, prayed constantly, and sequestered themselves high in the hills of Tibet for one moment of perfect clarity, selflessness, Nirvana. I don't know anything about their practices or their minds, but I'll tell you one thing—I knew I wasn't holy like that."

But you know differently now, don't you? You knew instantly that your revelation came from a higher power because your experience revealed Me to you on an intimate level.

"Yes. What happened to me that night in Mexico seemed like it involved the same truths that Buddha and Jesus taught. Why would something like this happen to an ordinary person like me?"

Did you ever stop to think that it happened to you because you're ordinary? Ancient spiritual doctrines are loaded with stories about how people were given divine guidance from non-physical realms, so why do you still doubt? If you believe that these things happened 2,000 years ago, what makes you think I would stop communicating with you between then and now?

"I never thought about it that way."

I no longer doubt where the voice is coming from. God's words are running down my spine like holy water.

"So you *do* hear my prayers?"

Always.

I shift my weight as I sit on the boulder and strain my eyes for any hint of the Great Being which seems to be communicating with me, but all I can see is the dry path leading up the mountain and blue sky. The bighorn sheep has turned his back on me now, revealing his cream-colored rump. The breeze is pushing the clouds at a faster pace and bouncing the little purple heads of the ground-clinging flowers. It's working its way into some kind of silent music.

"I've always been afraid of breaking the rules and making you mad, Lord. I was afraid you'd send me to hell if I didn't follow your rules."

I don't punish you. I am nothing but love.

Of course, I'd pretty much come to the same conclusion, but to hear it makes it all the more comforting. And it gives me hope. Maybe there's no such thing as hell after all. Maybe it's just something humans invented to control one another with fear. It's certainly worked on *me* all my life.

"I never would have married my first husband if I hadn't been so concerned about you punishing me for having sex before I was married. And look where *that* got me. How come you didn't save me, God? How come you let me suffer so?"

God doesn't seem to provide an answer, but the breeze blows stronger and the strange music grows louder; it's now almost a whisper. Maybe I'm committing blasphemy by interrogating the Almighty like this, but something about the situation makes me feel safe enough to let it all out, because now I'm getting angry. I want the real answers, not just fluff and ambiguity. I no longer care if God will strike me down for my insolence.

"Where were you when my parents died, God? Hm? Why did you take them both from me like that?" I'm shouting now. "I don't know if I can ever forgive you. All my life you let me go on believing I was safe. And even though my brain tried to prepare me, my heart knew that other people lost their loved ones, not *me!* You deserted me when I needed you most *again!*"

Agony rises inside of me like a raging fire, the likes of which I've never known before. The fury breaks loose. Tears run like rain from my eyes and I can't stop them. I don't want to stop them. I suddenly don't care if I live or die.

"Why don't you answer me, you son of a bitch?" I cry.

The wind begins to sound like a variation of some Middle-Eastern tune—drums, flutes, sitars, tambourines. It spins itself through the canyon below and rolls over the sparse shrubs clutching the hillside for dear life. It whips my hair and slaps me with the side of my jacket. I cry and cry and cry and cry until I'm spent.

And then I feel . . . calm. The wind has ceased. When I look up, I see that off in the distance, the meadow is filled with bighorn sheep. There must be a hundred or more. They act as if they don't even notice me, as if I'm just another ewe or ram like the rest of them. Maybe I am.

You do not walk this path alone. I am with you always.

I'm filled with warmth as if there are great arms around me, holding me, and I sit there for a long time, taking it in, trying to hear what God will say next. But nothing further comes. I finally gather myself up and slip down off the rock. With my own arms wrapped around my body, I walk back down the trail to my car. I feel numb and my face is tight and puffy from dried tears.

Lao Tzu wrote:

Since before time and space were,
the Tao is.
It is beyond is and is not.
How do I know this is true?
I look inside myself and see.

I look inside myself and see. Yes.

CHAPTER 30

Past Lives

Nothing splendid has ever been achieved except by those who dared believe that something inside of them was superior to circumstance.
—Bruce Barton

May, 2007

If there is anyone who is a genuine psychic, it's Sonia Choquette. I've heard her speak once before and I've read most of her books. And now, with all the synchronicities and psychic episodes coming into my life on a regular basis, I feel like I need to ask her if it's possible that I've known Sammy in a previous life. I can't come up with any other way to explain it, although I'm still not sure I believe in such things.

Some friends and I get tickets to her presentation. The night of her lecture, there isn't an empty seat in the auditorium. Sonia comes onstage as lively and vibrant as ever. She talks about listening to your intuition. She talks about how to feed your spirit. And she says that the time of spiritual awakening is upon us—that there is an enormous shift in consciousness beginning to take place all over the world, and she mentions something about the Mayan calendar and the year 2012. I've been hearing the same thing lately, from many different sources, so maybe there really is something to it.

Sonia says all you have to do is look around and you will notice things changing. Her words hit me like an arrow piercing my heart. I'm not sure how all of this relates to me, but something tells me that it does, because this is exactly what's been happening to me—a shift in my spiritual awareness. I *know*— I have seen—that there is something better out there (and in here) and it *is* attainable. I feel a small grin/grimace spreading over my face and tears welling up in my eyes and I glance over at my friend Lois who's sitting next to me. She nods and smiles, then reaches over and gives my hand a reassuring squeeze.

Sonia's words make me think about the recent earthquakes and tsunamis and how they seem to be more frequent and destructive than ever. And global-warming. Could these things also be part of this world-consciousness shift? Because our thoughts literally affect our environment. I know a lot of people who would say that all the natural disasters are indications of the commencement of Armageddon—the Bible's prediction of the end of the world—fire and brimstone and fear. And while all these earth-changes may very well signal the end of the world *as we know it*, I don't think they're about the complete annihilation of our planet. I agree with Sonia. I think all these things are happening to herald the dawn of a new spiritual awareness, but maybe a lot of our archaic notions, such as how we allow ourselves to be controlled by fear, and all our other beliefs that keep us down—including ideas we cling to simply because that's how we were raised—have to drop away before we can fully embrace it.

Sonia then sits on a small stool, closes her eyes, and allows her guides to speak to us through her.

As I listen to what Sonia's guides are saying, at first I feel kind of silly—how easy would it be for her to fake this? But when I think about the universal spiritual awakening she has just described, I relax a bit, and before long, I literally feel a change in the vibration in the room. It's not eerie. It isn't threatening, dark, or mysterious. It's as if the air is swirling around each of our bodies like how your skin feels when someone walks past you when your eyes are closed. Her voice drops to a lower pitch and into a different cadence. Her guides talk about love and how we can make a difference in the world. They say it's up to us.

I'm still not quite sure what to think about this; coming from someone else, I may not have believed that spirits could actually speak through human beings, and yet, coming from her, it feels real. And the things she's saying make sense.

At the end of her talk, Sonia announces that she'll take questions from a few members of the audience. About a year ago, I had a premonition of her answering my question, so I'm ready. It's the whole reason I came here tonight. First, she calls on a man on the opposite side. Then she chooses a woman near the back of the room, then a woman in the front. I'm starting to worry now. Maybe I was wrong about my vision because time is running out.

"She doesn't even look over here," I whisper to Lois.

"Have faith," Lois tells me. "Don't let anything interfere. You know it will happen. Believe it."

The palms of my hands are beginning to sweat, but I try to hold on to the spirit that previously showed me the outcome.

"We have time for one more," Sonia says looking around.

My hand is in the air. I'm sending her vibes as strong as I can, "Please pick me!"

She finally turns her head in my direction and we connect.

"Yes, you in the red sweater; please stand up and tell us your name." She's pointing at me.

My heart is pounding as I rise to my feet. A middle-aged woman appears out of nowhere and hands me the microphone. Before I can say anything, Sonia takes one look at me and announces, "You have fire in your eyes, girl!" Then she turns to the audience. "Can you all see it? Wow!"

She asks my name and I tell her.

"Pat, get back in your body," she says. "Your spirit is all over the place."

I'm not sure what she means by this and it almost throws me off, but I bring my mind back to what I want to ask and relay my practiced words, the words I've so carefully chosen so as not to influence what she might otherwise "see."

"There's a very famous person who has come into my life in the past few years," I begin. I know I'm taking a big risk asking this question in front of all these people. My mind screams, "You idiot, what if she tells you something you don't want to hear? You'll be so sorry. Then what are you going to do? Will you believe her over what your Higher Self tells you?"

My spirit says, "Ask her. You already know the answer. There's nothing to be afraid of. When are you ever going to learn to trust me?"

I planned on asking her why I keep having so many psychic connections to a person I don't even know, but I don't get the chance. Sonia interrupts me before I can finish my question.

"You have shared several previous lifetimes with that famous person; I think twelve. But you have always been in the background boosting *his* ego. It's your turn to step out and be seen. You are like the man behind the curtain in *The Wizard of Oz* and this has been true for several of your past lives with this person. Now it's your turn to shine."

I feel myself blushing. I'm not surprised to hear that Sammy and I shared a past life, but I'm shocked to hear it was twelve previous lives. Could this be why he keeps going out of his way to encourage me?

She continues, "This person is fire in your life, and is the type of person who lives his spirit and has an open heart. Because of this, he opened this up in you."

How does she know all this stuff? I haven't told her a thing. *I've got to remember this.*

"Oh, and you should take up boxing," she adds.

My mouth drops open. My heart quits beating for a few seconds. Sammy's father had been a professional boxer and Sammy himself had dabbled in it quite a bit. He even considered making a living out of it in his younger years.

At this point, I don't even notice that the room is filled with people and all eyes are on me. I'm dumbfounded.

"That's all we have time for tonight," Sonia says to the crowd. "But Pat, you have many, many talents to share with the world; you must allow them to come out now. Don't be afraid; stop hiding. You can't go wrong." She looks directly into my face, her dark eyes burrowing into my soul.

"Thank you, Sonia." I nearly collapse back into my seat.

After Sonia leaves the stage and the audience begins to file out of the room, I try to blend in with them, try to pretend that I'm just like them, but I don't feel like I am. They're all chatting about the evening; I want to burst out of my skin. It feels like my soul has been splayed open and glitter poured in. And my heart is still pounding.

As my friends and I drive home, I ask them, "So if this past-lives connection is true—and I believe it now—then why am I back in touch with Sammy in this lifetime? It's not just to show me that we've shared past lives. It's also something greater than his being an inspiration to me. I'm inspired by lots of people, books, and music, but they don't linger in my life and have such a profound effect."

"You may never know the answer to that," Jill says. "But at least now you know the truth about the past lives."

The universe then provides more encouragement: a regional magazine publishes an article I wrote about my parents. Shortly thereafter, our local hospice organization invites me to read some of my poetry at a memorial service. Afterward, the director approaches me for permission to publish another of my poems in a book of poetry.

My dream is coming true.

CHAPTER 31

Open Up Your Heart

As you sit on the hillside, or lie prone under the trees of the forest, or sprawl wet-legged by a mountain stream, the great door, that does not look like a door, opens.
—Stephen Graham

June, 2007

I've never gotten an e-mail from Sammy before, so when I log onto the computer and see this one, my heart skips a beat.

His message is short and to the point. The letters "CH" represent the number 11. And "SH" represents the number 9. Then he says that CH0142 = 9.

These numbers represent everything that defines him, he says.

I sit back in my ergonomically incorrect desk chair and squint my eyes at the text on my computer screen. *What does he mean by that?*

Several years ago, after a particularly unremarkable meditation, the characters SH/CH0142 came to me. As I tried to figure out what it meant, I kept seeing the image of a rocket launching. After a lot of investigating, I decided that the significance of the rocket was that when I finally understood the meaning of the letters and numbers, it would be the key that opened the door to the purpose of my life, thereby "launching" my career and bringing me a joy greater than I ever could have imagined. Although it seemed lofty, I knew it in my sleep. I knew it in my toenails.

Since then, I've looked everywhere for CH0142—license plates, addresses, and phone numbers, but I didn't see it anywhere, other than when I saw 0142 on that van that time. That was weird too.

I even did an Internet search, thinking it might be some kind of chemical formula. Nope, but that was another place the rocket kept showing up. Every time I looked.

I had a very strong feeling that Sammy understood a whole lot more about what was happening to me than he was saying, so I finally wrote and asked him if he knew what it meant.

And now he sends me this e-mail. I don't understand.

When I get over the initial shock that he actually contacted me *again*, I realize that the message was sent ten minutes ago. Maybe he's still online.

"Are you still there?" I type onto the screen, then lean back and wait to see if I get a response. But cyberspace doesn't cough up a reply.

A heavy sigh comes out of me. If he answered right away, that would be too easy, wouldn't it? Oh, quit indulging yourself. The man simply gave you information. Do your own research.

I don't know anything about numerology, so I do an online search and find that CH0142 does, in fact, equal nine just as Sammy said. And since nine is the highest single digit number, it signifies rebirth and the attainment of goals. Did that mean my rocket was right? But I can't figure out how Sammy adds the corresponding numbers and letters in his name to get nine. That's what you're supposed to do to figure out "your" number. Then I remember about the aliens he attributed with changing his life; he said they came from the ninth dimension, even named his publishing company after them.

I type "Ninth Dimension" into my computer's browser bar and the screen pops up with, "a love that transcends earth and human beings." And it says that the ninth dimension is "linked with the spiritual worlds of other planets beyond the Solar System," and that its inhabitants often act as guides to those of us on Earth. It goes on to say, "The highest form of love available to humankind is that of the ninth dimension. This love may be described as *God Incarnate as love*, or *the love of the Saviour* . . . ."[7]

As I sit here trying to digest those words, a shiver runs through me like icy fingernails—when I had my mystical experience during Sammy's show, that was exactly how it felt—a love that transcended earth and human beings. Was it possible that I tapped into the ninth dimension that day?

My insides feel like they've turned to mush and I notice that I'm clenching my jaw so I take a deep breath to help me relax. All of this just seems to get more complex and mysterious by the day. Since those characters came to me so vividly that time, they must have been bringing some message for me, but what? Am I reaching if I conclude that CH0142 represents Sammy, or maybe the spiritual force that came through him to me? Over the past few years, has the Universe been giving me hints of this all along? A kind of validation that I should believe in this force and trust it because it was indeed responsible for my self-realization? My definition of self-realization not only means accepting myself for who I am, but also finding the purpose of my life. I now know what that is—to pursue joy with all my heart and to share it with others. For me, that translates into being a writer. And combined with Sammy's e-mail, it all makes sense—Sammy and his music, and the spirit that came through him, provided the means for my self-realization to happen.

They provided the initial experience and the story to tell, then Sammy kept encouraging me to tell it.

I've heard it said that what we're meant to do with our lives is something that's been tapping us on the shoulder forever. It's something we feel passionate about and brings us joy. Joy is God. What we feel most passionate about brings us to God. God is love. And isn't that what it all really boils down to anyway? —love? We all just want to be loved. It makes more sense to me to think that I'm spending my whole life trying to realize that God is a part of me, than to believe I'm spending my whole life trying to *please* God, as if God were separate from me.

For some, religion satisfies their spiritual needs. I admire people like that—my parents were among them. I think it must be easier for them though. They don't have to go around questioning and turning over every stone; they just accept what's been laid out for them. But it didn't happen that way for me, and since I was taught that it was a sin to look in other directions, I felt trapped and frustrated.

And now that I'm giving myself permission to seek my own answers and to adapt them into my life, I've never been happier. I have seen for myself that there's more than one way to God, be it Buddhism, Christianity, Hinduism, Islam, Shamanism, discovering-one's-self-in-nature-ism, or little bits taken from all of these, or some of these, or none of these, or whatever else is out there, whatever works for you—as long as love and kindness to others are at the core. I get so turned on when I hear devotees of one belief system actually considering the tenets of another. I wish we could all just do that, instead of fighting over whose beliefs are the truth.

I do know one thing, though—I've discovered *my* truth. And maybe it doesn't always make sense to my brain, but it sure does to my heart: I found God through Sammy's music. And within that music, I found God in me. I read somewhere that music affects us so deeply because it stirs emotion and emotion is the language of the soul—it's that which connects us to the Divine. And often when people experience Nirvana, it happens to them through music.

Shuffling a pack of ordinary red and white playing cards, I spread them out in front of me on the floor. I'm curious to see what will happen, if they really can give me advice. Dee and I are getting ready to take a trip to Tahoe to see Sammy in concert and lately I've been getting the feeling that something big is about to break loose. At the same time, my Catholic voice hisses, *You're not supposed to be doing this; in the Bible, God said fortune-telling was evil.*

Ah, it's just for fun. I won't take any of it seriously.

I meditate first to clear my mind and pray for God's protection, then I ask the cards to tell me what I need to know for the trip. As I turn them over one by one, consulting Sonia's book for interpreting their meanings, what I see makes me smile: three out of five cards say the same thing. Even though part of me considers it a game, I also know the messages are coming from a higher part of *me*, God, or my spiritual helpers not in physical form, because the edges of what I consider God and what I consider "me" seem to be blurring together lately. "The unanimous message here is *open your heart*," I write in my journal. "I've never seen such an overwhelmingly explicit message before."

At the concert, Dee and I manage to get in the front row.

About halfway through the show, Sammy introduces a new song he wrote. He says it's called "Open." It doesn't occur to me that that's exactly what the cards said, until I look back on it months later. As Sammy starts singing, it seems as if he's looking right at me, then he makes a circle with his fingers and gestures to me. I figure it's my imagination. He doesn't mean *me*. There must be someone behind me he's referring to.

Several songs later, he comes to the edge of the stage and bends over in front of me. His red guitar is strapped across his chest and I notice that it has a sticker of an alien face on the front. *Wow, he's really serious about this stuff.* I'm sure he must have had that sticker there for years but I never noticed it before. He tips his guitar to the side so it doesn't slam into me and holds the microphone away from his face. The other musicians are milling in the background, waiting for him to decide what to play next.

"Do you like the new song?" he asks, looking me right in the eye.

"Oh yes," I say. Why is he asking *me?* Why does he care if *I* like the song and why didn't he say that into the mic and ask the whole audience if they liked the song?

He wipes the hair out of his face. "That first part, you understand all that, don't you?"

I nod, but I have no idea what he's talking about. Maybe he's asking if I understood the first few words, maybe they have some significance. But I couldn't make out the lyrics when he sang them. From where I'm standing, the sound is all distorted and Sammy's voice isn't top-notch tonight; he's been sick for months and still sounds like his head is clogged up. Now there's no time to ask him—he's already in the middle of the next song.

I get caught up in the music and forget all about it until afterward, as Dee and I are walking to our hotel room. When I mention it, Dee tells me that I'm making way more out of this than it really is. I'm sure he must be right. I'll just drop it.

Several weeks after we're back home, someone sends me a video she took of Sammy's show that day. Plugging the disc into my computer, I watch portions of song after song unfold on the screen, and then my whole body seems to come alive at the sound of one guitar accompanied by a simple drum beat—the intro to "Open." As the song takes off, the video shows Sammy pointing to someone in the audience. He gestures back and forth between himself and the other person several times, as if to say "me and you, me and you, me and you," then he makes a circle with his fingers, like the sign for "okay" or "connected" and directs it to them. Although the video doesn't show the audience in the picture, I know the person he pointed to that night was me.

Nah. It can't be. Am I really seeing what I think I'm seeing?

I watch it again. There is no doubt. He was clearly trying to tell me something. The night of the concert, his last gesture was the only one I saw. And on the video, he did it so fast it was easy to miss, but once I saw it, and combined with what he said to me that day, it was obvious. Why did he ask me if I understood about the song? There must be something in the lyrics I'm not catching. I watch it again, but all I can make out is "whispers," "stranger," "open up your eyes." There are no answers here. Dammit! Why does all of this have to be such an enigma every step of the way?

A few days later, a package arrives on my front porch. It's a case of Cabo Wabo tequila from Sammy.

None of this feels real.

About a week passes and the professional studio version of "Open" becomes available for download. I can hardly wait to hear it. I figure if I know what the words are, it will explain everything.

There is a story about this song. Someone snuck a video camera into the studio when Sammy and his band were rehearsing. Part of the song was recorded and leaked to the public on Youtube well before the studio version was released. Apparently, the person who did this hid his camera under his coat, which muffled the sound. And yet, the first time I heard it, although I couldn't understand the words, I got goose bumps all over me. It was as if the song knew me and I knew it, even though I'd never heard the melody before. I remember thinking, *this song tastes like me,* but I couldn't say why. I even mentioned it to Dee. He just rolled his eyes.

After I download the song, I grab a pen and paper and attempt to decipher the lyrics. Nancy is on the phone trying to help. After a few minutes of playing it back, she speaks in a hushed tone, sounding as if she can't believe what's coming out of her mouth, "This song is about *you*—and everything that's been happening to you!"

"Yeah right, and I'm also the queen of England," I say, laughing. I don't want to believe it because then all of this will become even more complicated and it's already way too complicated to begin with.

I stare at the scribbled lyrics on my paper:

Start with your eyes closed,
let green and red shadows
start drifting you downstream;
just open up your eyes and you'll be there.

Listening so closely to
every sound you see inside your mind. (I swear)
Open up your arms and you'll be there. (I swear)
Open up your eyes and you'll be there. (I swear)
Open up your eyes and you'll be there. (I swear)
Open up, your heart will take you there.

And there on your shoulders,
your guide starts to whispering
some new things, some old dream,
some strange things, so quietly to hear.

Watch for a stranger;
some unsuspecting messenger appears. (I swear)
Open up your arms and you'll be there. (I swear)
If you open up your eyes, then you'll be there. (I swear)
Just open up your mind and you'll be there. (I swear)
Open up, your heart will take you there.

Open up your mind,
open up your dreams,
open up your world . . . .[8]

We agree that the song is about a person who doesn't under-stand what's going on in the beginning, and maybe the color green represents aliens and "red shadows" represents Sammy's indirect influence (since he calls himself the Redrocker). It sounds reasonable enough. And it's about how the person in the song is being taken somewhere beyond his or her control, but the line, "Let green and red shadows start drifting you downstream," really throws me for a loop.

"These are the same words I wrote in my journals and in my book a whole bunch of times," I say in slow motion because I need to slow everything down so I can get a good look at it. "That was exactly how I described the force that came to me through Sammy's music, Nanc. I remember it because I used those words so often. I wrote, 'I feel adrift on a raft without oars, being swept swiftly downstream,' and now that I think about it, a few years back, I had a dream about a stuffed eagle and a red light bulb casting its red shadow over me. That's precisely how I wrote it. How strange."

"Did you ever tell that to Sammy?"

"No, but I did tell him that he opened my eyes." It feels like it's not even me that's controlling my mouth.

"And remember when you told me how you wrote his words on your paper, your poem you were writing a few years ago? You wrote them at the exact moment he was singing them in another state." Nancy's voice trails off. "Wow. You wrote his words; now he's writing yours. *Unbelievable!*"

This can't be real. I must be allowing her to influence me into jumping to conclusions. I feel kind of panicky, as if I'm trying really hard to cling to my sanity because this is absurd. I force myself to focus.

The rest of the song seems to be about someone who is desperately trying to figure out what's going on, then there's a reference to past lives and supernatural stuff—"guide, whispering, new things, old dream, strange things." And then, as I'm skimming the lyrics, it jumps off the paper and grabs me by the throat.

Watch for a stranger, some unsuspecting messenger appears.

That does it. Tears stream down my face and fall onto my keyboard. This song is about me. The mystical experience I had came to me through Sammy although I didn't know who he was when it happened. And he knew this, because I told him.

Emotions run through me in waves—fear, confusion, honor.

"He's saying that aliens, directly or indirectly, came through him to me and opened me up to something wonderful. That's what he was trying to tell me from the stage in Tahoe, that this song is about him and me and how we're connected." My voice is so small I can hardly hear it myself.

"Yeah, he is." Nancy says with a sigh.

"Now wait a minute, Sammy Hagar—former lead singer of the legendary rock band Van Halen, Sammy Hagar—multimillion-dollar tequila entrepreneur, Sammy Hagar—world-renowned rock star and inductee into the Rock and Roll Hall of Fame, *has written a song about me?* Little nobody me? Uh uh."

"I'd say you've got that right—one hundred percent." She sounds like she's fighting back tears because she's so shocked and overjoyed for me. Friends like her don't just come along every day. I've always said that we're like two halves of the same person because we keep each other in line. When life pulls one of us too far in one direction, the other gently balances everything out, reminding her of the other side of the big picture: come down from the clouds when you're being too lofty, hold your hand when you're sad, whatever it takes. "And you're not a nobody," she says, then takes a very long pause. "Sammy's telling you, 'I promise you that if you stop fighting it and allow this energy, this spirit to come to you, it will bring the answer to your dreams.' Damn, girl, he has given you quite a gift here."

I write in all caps across the bottom of the page, NO FUCKING WAY!!! and underline it three or four times so heavily that the pen almost cuts through the paper.

Six years ago, I didn't even know who Sammy was; now he's writing a song about all the mystical things that have happened to me? *Me*? I wonder what was going through his mind when he wrote it. The lyrics don't sound like he's the least bit freaked out about any of it; he sounds confident, as if to say, "Don't worry, let it come to you; it's all good." Oh man, I wish I could talk to him. I need him to reassure me some more. It's not as easy for me to accept this stuff as it seems to be for him.

I'm so lost in my thoughts, I almost forget Nancy's still on the line.

"Are you there?" she finally asks. Her question doesn't really demand an answer; it's more of a validation, telling me that she's here for me.

Am I there? Am I here? Am I *where*? I don't know anymore. I lean back in my chair, away from the desk, and rub my hand across my forehead and into the hollows of my wet eyes. If I've been astonished by all the bizarre incidents over the past few years, this one makes everything else seem insignificant. Part of me wants to run away from it, deny it, but another part of me wants to dive in with everything I've got. It's shocking. It's thrilling. It's . . . wow.

"*These things just don't happen,* Nanc. Not in my life anyway. Nor in the lives of anyone I've ever heard of. Rock stars do not write songs about Mrs. Frumpingtons like me." But deep inside, my heart knows. Has always known. A small empty ache pierces the pit of my stomach. Something hot surges out my pores. Spirit has revealed concepts more incredible than I can grasp—Sammy and I are connected on a spiritual level; we are *all* connected; there is a God; there is a realm of otherworldly beings that exists and we are all connected to that as well. And anything we can dream, we can be. "This is freaking huge. What am I supposed to do with all this?"

"Write your book, Honey. You've got an amazing story to tell," she says.

"Yeah, *but who's going to believe me?* I'm going to sound like some crazed fanatic blowing things out of proportion, you know, like the 'Paul-McCartney-is-dead-and-you-can-tell-if-you-play-the-record-backwards' scam. And if people think that about me, they aren't even going to hear what's really important about all this—how I arrived at enlightenment, self-realization, through all these supernatural and fascinating events that continue to surprise even me. Like this one!"

"It's none of your business what other people think of you. The ones who need to hear your message, will. Besides, *Sammy believes you!*"

"Yeah, I guess that's pretty obvious now."

I know Nancy's right. People are going to judge me no matter what I say or do, so I'll just tell the truth and "let the chips fall where they may," as my dad used to say.

When I go to write all this down, I find two tiny pieces of paper taped into my notebook from several years earlier: "The world is always ready to receive talent with open arms." And above this, there's a description of how a spirit voice came to me a few weeks before I received those fortunes, saying, "The universe is welcoming this with open arms."

"Oh my God," comes out of me in a whisper.

Journal entry dated August 12, 2004

CHAPTER 32

Celebrity's Song

There is a vitality, a life force, an energy, a quickening, that is translated through you into action, and because there is only one of you in all time this expression is unique. And if you block it, it will never exist through any other medium and will be lost.
—Martha Graham

May, 2008

Tonight Dee and I bought onstage tickets for the show in Tahoe. I know, we're beginning to sound like all those fans I once laughed at because they planned their entire vacations around Sammy's concerts. But we don't just go to see Sammy; we go to see all our friends too because now we have friends from all over the world—Japan, The Netherlands, England, Scotland, Italy, Mexico, Canada, Australia. I love hearing all the different accents and about their cultures. And I'm not sick of hearing Sammy play the same music. Not yet anyway.

We haven't been to any live concerts in over a year though, so this is an extra-special treat because we're standing in the very middle of the top riser behind the drums. The top of the top. Something in my bones says this is going to be a great night.

The concert bursts open with the song "Mas Tequila" and Sammy runs up and down the stage singing to the thousands of cheering faces. Young girls in string bikinis and shiny belts strut their stuff and deliver tequila to him from the palm-thatched bar on the side of the stage. He takes a sip of his drink, then flings the rest all over the crowd.

Still singing into the mic, Sammy comes up onto the risers, where Dee and I and about seventy-five other fans are rocking out onstage behind the band. He's wearing a silly hat and a few strings of Mardi gras beads, along with a necklace made of fake pot leaves someone in the front row gave him. He stops every now and then to pose for pictures or to sign autographs, then as he makes his way through the onstage mob, with bodyguard in close pursuit, he slides up beside me and shoves Dee out of the way to get next to me. At first I feel sorry for Dee, like, "Hey! That's my husband! What do you think you're doing?" But then I figure maybe Sammy's going to give me a hug. But no. He puts his arm around my neck and pulls me into his chest, then spins me around to face us outward, toward the audience.

I feel like the sacrificial lamb being presented to the world before the big feast.

His whole body is pressed up against mine but I didn't even feel him do it. It's a moment caught in a vacuum somewhere between slow motion and a speeding blur. I have a friend who drives a drag-racer—the kind that shoots out a parachute to help slow down the car. He once told me that the car goes so fast, it feels like your guts are being smashed into the seat. That's how I feel right now, like things are moving so fast, my guts have fallen into my feet, and I'm exploding in every direction in some kind of helpless awe/elation that only happens to other people. Or in dreams. I'm thinking this is how it must feel to be a celebrity—the non-blinking eye of the public seeing everything—every pore on your face. But I'm so shocked, so stupidly dazed that this is happening, I don't even care.

When I look out at the crowd, it's hard to see at first because there's a huge, white light shining on Sammy and me. Then I notice how bright the colors are—on the walls, the curtains, the platform, the stage below, and splashed throughout the audience, whose potpourri of shirts looks like confetti. Red, blue, and green lights flick on and off and cameras flash like strobes. Sammy's son Aaron, who's recently been doused with a cup of tequila by his dad, has made his way up the other side of the platform and is standing directly behind us, singing along.

The whole room looks different now, the whole *world* looks different—like it's on fire and I have to react somehow, only I'm not sure what to do because the fire's not the destructive kind, it's the lively kind with flames dancing all over the place. And Sammy's not giving me any cues either, so maybe I'm not supposed to do anything except stand here looking like the proverbial deer in the headlights. I think I must be doing a pretty good job of that.

Sammy's still singing into the mic and it's a good thing he's holding onto me because I'm shaking so bad that if he were to let go, I'd probably fall down. And my cheeks hurt; I haven't smiled this hard since the day I received my college degree. I'm shimmering, shining like the sun and it feels like it's pouring out of me. I think my heart has turned to liquid.

Sammy's acting like this is no big deal, like it's part of his performance and I know it is, but I wonder how many people get to experience this feeling—being in the spotlight with a big star. And maybe it all sounds so lame, but *there is no feeling in the world like this*. Something in me says, "Quit being so afraid to let yourself be a fan. It isn't necessarily a bad thing—as long as you keep it in perspective."

I've beat myself up about this from the beginning, fought against being swept up in the fan role like it's a degrading thing, and analyzing every detail to make sure I wasn't just inventing all this for that reason. Because to me, it was a symbol of relinquishing my power over my life. But I guess there's nothing wrong with appreciating Sammy's music and how it makes me feel. I can be so strong when I'm not around it, but the minute the lights go out and the band strikes that first chord, I'm gone. All over again. It gets to my soul. Anyway, we're all fans of something, right? —football, baseball, dogs, horses, the pope, cooking, eating. . . . Even famous people are fans of other famous people. I once read that Keith Richards was a huge fan of Chuck Berry and Elvis and they were the inspiration for his wanting to become a musician.

The truth is, I wouldn't have gotten where I am without Sammy. Sure, my awakening might have come to me in an entirely different way, but it didn't. And Sammy could have chosen not to get involved, but he didn't. I'm truly grateful for everything he's done for me.

And now he's singing the song "Rock Candy" in my ear, and the voice I hear coming out of the speakers behind the crowd seems to be a different voice than the one I hear coming out of him. What a strange sensation; it's like his physical presence is disconnected from his voice. I wonder how he can hear himself. Then he puts the microphone in front of me. He wants me to sing. I can't sing. A split-second thought: *What if I screw up the lyrics?* Aw, who cares—*relax! Enjoy it!*

I sing the next line of the song into the mic. I can't hear myself; it's like I'm singing into Sammy's hand, so I'm sure I'm off-key, but my entire soul is beaming. It feels like all the thousands of watts of power that are driving the sound system and the lights are being forced into me with an enormous jolt and the blood in my veins is being replaced with electricity. I think

I must have entire galaxies spinning around my head, and it's suddenly really, really warm.

Dee is leaning over the rail next to us and trying to snap pictures, but he might be too close to get a shot. And he looks kind of like how I feel—completely astonished.

Sammy keeps standing there with his arm around my shoulder and singing for a bit longer. Then he gives me a hug and whispers something into my ear, but it doesn't register in my brain.

I don't see him walk back through the rest of the onstage crowd and I hardly feel the hands patting me on the back and the smiles and words of congratulations being hurled at me from all around me. I feel like a peasant unexpectedly having been crowned queen—no, *king!*

At the end of the show, from center stage, Sammy turns around and comes over to where he can see me on the risers. He points at me, making sure I know he's talking to me. Then he brings his hands up as if he's holding a book, moving his index finger up one side and down the other, as if he's reading it. Licking his finger, he pretends to turn the pages. Then he turns around, grabs the microphone off the stand, and points to me. I hear him say my name. He's telling the audience about my book.

I put my finger to my lips. "Shhhhhhh—" I'm not ready for everyone to know about it yet. But he pays no attention; he just keeps on talking. I feel like he's just pushed me off a pier into a very big lake and I don't know how to swim, but at the same time, something about his demeanor feels reassuring, as if he's telling me, "Don't worry; it doesn't have to be perfect—let it go!" He never seems to worry about being perfect. He does what he wants, and it's like he's giving me permission to do the same.

I've been procrastinating in the name of perfectionism, telling myself that no matter what I do, my writing will never be good enough. I know I need a push or I might never turn this thing loose on my own. I read something about that once. When we get very close to realizing our dream, we often back away because deep down, we don't believe we deserve it. Then all sorts of demons come out of the woodwork to make it easy for us to give up. And they're usually damn good ones too, justifiable, like the deaths of my parents. Not only that, but if our dream were to come true, the world as we know it would change. And although our current situation may be unrewarding, it's comfortable and familiar. For a lot of us, change is frightening because it's the unknown, so rather than risk what's familiar—even to realize our dreams—we often sabotage ourselves.

"And Pat will be coming out with a book soon for y'all," I hear Sammy say.

Oh God, now he's said it out loud, handing me *his* captive audience, dropping them in my lap like I've earned this right. What do I do now? A raging bull is suddenly delivered to my backyard and I'm the matador armed with only a pen to subdue the great beast. What *can* I do? Appreciate how colorful the spears are that are sticking out of its sides? I know the spotlight is on Sammy, but it sure feels like it's on me too. I'm suddenly aware that a world of limitless possibilities is before me. My ability to make of my life anything I want is now within my reach. It's *always* been within my reach—but I can feel it, taste it, smell it, now more than ever—and not just because of what's happened here tonight, but from the accumulation of events over the past few years. When I surrender to that higher power within me, that joy I'm feeling right now, even though my ego mind screams that I'm being ridiculous, when I completely let go and follow my Higher Self, I find my truth. Every time. But maybe only those who are more highly evolved souls than me, the ones who've trained their minds through meditation and lifetimes of selflessness can fully grasp these things—like Jesus, Buddha, Gandhi, and the Dalai Lama, because the deeper I look, the deeper it gets. Which is why before all of this started, I didn't allow myself to think. I didn't have the courage to let myself explore my heart like this; it was just easier to float along with the current.

Standing here tonight on this stage, when I look around me at everything Sammy represents—music, excitement, tequila, unlimited resources, power—I finally understand his role in all this. It's not just Sammy Hagar, the rock star, that's important in my transformation, it's what he represents *to me*—a side of myself that I never knew existed. And not all of it, but a lot of it, has been sexual. My journey has had sexual undertones from the start and Sammy's a sexy man. But I also knew from the beginning that whatever it was that was happening to me was not about Sammy; this was coming from something beyond him. If I gave him all the credit, then I'd be focusing on him and I'd be stagnating. His purpose was to show me the path, but I had to step out from there and find my own path. There's a Buddhist proverb that says, "How do you show the way to The Way? It's like a finger pointing at the moon. If you're looking at the finger, you can't see the moon." So true. The Rolling Stones might never have happened if Keith Richards had simply remained a fan of Chuck Berry and Elvis.

And if I said I never entertained thoughts of having sex with Sammy, I'd be lying. Sammy writes explicit lyrics and he can get really nasty onstage sometimes; he's gotten pretty nasty with me more than once. He still does. And although at first, it was kind of hard not to take it personally, I don't anymore. I realize the way he treats me when he's onstage is part of his image as a rock star and it's part of his act, so I just play along too.

Besides, all the supernatural events would not have brought me all this way merely for a ten-minute fling with a rock star. God has better things to do with her time. And so do I. I don't need to have sex with a celebrity to prove to myself that I have value as a human being. I'd much rather sit down with Sammy and get his opinion on all this mystical stuff and discuss his spiritual concepts, because from the little I've seen of him on a personal basis, I think there's more to him than he allows the public to see—being a passionate musician and all. People like that feed my spirit like nothing else can.

I think the reason my journey has been so sexual is because that was one of the areas where I needed to heal and grow since the Catholic Church and my first husband had really messed up my head in that respect. I now know that sex is one of those amazing, wonderful joys of life I'd been missing out on all those years and because of this mystical journey, I've finally gained a healthy and confident attitude about it.

And that's another thing Sammy represents to me—confidence. Here's this big star going out of his way for me time and time again, like he did tonight, making *me* feel like a star. It's as if he's saying, "Yeah, I'm famous, but I'm no more important than you. I haven't accomplished anything you can't also accomplish."

A mixture of panic and pure joy fills my entire being. I am whole. I'm deserving. I'm good. I'm intelligent. I'm sensual. I'm beautiful. I'm talented—I just never knew it. My soul is on fire with a flame big enough to light the world. *Bring it on!*

As I walk off the stage, people I've never seen before approach me. They introduce themselves and hug me as if I'm somebody famous. Then they introduce their friends as if they want to impress their friends by showing them that they know someone who's famous. I want to say, "*I'm not a celebrity. Stop it! I'm no different than you.*" But I don't because I can't get hold of the words. I'm still in shock. Then they say they're proud of me and can't wait to read my book. The questions come in droves.

"What's it about?" *Uh, that's a long story.*

"When will it be out?" *Um . . . what was that again?*

"Can I have your autograph?" *My autograph? Are you kidding me?*

"That was really nice of Sammy to plug your book." *I can't believe it.*

I think I must be standing still and the whole world is swirling around me. What irony—*I have fans!* Only because of Sammy of course, but still . . . I don't know how to act or whom to talk to first. "Just be yourself," I tell myself. *Yeah, but my self feels like it's just been peeled open like a banana that's not quite ripe yet.*

As I'm taking all this in, it suddenly occurs to me that I foresaw this entire night years earlier, several times—Sammy introducing me to his audience exactly like he did tonight. I saw the crowd, the lights, him holding the mic for me to sing, the stage—everything, right down to the part where I felt kind of embarrassed.

As Dee and I walk through the casino, I tell him about my premonition and instead of informing me that I'm imagining things like he usually does, he nods and gives me a soft smile, as if he's actually considering, for the first time, that all this mystical stuff just might be real. He's certainly been there every step of the way as it's unfolded in our lives. Maybe he's afraid to admit it though, because he always likes to be in control. Even when we go somewhere, he insists on driving; that way he doesn't have to depend on anyone else's judgment. So if he were to acknowledge that there really is such a thing as a spiritual realm, maybe he thinks that would be like admitting he doesn't have complete control after all and he just can't accept that. I can sure relate. But perhaps when we recognize that other realms really do exist, such as the power of the mind, and other levels of consciousness that connect us to one another and to what I call God—maybe even to other worlds, and when we realize they aren't separate from us, but an important part of us, that's when we really tap into having control over our lives, like letting go to gain control. Because we're not just measly, frightened human beings floundering through life all alone; we're so much greater than we think.

Wow, I swear these thoughts are not coming from me.

Dee grabs my hand and squeezes it. *Can this night get any better?*

As we enter the Cabo Wabo bar, an attractive woman approaches me. "I saw you up there onstage with Sammy—bitch," she says.

I laugh. I guess it's a compliment.

Then a dark-haired woman stops me and asks for a picture. I assume she wants me to take a picture of her and the man she's with. "Sure," I say, reaching for her camera.

"No—you and him," she says, stepping back to aim the camera.

Before I can say a thing, the man hands me a double shot of tequila and takes one off the bar for himself. We pose together and the woman snaps the picture.

"Down the shot," she says. *"¡Salud!"*

The man, a rather short, olive-skinned gentleman in a freshly pressed, button-down shirt and black-rimmed glasses, and I clink glasses and throw down the shots.

"He's the owner of Cabo Wabo tequila," she whispers in my ear as if it's a secret.

Yeah, right, whatever. The owner of Cabo Wabo tequila would not want a picture with *me*.

I later found out it was true. Skyy/Campari had recently bought 80 percent of Cabo Wabo tequila from Sammy for $80 million and this guy was one of the new owners.

How am I supposed to deal with being a middle-aged wife and mom running through the motions of everyday survival one minute, to being onstage with a famous rock star who actually wrote a song about me and is promoting my book without even being asked? From ironing my husband's shirts and fixing casserole for dinner to having people I've never met before buying me drinks and asking for my autograph? *Me,* your next-door neighbor.

CHAPTER 33

Flight of the Hummingbird

There is no place to seek the mind;
It is like the footprints of the birds in the sky.
—The Zenrin

September 26, 2009

It's so weird. We go to these concerts, and mixed in with us regular folk are all these celebrities and millionaires, and the whole time it's one big party—over-the-top, non-stop excitement—and then we come home. And like today, as I'm taking a walk through my neighborhood, I notice parked cars in front of pastel-colored two-story houses, kids wearing little purple helmets riding their bikes on the sidewalk, and it feels like two different worlds. I enjoy going to Sammy's shows, but that's not my whole life, so it's hard to believe that both worlds can exist like this. It feels like the concert atmosphere was all just a dream and now I'm back to reality.

As I walk past all these little kids today, it brings back memories of when my boys were that age. It doesn't seem that long ago, but I sure miss those days. Life was so much simpler then. Now the only one still living at home is our youngest, Michael, and I know it won't be long before he'll be leaving too. John lives in an apartment with friends and David is married with a beautiful baby boy of his own. Sometimes I wish I could just keep them all here with me forever, but I guess I must have done something right because they visit us often and I love that.

When I think about everything that's happened to me though, I realize that LIFE IS GRAND in so many ways. I have so very much to be thankful for. The joy that sprang from my mystical experience during one, simple concert more than six years ago, still bubbles over inside of me, and because of it, I now know who I am and *I love being me!* I love being a mom, a wife, a grandma. And I love being a writer, although the process of writing a book is wearing me out. But I guess it's the *process* that's important, right? The act of doing what we love most. And in that regard, I wouldn't change a thing, although Dee still hounds me to be done with it.

As I walk past the aspens in my neighbor's yard, I notice their leaves are rustling, swinging and clicking, holding fast to their branches, but not for long. Fall is almost here. I can smell it. And as I'm taking in all these wonderful scents, I feel the presence of an immense power within me, as if its influence connects me by a golden cord to something even greater. Or maybe it's not only a golden cord but also a golden "chord." Yes.

My friend Jill, who lives a few houses down, waves me over. She's pulling weeds in her yard while her beagle rummages through her neighbor's shrubs and pounces on unsuspecting grasshoppers. Since the Zen lecture, Jill and I have become close friends. It's so great to have someone to talk to about all my mystical stuff, someone who doesn't judge me. "Cosmic," she calls it. I think that's about as good a description as any.

"Hiya, Pat, how's it goin'?" She straightens up and pushes her hand into her lower back as if it hurts, then she notices a small stain on the knee of her beige capris and attempts to brush it away, but it doesn't come off. She's always so tidy, even when she's outside working in the yard. I don't know how she does it.

"Great! How about you?"

"Same ol', same ol'." Her gray eyes always seem to harbor a bit of sadness but she tells me all the time what a kick she gets out of my adventures. "Whatcha doin'?"

"Just taking a break and going for a walk."

"Well, it's a nice day for it." She calls to her dog, but the dog ignores her. She turns back to me. "So, what's new? How's your book coming?"

"I think if someone would have told me in the beginning how much time and effort were involved, I wouldn't have even started it."

"Yeah, right, who do you think you're kidding? You couldn't have stopped it if you wanted to."

I kick a small stone and send it bouncing across the street because I know she's right. "Okay, then, can I get your opinion? What would be the best way for me to describe the source of my mystical transformation? People may not take me seriously if I use the word aliens. Anyway, I don't think all of this is caused by aliens. Of course, I could be wrong."

She's just nodding her head in agreement, so I keep going. "And I'm sure there are many who will object to light beings, angels, a supernatural force, or Spirit Guides, maybe even Higher Self, an altered state of mind, or Sammy Hagar," I say. "'Cause it's my mind that created my definition of all these things in the first place, right? —my definition of God, my definition of reality—even my definition of what it was I needed to make me whole. So maybe it's *all* those things, and I should just say that it was brought about through my Sunday night tuna casserole, because it really doesn't matter what you call it. It happened. It opened my eyes. It opened my mind—that's all that matters."

Hummingbird.

"What?" I lift my eyes to hers, wondering why she would say something so random and off-the-wall. Maybe she's referring to her new birdfeeder that's swinging near her front window.

"I didn't say anything," she says and gives me the strangest look. I can't figure out what she means.

"Yes, you did, you said hummingbird."

She shakes her head. "No, I didn't."

"Uh huh, I heard it clear as a bell."

"I didn't hear anything."

I know I heard someone say "hummingbird." When I think about it, the only thing that comes to mind is something I asked Sammy when he performed in Denver a few years ago. I asked him if he were to describe his spirit as an animate object, what would it be? I have no idea where the question came from at the time. Maybe I was hoping he'd say an eagle, because eagles kept coming to me since all this started. But he said a hummingbird.

I tell this to Jill.

She looks closely at me, so closely that it makes me wonder if I have food in my teeth or something. Then she says, "I wonder why *hummingbird?*"

"He told me, but I don't remember. Anyway, I didn't think anymore about it until about a year later. I was trying to come up with a title for my book and something told me to investigate the word hummingbird, since Sammy's spirit did have so very much to do with all this, so I looked online to find out what a hummingbird symbolized. It's considered a very spiritual symbol in a lot of cultures and represents energy, unlimited joy, and the accomplishment of things that are said to be impossible. The hummingbird supposedly teaches us how to find miracles in our everyday lives. It's also a type of dreadnought acoustic guitar."

"Cool."

"Yeah, I thought it was a fitting title. So before I drifted off to sleep that night, I asked the source of this force, 'Please provide me with a title for my book and let me recognize it when I see it.' In the morning when I checked my e-mail, the screen pulled up an ad for a holistic bookstore. I deleted it, but then I got the feeling I should look at it again, so I pulled it back out of my deleted files. And there was a red hummingbird on my screen, sipping nectar from a green flower. It was the sign I asked for! I 'bout crapped my pants."

"Wow, you never told me about that."

"Oh, there's more." I explain about how on that same afternoon, I had been talking to my brother on the phone and telling him about the hummingbird. "He doesn't believe in psychic or otherworldly stuff, but he listened anyway. An hour after we hung up, he called back. He said that after he and I talked, he was working in his garage when two guys came up his driveway and handed him a pamphlet for some religious group. He was about to throw the pamphlet in the trash, but something made him look down at it. There was a picture of a *red hummingbird* on it and it said, 'Happiness for life!' Can you believe that? My brother was really freaked out because he and I had just been talking about a red hummingbird, and we hadn't talked to one another in over two months. I said to him, 'See what I mean? There's some kind of supernatural force involved here and now it's affecting you too!' As we talked, Tim kept saying, '*How can this be?*'

"That's happened to me *a lot* over the past few years," I continue. "Just when I would chalk everything up to being just my imagination or whatever, something really weird like that would happen and make me wonder all over again."

"That's wild," Jill says, bugging out her eyes and smiling. It's kind of her trademark expression. I love it. "And just now you asked what to call the source of your transformation, and you heard the word hummingbird. I swear I didn't say it, Pat. Honestly. I swear." She's still looking into my eyes but something about the way she's acting makes me uncomfortable all of a sudden. Then she leans toward me and lowers her voice as if she's about to let me in on a huge secret. "And you know what? I have a feeling you've just uncovered the tip of the iceberg with all this stuff."

I'd been feeling the same way lately, although I wasn't going to admit it, not even to myself because what would that mean? That there was more to come. I didn't know whether to feel blessed or terrified, so I just pretended I didn't have those feelings. "Yeah, me too," I finally confess.

Still feeling awkward, I start combing my fingers through the hair on the back of my head, when something moves and catches my eye. The sky is suddenly swarming with white gulls. "Look at all those gulls! There are hundreds! Thousands, maybe. I've never seen this many before, have you? Well maybe at the lake, but not here. What do you suppose they're doing here? There's no water around here for them."

She raises her eyebrows and makes a slow and thoughtful gesture of sliding her hands into the pockets of her capris as if she's looking for a way to make sense of all the birds. "I don't know. They're all congregating above your house."

My back is toward my house, so at first, I don't believe her— why would hundreds of gulls be hovering above my house? But her voice sounds breathy, the way it does when something inexplicable has happened and she doesn't quite know how to take it. I turn around to look at the birds, mostly to convince myself that Jill is imagining things. Instead, I see gulls—thousands of them—flying in tight circles like a swirling tornado of white wings above my house—*just* my house, and not the houses on either side of it. "Yeah, they are."

We stand there watching for a few minutes.

Ever since this mystical journey of mine began, I've been seeing lots of birds and symbols of birds—eagles, blackbirds, bluebirds, flickers, robins, hummingbirds, and now gulls. I wonder if they're a representation of my Spirit Guides. A lot of people believe in that and so do many spiritual principles, like Shamanism and Native American philosophies. Some people might even think of them as angels.

Jill breaks the silence. "Aren't you and Dee leaving for Cabo to see Sammy pretty soon?"

"Three days. Why?"

She nods at the birds. "Pat, it's a sign."

Okay, well, I guess it's time for me to stop questioning. To trust and believe. In this force. In myself. And in the power of my spirit. When I think about it, it befuddles even me, to realize how great the depth of my disbelief after everything that's happened to me. And while all my doubt and analyzing of events were, in my opinion, admirable, like the Zen master told me, if I focused too much on the means, it could cause me to stray off the path to self-realization.

It's time for me to fly.

Author's Note

This book is based on the journals I've kept over the past fifteen years. It contains only an infinitesimal number of the supernatural incidents that have happened to me since October, 2003. Actually, there have been so many, it was difficult to decide on which ones to include.

And they're still happening.

Like all accounts, this book is somewhat slanted toward my recollection and personal interpretation of events. It does not reflect the opinion of Sammy Hagar or anyone else involved.

In some places, I have changed people's names to protect their privacy.

Many people have told me that simply hearing my story has affected their lives too, in extremely positive and unusual ways, as if there is powerful magic in the spirit beneath the words. And it's not even necessary to believe any of it. If it hadn't happened to me, I'm not so sure I would have believed it either. If you do happen to notice anything, I'd love to hear from you.

For more information, please visit www.bajarockpat.com.

Endnotes

[1]http://wordnetweb.princeton.edu/perl/webwn?s=koan

[2]"Eagles Fly." Words and music by Sammy Hagar, 1987. Used by permission.

[3]http://en.wikipedia.org/wiki/Mysticism

[4]Rhea A. White, "Exceptional Human Experiences and the Experiential Paradigm," in *Body Mind Spirit: Exploring the Parapsychology of Spirituality*, edited by Charles T. Tart, Charlottesville, VA: Hampton Roads Publishing Company, Inc., 1997, p. 98.

[5]*Introduction to Contemporary Music Review, Music & Mysticism Issue* by Maxwell Steer, www.musicpsyche.org/mmintro.html.

[6]White, "Exceptional Human Experiences," p. 86.

[7]www2.gol.com/users/utopia/variety/multiuni/multi9.html

[8]"Open." Words and music by Sammy Hagar, 2007. Used by permission.

Acknowledgments

To my parents, John and LaVerne, especially my dear mother, whose faith in me never wavered. You knew someday I would be a writer long before I did. You are my guiding light from heaven. I miss you more than words can say.

To all my dear friends and my brother who stood by me and held my hand. I am so blessed to have you.

To Dr. Blair Oliver: Thank you for believing in my abilities by publishing my first poem and giving me the chance to share my work before a live audience. You told me, "Poets wear whatever they want!" I will never forget it.

To Dr. Robert Mines: Your professional expertise and inspiration have been a tremendous help to me. I am paying it forward.

To Father Bert: You are one of the greatest sources of light in my life and always have been. All those who have the pleasure to know you are truly blessed.

To Christopher Romero and Joanne Hedleston: Thank you so much for your time and your help.

To Gayan: God bless you for your invaluable wisdom, talent, and your wonderful mind.

To Favazz: Thank you for taking your valuable time to advise me on this book.

To Jan Garrett: Your music is an inspiration. Thank you so much. I will never forget "The Great Mother."

To Sharon Hamm: Thank you for your help and expertise.

To Gerry Shishin Wick Roshi: You are a mountain; thank you for allowing me to sit for a few moments in your great shadow.

To Julie Piotraschke: You have been invaluable. I couldn't have done this without you.

To Troy Cook: For all your advice, thanks so much.

To Veronica Patterson: Your poetry and your generous spirit have been an inspiration to me from the first time I heard you read about paper lanterns.

To the members of Word-By-Word: Without your help, this book would not be. Your inspiration and honesty have helped me more than you will ever know.

To Renata: Your help and willingness to make things happen have been invaluable. I can't thank you enough.

To Paula Rowan: Thank you for everything you did for me. I couldn't have done this without you.

To Aaron Hagar: You are amazing! Thank you, thank you, thank you . . . .

To Vic Johnson: Your outstanding talent as a musician is only exceeded by the wonderful person you are. Thank you for everything.

To Jon Ostrin: Thank you for your help and input, and your incredible talent.

To Laura Pritchett: Thank you from the bottom of my heart. You made this happen by bringing out the *best* in me!

To Jen Henrichsen, Colleen Barry, Theresa Kunis, Nancy Reighter, Patricia Stoltey, Carrie and David Pinsky, and Kristin Hungenberg: Your honesty and feedback have helped me make this manuscript better than it ever could have been without you.

To the REDheads: I wrote this book to share with the world the strange and wonderful things that have happened to me. I wrote it to give people hope. My life has become a living example of the things Sammy sings about—follow your heart and pursue your dream with all your might. I hope my joy becomes your joy as well, because you, of all people, as Sammy says, "Get this shit." I am proud to call you my friends for life. A special thanks to those of you who put the word out about my writing. I am humbled and honored by your undying support—it is *everything.*

To my husband, my children, and grandchildren: Thank you for your patience in putting up with my countless hours of reading, writing, and searching for my inner soul when maybe I should have been cooking, cleaning the house, or bringing in a paycheck. My love for you is beyond limit.

To Sammy Hagar: I wouldn't have realized any of this if it hadn't been for you. Through you, I saw my soul. You stood by me and believed in me even when I didn't believe in myself. You helped me find my voice and repeatedly encouraged me never to give up on my dreams. There are no words to describe the depth of my gratitude.

References and
Recommended Reading

Websites:

www2.gol.com/users/utopia/variety/multiuni/multi9.html

www.americaneaglerecords.com/programs/eagle-facts/
american-indian.php

www.bachmans.com/retail/tipsheets/indoor_plants/
CactiandSucculents.cfm

www.cabowabo.com

www.jpl.nasa.gov/news/news.cfm?release=2005-009

www.metallica.com

www.nuradeen.com/reflections/ElementsOfSufism11.htm

www.redrocker.com

www.rootsworld.com/reviews/iz.shtml

www.tastings.com/spirits/tequila.html

http://en.wikipedia.org/wiki/Mysticism

http://wordnetweb.princeton.edu/perl/webwn?s=koan

www.zentourage.com/uncategorized/
bittersweet-love-poem-by-rumi/

Books, Films, Interviews:

Bays, Brandon. *The Journey: A Practical Guide to Healing Your Life and Setting Yourself Free.* New York: Fireside, 2002.

Braden, Greg. *The Divine Matrix: Bridging Time, Space, Miracles, and Belief.* Carlsbad, CA: Hay House, 2007.

Brown, Dan. *Angels & Demons.* New York: Atria Books, 2000.

Buffett, Jimmy. *A Pirate Looks at Fifty.* New York: Random House, 1998.

Bouchez, Colette, Reviewed by Louise Chang, M.D. *A New Age of Celebrity Worship: Experts Dissect The Good, The Bad, And The Ugly Of Being A Fan.* March 3, 2006, www.cbsnews.com/stories/2006/03/03/health/webmd/main1366162.shtml.

Buksbazen, John Daishin. *Zen Meditation in Plain English.* Boston: Wisdom Publications, 2002.

Cameron, Julia. *The Artist's Way: A Spiritual Path to Higher Creativity.* New York: Jeremey P. Tarcher/Putnam, 2002.

Castaneda, Carlos. *The Active Side of Infinity.* New York: HarperCollins, 1998.

Chilson, Fr. Bert. Personal interview.

Choquette, Sonia. *Ask Your Guides: Connecting to Your Divine Support System.* Carlsbad, CA: Hay House, 2006.

Choquette, Sonia. *Diary of a Psychic: Shattering the Myths.* Carlsbad, CA: Hay House, 2003.

Choquette, Sonia. *The Psychic Pathway: A Workbook for Reawakening the Voice of Your Soul.* New York: Three Rivers Press, 1994, 1995.

Coelho, Paulo. *The Alchemist,* translated by Alan R. Clarke. New York: Harper San Francisco/ HarperCollinsPublishers, 1993.

Coelho, Paulo. *The Pilgrimmage.* New York: HarperPerennial, A Division of HarperCollinsPublishers, 1998.

Cohen, Alan. *I Had It All the Time: When Self-Improvement Gives Way to Ecstasy.* Haiku, HI: Alan Cohen Publications, 1995.

Contact. Dir. Robert Zemeckis, Warner Bros., 1997. Video.

DeMarco, Frank. *Muddy Tracks: Exploring an Unsuspected Reality.* Charlottesville, VA: Hampton Roads Publishing, 2001.

Des Barres, Pamela. *Let's Spend the Night Together: Backstage Secrets of Rock Muses and Supergroupies.* Chicago, IL: Chicago Review Press, 2007.

Dyer, Dr. Wayne W. *The Power of Intention: Learning to Co-create Your World Your Way.* Carlsbad, CA: Hay House, Inc., 2004.

Favazzi, Guy. Personal interview.

Freke, Timothy, and Peter Gandy. *Jesus and the Lost Goddess: The Lost Teachings of the Original Christians.* New York: Three Rivers Press, 2001.

Freke, Timothy, and Peter Gandy. *The Jesus Mysteries: Was the "Original Jesus" a Pagan God?* New York: Three Rivers Press, 1999.

Garrett, Jan. Personal interview.

Hart, Mickey, and Fredric Lieberman. *Spirit into Sound: The Magic of Music.* Petaluma, CA: Grateful Dead Books, 1999.

Hagar, Sammy. Selected song lyrics used by permission.

Hedleston, Joanne. Personal interviews.

Kelley, Mark, N.D. LAc. Personal interview.

Khan, Sufi Hazrat Inayat. *The Mysticism of Sound; Music; The Power of the Word; Cosmic Language: The Sufi Message of Hazrat Inayat Khan.* International Headquarters Sufi Movement, Geneva, 1979.

LaGrand, Louis E., PhD. *After Death Communication: Final Farewells, Extraordinary Experiences of Those Mourning the Death of Loved Ones.* St. Paul, MN: Llewellyn Publications, 1997.

Long, Gayan Gregory. Personal interviews.

McIntosh, John. "The Healing Power of Art." *Remedy MD.* New York, (Summer 2007).

Millman, Dan. *Way of the Peaceful Warrior: A Book That Changes Lives.* Novato, CA: HJ Kramer Books in joint venture with New World Library, 1980, 1984, New Revised Edition 2000.

Mines, Robert A., Ph.D. Personal interviews.

Ming-Dao, Deng. *365 Tao Daily Meditations.* New York: Harper San Francisco, 1992.

Mitchell, Stephen. *Tao Te Ching.* New York: Harper Perennial, 1992.

Montgomery, Ruth. *Aliens Among Us.* New York: G. P. Putnam's Sons, 1985.

Nassar, Carl R., Ph.D. *The Spirit of Joy: A Transformational Journey to Awaken the Soul.* Fort Collins, CO: Miracle Books, 2001.

Ostrin, Jon. Personal interview.

Peart, Neil. *Roadshow: Landscape with Drums: A Concert Tour by Motorcycle.* Cambridge, MA: Rounder, 2006.

Peck, Dr. M. Scott. *The Road Less Traveled: A New Psychology of Love, Traditional Values and Spiritual Growth.* New York: Touchstone, 1978.

Perry, Frank. *Temple of the Ancient Magical Presence.* January 10, 1999. www.musicpsyche.org/index.html.

Rand, Ayn. *The Fountainhead.* New York: Signet, New American Library, a division of Penguin Group, 1952.

Romero, Christopher. Personal interviews.

Rothschild, Joel. *Signals: An Inspiring Story of Life After Life.* Novato, CA: New World Library, 2000.

Sammy Hagar & the Waboritas: Cabo Wabo Birthday Bash Tour. Dir. Jeb Brien. Image Entertainment, 2001. Video.

Sohl, Robert, and Audry Carr, eds. *The Gospel According to Zen: Beyond the Death of God.* New York: Mentor, 1970.

Steer, Maxwell. "Introduction," *Contemporary Music Review, Music & Mysticism Issue.* www.musicpsyche.org/mmintro.html.

Storm, Hyemeyohsts. *Seven Arrows.* New York: Ballantine Books, 1972.

Suzuki, D.T. *An Introduction to Zen Buddhism.* New York: Grove Press, 1964.

Tame, David. *The Secret Power of Music: The Transformation of Self and Society Through Musical Energy.* Rochester, VT: Destiny Books, 1984.

Tart, Charles T., ed. *Body Mind Spirit: Exploring the Parapsychology of Spirituality.* Charlottesville, VA: Hampton Roads Publishing Company, Inc., 1997.

The Healing Path: Magazine for Earth, Body, Mind & Spirit. Fort Collins, CO, (Jan./Feb. 2007).

Tolle, Eckhart. *The Power of Now: A Guide to Spiritual Enlightenment.* Novato, CA: Namaste Publishing and New World Library, 1999.

Visocky, Donna. Personal interview.

Walsch, Neale Donald. *Conversations with God: An Uncommon Dialogue,* Book 1. New York: G. P. Putnam's Sons, 1996.

Walsch, Neale Donald. *Conversations with God: An Uncommon Dialogue,* Book 2. Charlottesville, VA: Hampton Roads Publishing Company, Inc., 1997.

Weiss, Brian L., M.D. *Many Lives, Many Masters: The true story of a prominent psychiatrist, his young patient, and the past-life therapy that changed both their lives.* New York: Simon & Schuster, Inc., 1988.

Weiss, Brian L., M.D. *Messages from the Masters: Tapping into the Power of Love.* New York: Warner Books, 2000.

Wick, Gerry Shishin Roshi. Personal interview.

Yogananda, Paramahansa. *Autobiography of a Yogi.* Los Angeles, CA: Self-Realization Fellowship,1998.

Ziemann, Greg. *Baja Legends: The Historic Characters, Events and Locations That Put Baja California on the Map.* San Diego, CA: Sunbelt Publications, Inc., 2002.

For further enhancement of this book, you may enjoy these songs:

"Open" by Sammy Hagar

"Dreams" by Van Halen

"Crush" by Dave Matthews Band

"Pages" by 3 Doors Down

"Can't Stop Loving You" by Van Halen

"Nothing Else Matters" by Metallica

"A Gift of Love: Deepak & Friends Present Music Inspired by the Love Poems of Rumi" by Various Artists

"Imagine" by John Lennon

About the Author

Photo by Mike Barry

PATRICIA WALKER lives and writes in northern Colorado. Her poems have appeared in published poetry compilations and many articles she has written are featured on the Web. She authors a personal blog, writing primarily about traditional and nontraditional spiritual approaches to life and ways to enhance one's journey through music, nature, and personal introspection. Patricia is currently working on her next book.

Visit her at: www.bajarockpat.com or www.bajarockpat.net

Related Titles

If you enjoyed *Dance of the Electric Hummingbird*,
you may also enjoy other Rainbow Ridge books:

The Cosmic Internet: Explanations from the Other Side
by Frank DeMarco

Conversations with Jesus: An Intimate Journey
by Alexis Eldridge

Dialogue with the Devil: Enlightenment for the Unwilling
by Yves Patak

The Divine Mother Speaks: The Healing of the Human Heart
by Rashmi Khilnani

Difficult People: A Gateway to Enlightenment
by Lisette Larkins

When Do I See God: Finding the Path to Heaven
by Jeff Ianniello

Rainbow Ridge Books publishes spiritual
and metaphysical titles, and is distributed by Square
One Publishers in Garden City Park, New York.

To contact authors and editors, peruse our titles, and
see submission guidelines, please visit our website at:
www.rainbowridgebooks.com.

For orders and catalogs, please call toll-free:
(877) 900-BOOK